A Game of Moments

A Game of Moments
*Baseball Greats Remember
Highlights of Their Careers*

RON GERRARD

McFarland & Company, Inc., Publishers
Jefferson, North Carolina

All photographs are by the author.

ISBN (print) 978-1-4766-7194-9
ISBN (ebook) 978-1-4766-3205-6

LIBRARY OF CONGRESS CATALOGUING DATA ARE AVAILABLE

BRITISH LIBRARY CATALOGUING DATA ARE AVAILABLE

© 2018 Ron Gerrard. All rights reserved

No part of this book may be reproduced or transmitted in any form or by any means, electronic or mechanical, including photocopying or recording, or by any information storage and retrieval system, without permission in writing from the publisher.

Front cover: 1957 Braves and World Series reunion. From left, Johnny Logan, Eddie Mathews and Lew Burdette (photograph by the author).

Manufactured in the United States of America

*McFarland & Company, Inc., Publishers
Box 611, Jefferson, North Carolina 28640
www.mcfarlandpub.com*

To Margie E. Gerrard for her love,
support, patience and encouragement,
and Robert, my canine companion while serving
in Phu Bai, Viet Nam. I thank you for leading me home.

Acknowledgments

I wish to thank Rocky Van Blaricom II for valuable assistance rendered during the creation of this book. He is the person responsible for helping me stay afloat with his Computer literacy which encompasses applications, workflows and anything else remotely compatible with a computer or smartphone. When I would ask something stupid, which I can assure you happened on numerous occasions, he would never embarrass me but simply tilt his head in a quizzical fashion and mutter: "Dude."

I also wish to thank Robert X. Modica, who was and is to me, the Iron Man of acting coaches, for shining his light on my life. I may have disagreed with him on more than one occasion during an acting exercise in his studio but in the end he was always right. You are with me every day.

A heartfelt thank you to the McFarland team for their guidance and keen eyes. Your kindness will always be appreciated. So many times in life we encounter closed doors. You opened one for me.

I wish to thank The Church of the Blessed Sacrament in Valley Stream, New York, for putting me in the starting lineup after I was cut by every other denomination of Church League teams on Long Island. Your kindness kept my young dream alive and taught me to believe and be a grinder long after baseball.

I extend my gratitude to the Cleveland Indians and Pittsburgh Pirates organizations for their kindness and assistance through the many seasons I arrived early and left late from their ballparks.

Finally I thank all the subjects, players, managers, and broadcasters who were gracious and kind enough to give of their time. Each of these gentlemen is an inspiration. They struggled and despite hardships put it all on the line, making it possible to live their dream and in a number of instances forged change in our society. At times the journey directed them on another path but they returned like the champions and competitors they are. The game is better, we who appreciate it are better because of you, and I extend my heartfelt gratitude and respect. It is my hope that through these interviews, their exploits on and off the diamond will inspire others.

Table of Contents

Acknowledgments vi
Preface 1

Hank Aaron	3	Elroy Face	60
Sparky Anderson	7	Bob Feller	62
Bobby Avila	10	Wilmer Fields	64
Ernie Banks	11	Rollie Fingers	66
Dick Bartell	13	Tito Francona	69
Joe Black	15	Steve Garvey	70
Ewell Blackwell	17	Bob Gibson	72
Lou Boudreau	19	Al Gionfriddo	77
Ralph Branca	20	Jim "Mudcat" Grant	78
Lou Brock	23	Tony Gwynn	80
Gates Brown	24	Harvey Haddix	83
Lew Burdette	27	Bud Harrelson	85
Rod Carew	29	Ernie Harwell	87
Gary Carter	32	Tommy Henrich	89
Rico Carty	33	Ralph Houk	93
Chris Chambliss	36	Monte Irvin	95
Ed Charles	37	Ferguson Jenkins	98
Jerry Coleman	39	Harmon Killebrew	99
Babe Dahlgren	41	Ralph Kiner	101
Alvin Dark	45	Bob Lemon	103
Tommy Davis	47	Al Lopez	105
Leon Day	49	Juan Marichal	106
Bucky Dent	51	Eddie Mathews	108
Larry Doby	53	Bill Mazeroski	110
Bobby Doerr	54	Rick Monday	113
Don Drysdale	56	Manny Mota	116
Carl Erskine	59	Ron Necciai	118

Buck O'Neil	120	Ted Simmons	152
Tony Oliva	121	Enos Slaughter	156
Mickey Owen	123	Hal Smith	157
Gaylord Perry	125	Willie Stargell	159
Johnny Podres	126	Ron Swoboda	162
Dick Radatz	128	Gene Tenace	163
Dusty Rhodes	129	Bobby Thomson	165
Robin Roberts	134	Cecil Travis	167
Brooks Robinson	135	Johnny Vander Meer	170
Cookie Rojas	138	Mickey Vernon	172
Al Rosen	139	Bob Watson	174
Joe Rudi	141	Billy Williams	175
Ron Santo	142	Dick Williams	178
Mike Schmidt	144	Maury Wills	180
Red Schoendienst	146	Jimmy Wynn	181
Roy Sievers	150		

Index   183

Preface

My introduction to baseball came through a photograph of Joe DiMaggio taken by my father at Yankee Stadium on June 6, 1940. My father would later become a professional photographer, but this day he was as enthusiastic about baseball as he was about photography. As he explained to me years later, the Yankee Clipper was walking towards the dugout prior to the game versus the White Sox when my dad asked if he could take a photo, and the Yankee Clipper obliged. It was a special moment as a great player stopped and posed unassumingly. The film was developed and printed at home in my dad's bathroom, which also served as his studio. It was a black and white photo, two and a half inches by three inches. Years later it would be displayed in our breakfast nook, where I would stare at it and imagine that I, too, would play the game like Joltin' Joe. The baseball gods must have been looking down and smiling at my father that afternoon as he later would retrieve a foul ball hit by Frank Crosetti, which he gifted to me and which I still have. The only blemish is a scuff mark I was responsible for when, against his instructions, I threw a pop-up to myself in our driveway only to have it carom off the web of my glove and hit the pavement. Even at that early age, I suspected I would end up chasing far more dreams than I would fly balls. So much for me being another Joe DiMaggio.

As a sports reporter and producer of radio broadcasts, I have been fortunate enough to speak with many former major league players. When you break the game down it's easy to see how a player with a single at-bat or a spectacular defensive play can suddenly place himself in select company, and that is what I have done with *A Game of Moments*. *A Game of Moments* features many of baseball's great or pivotal moments, told by the players who were center stage, performing and defining our national pastime. The interviews serve as first-hand testaments of clutch hits, home runs and defensive plays in an era that will never come again. The interviews are illuminating and related by men who were gracious and happy to express themselves years after leaving the diamond. The majority of interviews took place in Pittsburgh and Cleveland, with several others conducted in Baltimore and Toronto. The years when I spoke to the subjects ran primarily from 1988 to 1992, with the exception of Rollie Fingers and Steve Garvey which were conducted in 2007. Exact years when known are posted on each interview. Most conversations were taped on the field at the ballpark or in the dugout at Old Timers Day games. Hank Aaron and Bob Gibson were recorded in studio. Cecil Travis, Babe Dahlgren, Tommy Henrich, Gates Brown and Tommy Davis were recorded via telephone.

Through these former players we are afforded the opportunity to hear about Bobby Thomson's "Shot Heard Round the World," Mickey Owen's dropped third strike, Johnny Vander Meer's back-to-back no-hit games, and Al Gionfriddo's amazing catch to rob Joe DiMaggio in the 1947 fall classic. Chris Chambliss and Bucky Dent recount their dramatic playoff home runs, while Bill Mazeroski reveals his thoughts as he watched his dramatic

Game 7 walk-off home run clear the left field wall of Forbes Field and propel the underdog Pittsburgh Pirates to a stunning 1960 World Series victory over the powerful New York Yankees. The "Hammer," Hank Aaron, speaks candidly about the elation and pain that followed his breaking of Babe Ruth's all-time home record, and big game pitcher Bob Gibson looks back at 1968, the year of the pitcher, and his 1.12 ERA. Through the pages of *A Game of Moments*, we hear from Larry Doby, the first African American to break the color line in the American League. Former Negro League players Leon Day, Buck O'Neil, Monte Irvin, Wilmer Fields and Joe Black speak about their experiences and some of their teammates who, because of racism, were forced to play in the shadows. Bobby Avila, the first Latin player to win a batting title in the Major Leagues, expresses the pride he felt after his achievement when there were few Latin players competing in the Major Leagues. *A Game of Moments* examines the effect that World War II and the Korean War had on players who felt it their obligation to enter and serve their country, the aftermath when they returned up to four years later, and how it affected their careers. You will read about famous and not so famous moments that are woven into the fabric of Major League Baseball and will better understand that statistics alone will never overtake heart as the true pathway to greatness.

"The Yankee Clipper," Joe DiMaggio.

Hank Aaron

Hank Aaron excelled in every aspect of the game but will always be associated with the long ball. He produced 20 consecutive seasons with 20 or more home runs, finishing his remarkable career with a total of 755. He batted over .300 for 14 seasons, with more than 100 RBI 11 times, and 15 seasons with at least 100 runs scored. He was chosen for 24 All-Star Games, a record he shares with Willie Mays and Stan Musial. In 1957 he was the recipient of the NL MVP Award. Hank Aaron drove in more runs than any other player with 2,297 and holds the major league records for total bases, 6,856 and extra-base hits, 1,477. On April 8, 1974, Hank Aaron eclipsed the record of 714 home runs held by Babe Ruth, a record that had stood for 39 years. Unfortunately, racism continued to plague our nation and he received over 900,000 threatening pieces of mail according to his autobiography, *I Had a Hammer*. He is a member of MLB's All-Century Team and was elected to the Baseball Hall of Fame in 1982.

This interview was conducted in Pittsburgh, Pennsylvania, in 1991.

I Had a Hammer's the book and we'll get right into it. You wrote it with Lonnie Wheeler. What made you want to write the book at this time? You could have done it years prior to this.

Well not this type of book, Ron. I had an opportunity when I retired from baseball in 1976 to write a baseball book. A book dealing with when Henry Aaron hit a home run in April of 1972, the 12th inning or how many innings you played. I didn't want to write that type book. I wanted to write a book that was dealing with more than just baseball. This is a history book having to deal with some of the trials and tribulations in which I went through. Some of the things and some of the pain I suffered during the 1973 and '74 season when I broke Babe Ruth's record. So I wanted people to understand that there's more, there was more to Henry Aaron than hitting home runs.

That is quite evident. You said in the book that there were painful aspects to breaking Babe Ruth's record, not the actual breaking of the record but what you had to put up with, and you don't like talking about it that much, but on the other hand you were one of baseball's greatest all around players. More than just a home run hitter, but that is what people know you by, Henry Aaron the all-time home run king.

Well that's true, that's true. But I also want them to know, that's fine with me, I'm not going to ever get rid of that stigma, you know as far as baseball, I enjoyed it. I just want people to understand that when I first started playing and went to the big leagues in 1954 of course and left home in 1953 I guess, somewhere, about '52 or '51 rather, I'm sorry. I just didn't walk out from Mobile, Alabama into a major league uniform. There were things that led me to doing that. I had a lot of, well let's just say I had problems. In Mobile growing up, didn't have a baseball bat, didn't have a baseball, didn't have pants.

So I to provide all of these things and pretend like I had baseballs, artifacts, I wanted kids, particularly minority kids, because they have to be bigger let's face it, those are the ones that have a lot of problems, and I wanted them to understand that they have to be bigger than just looking at some of the things, that some of the troubles that they may be going through.

"The Hammer," Hank Aaron, who, when he retired in 1976, had hit 755 home runs. What's in a number? Plenty!

You mentioned in the book, in the minor leagues, especially in Jacksonville, how tough it was, and you were with Horace Garner and Felix Mantilla and breaking the color barrier was very difficult. Was that the most difficult time for you in the minor leagues or do you think, even though Jackie Robinson had already broken the color line, it must have been just as difficult when you came to the major leagues.

Well, no question about it, and I want people to understand that when we start talking about things that happened in this country, or things that happened in the world, we're not talking about a hundred years ago. For example, if you start mentioning the Holocaust, you know you're not talking about a hundred years ago. When you start talking about Jackie Robinson breaking into major league baseball in '47 or '48, we're not talking about a hundred years ago. When we start talking about things that happened in Los Angeles just the other day, when you have 20 policemen cracking down on some black person here, we're talking about now. We're talking about things that happened in this century. People start wondering, and when they read that book they start saying, oh, that happened in '56, I mean '72, '73, '74. So people are amazed and astonished by these things. I'm not trying to say that I'm sitting here trying to make people feel sorry for me, by no means, baseball was great to me. But I paid my dues. It was very painful. I paid my dues unlike say some of the other white players, unlike the white players, simply because of the fact that I was black. I had to go through a lot of other things that some of the white players didn't have to go through.

You mentioned Jackie Robinson. There was one instance it was probably in the early spring, you were in a room with him, and you came to a point where you said you could not go along with the program, this was many years ago, you could never not address issues and you didn't really have any choice especially after speaking with Jackie Robinson.

Well Jackie was a person that I will never forget, just as Dr. King is a person I will never forget, Jesse Jackson, Malcolm X and all of these great civil rights leaders. Jackie is someone that you just can't forget because if it had not been for Jackie Robinson, there would not have been Henry Aaron and I feel like I just made a little contribution to the way things are today, but Jackie Robinson was the one that actually paved the way for all of us especially black minorities to be in baseball now.

I was listening to Wynton Marsalis and he was talking about Art Tatum and some of the greats and how he learned from them and it was a building block and so forth. It seems that in baseball there isn't as much an appreciation for the past. How do you look at this, how do you explain it? Why don't players have that reverence for the past?

That is one of the things I think that I have some great concerns with because too many times I think that blacks and black youngsters have lost our history. We have lost it because we're not taught it in school, that's number one. The other thing is that in our homes we're not taught it. When I hear someone say they don't know who Jackie Robinson is, they don't know who Dr. King is; it's something wrong with our country, something wrong with our society. And yet in some parts of this country you can go and people don't know who Jackie Robinson is or don't know who Dr. King is. That's absolutely crazy when people don't know who these great civil rights and people who have gone on before them who have paved the way for them to be where they are today. I don't have an answer; I really don't have an answer for it. The only thing I can say is that we got to keep, and when I say we I'm talking about black people, just gotta keep on pushing and keep on fighting and let people know that we would like to be included in the everyday academic studies in high schools, colleges and etcetera. Because we have had some great black people come through this country and we need to start paying tribute to them.

You have a mission in life. Where does that come from?
I don't know where it comes from but I can honestly say this: I just wouldn't be able to sleep with myself if I just wouldn't speak out on certain issues. I'm familiar with baseball, I know what the problem is that we have in baseball and it's my job to speak out on these issues. I have two sons that I feel like if I don't speak out and let people know what the issues are then I certainly can't look in the mirror at night and sleep well when I go to bed.

On the diamond, 1957 was a great year for you as a team and for you personally. Would '57 be the most gratifying outside of breaking the home run record?
Yes '57 was one but I would have to say '59 would have been the greatest overall year that I had. Although I didn't hit as many home runs but I almost ended up hitting .400, I hit .355, I had a high batting average and I also had a 39 home run total. So I would have to say if I had to put the two together I would have to say '59 was the year that I think that I had a better year than I had in '57.

Do you think that on the playing field there is equality in baseball today?
I have to let the players today answer that who's playing on the field, but I certainly don't believe that they've been equal quality as far as the front office is concerned. I still believe that in some areas that still need to be addressed, I'm speaking about the minor league system. We need black doctors through our minor league system, we need black coaches, instructors etc. All through the minor league system and we just don't have them.

You're known as Henry Aaron to your family, Hank Aaron to the fans. What do you like to go by?
It really doesn't make any difference. Good friends of mine like Donald Davidson, who's no longer with us, called me Hank, some baseball players who I played with called me Hammerin' Hank, some called me Henry. My wife calls me Henry when she's angry with me and Hank when she's not.

You likened yourself to a Stan Musial. You were a guess hitter; you guessed the location plus guessed the pitch. Obviously that worked very well for you.
That's just about it. I looked for the ball and I guessed curve ball, looked for a curve ball, and I looked for it in certain location and that was my way of hitting. Some guys look for a curve ball, no matter where it is they swing at it. I just had a lot of patience at the plate and guess it paid off.

The 715th, that was in '74, these many years later, you've spoken about it countless times, and do you ever look at it any different? Does it mean anything different to you now than say back in '74 or a few years after that? Has it set into you what an occasion that was?
No, really as I said before and I think I explained it in the book, those numbers don't mean anything to me. 715, 755, I realize that's a lot of home runs no matter how you look at it but still it doesn't mean that much to me in terms of numbers or whether somebody's going to break the record or whether somebody's going to come close to it. I never think about it.

How would you like people to think of you and to remember you?

I don't have any special notion of how people should remember me. I think that that would have to be left up to people who were going to try and identify a person with certain things. For an example, they look at me as a baseball player quite naturally. That's the first thing that's going to come to most people's mind. They're going to say well Hank Aaron the home run king, that's what they're going to remember me for. They're not going to think about Hank Aaron did everything humanly possible to help young people. They're not going to think about a Hank Aaron who was able to do other things on the diamond. So I don't know how I would want people to remember me. I just want people to remember me as being a complete man and doing the very best that I possibly could at all times.

◆ ◆ ◆

Sparky Anderson

George "Sparky" Anderson was the first manager to win the World Series in both leagues. Anderson won back-to-back in in the NL in 1975 and 1976 with the Cincinnati Reds, aka "The Big Red Machine," and then in the AL with the Detroit Tigers in 1984. He was also named "Manager of the Year" with the Tigers in 1984 and 1987. The man known as "Captain Hook" due to pulling his starting pitchers early managed in the Major Leagues for 26 seasons and won 2,194 games. All told his squads won three World Series, seven division titles and five pennants. His number 10 was retired by the Reds, and likewise his number 11 was retired by the Tigers. He was elected to the National Baseball Hall of Fame in 2000.

This interview was conducted in Cleveland, Ohio, in September 1991.

Sparky, you're in a pennant race now, we hear all this talk about managers making a difference or not making a difference down the stretch. Some people feel maybe they try to make too many moves to cost the team a game or this or that. What are your feelings on that because you're certainly an authority on pennant races?

I never have thought managers, once the season starts, I never thought managers have anything to do with it. I once told Lou Piniella the first game I ever managed against Lou when he took over the Yankees, as a young manager, I said when we were turning in the lineup card, I said, "Lou, are you finished?" He said, "What do you mean?" I said, "You have just done the last thing in this ball game tonight that will be anything important to the game. You turned in the lineup card. You are not going to have one decision that's going to win or lose this game. The only people that are out there are your players, and the only people you'll fear over in my dugout is my players." Players control the game. They win and they lose 'em. There's not such a thing as a manager going to outsmart somebody else. The personnel dictate what you do. For instance, I would manage 14 different ways in the National League. We have 14 different clubs, you have 14 different types of personnel. There's 14 different ways I would have to manage because all personnel has to be managed different, and no two clubs are identical. You couldn't possibly manage

George "Sparky" Anderson, the first manager to win World Series Championships in both leagues, shakes the hand of Cleveland's legendary pitcher Mel Harder.

any one club and then go manage another one, try to manage that the same way. You have to be able, I say, to be 14 different people. If you can't do that, you can't manage.

Now, in this league, you have the DH, you had such success in the National League, how do you feel about the DH?

    I never liked it from the day they started it period, and I was in the National League when it started over here but it was foolish, it's foolish now, it has nothing to do with the game of baseball at all. I don't know what bearing it has to do, I always thought the pitcher who was pitching must compete also with the bat, he must be part of the game. It's kind of funny that when you see the pitcher leave the mound, you never ever see him come up during an inning, ever. The only time you see him again is when he appears back on the mound. I don't know, I think our new commissioner has the right idea and I hope as I have no control over it, it will come to a vote. You know it's one and one, National and American League, commissioner can break that vote. All he has to do is vote and as soon as he votes, it's over one way or the other. I am hoping very much that this is decided one way or the other, and I hope it is decided this winter at the winter meetings.

On the personal side, the victories you've notched are at 1,900, I mean you are approaching 2,000 wins. This is mind-boggling. I'm sure it's mind-boggling to you, like when you started you never thought that would happen, but how do you feel that you're hitting these milestones?

I'm like you, I have to laugh but I was walking down coming to the ballpark today, walking down the street and I was actually thinking about what you're saying. I said, here's a boy that came from Bridgewater, South Dakota, I was nine years old, to Los Angeles. I finished high school by looking out of the corner of my eye at a test, enough to get through, you know, finding any way I could to make it through, and to think that here I am roughly 80 some games away from 2,000. I said you know, I reminded Andy Allanson about that, one of our catchers. I said, "You know Andy, I remember my first year in 1970 looking across the dugout, my first trip into Dodger Stadium and there stood Walter Alston. And Andy, he looked like he reached the sky. He looked so tall to me. To think what a giant he was in the industry at that time and I said here I was 35 years old, looking across at this guy that has records on top of records and I said to myself, what am I doing managing in the same ballpark with this guy. And yeah, it is, it's very mind boggling and it is funny. I don't think I will ever think of it any other way than funny. How can these things happen, I don't know, but that old saying about only in America, it's very true. Only in America do crazy and weird things happen.

I think you had a lot to do with that, I don't know that it's that weird, many people have had the opportunity and didn't put the wins up. What keeps the game fresh for you? What is it that makes you want to push forward, because you have nothing to prove.

Players. Players are marvelous. Today I have had four guys in to see me today. Two of them on personal things and two of them on baseball. A personal thing never leaves me, and they know that. I have some personal things over my career that if I would ever tell, they would just be disastrous to people. They know that I will never leave them. They come in and close the door, that's gonna be the end. The other two things were on, one's about signs, what to do, this and that. Another one was that just feeling low about his year and that to me is so marvelous. I told the one, I said you know what, I think I really should have taken up psychiatry, I said I think I should have been a psychiatrist 'cause my head right now is pounding because you cannot talk to four different people, and get that deep into things without really using a lot of strain and you're trying to help them and you just, your head starts to pound, but that's what does it. The players. I don't think there's anything more marvelous than guys and I call them warriors, that are going out there to battle and all you gotta do is sit there and watch them. But I think your job is to help them when they need your help, as far as from the mental standpoint.

Finally Skip, I remember the great years in Cincinnati. You've been here for great teams over the years but is there one team, I know you're a Tiger currently, that you feel closer to if you had to walk away today, how would you feel about either team or ...?

Okay, the Reds clubs were tremendous people, they were professionals, great talent, uh! The '76 club I will never live long enough to see another team like it, I myself personally. It might come 30 years from now but I won't see it. The '87 club was a tremendous club to watch go about their work because it didn't deserve to win, that was a fifth-place club, really and truly it was. I picked the fifth with my wife and I always tell her every spring when we leave where we will finish and I picked the fifth and we finished first and how, I don't know yet, I told Roger Craig, we don't have enough time or years to try to describe but this year, 1991, I didn't know it when we started but will be my favorite no matter what. This club had more all-around, outstanding good people. I have never had one disciplinary thing, now that's crazy. Now, we got, I know three weeks to go and it could happen, you know it could happen, but I've never had to discipline a player on this club in 1991. Now that is unheard of. I have never been on a club in my life, including the Great Reds Clubs, that I didn't have to discipline some.

I appreciate you taking a few moments of your time and we wish you and the ball club all the best the rest of the way and hopefully we will see you in the post-season. Thank you Skip.

Thank you and it is mind boggling about 2,000. It scares me.

◆ ◆ ◆

Bobby Avila

Mexican-born second baseman Bobby Avila played the majority of his 11-year big league career with the Cleveland Indians (1949–1958). The three-time All-Star became the first Latin player to win a batting title when he led the American League with an average of .341 in 1954. In 1953 he led all Junior Circuit second baseman in fielding percentage. He later served as Mayor of Veracruz, Mexico, and as president of the Mexican Baseball League. For his career, Avila hit .281 with 80 home runs and 467 RBI while collecting 1,296 hits.

This interview was conducted in Cleveland, Ohio, in 1993.

Bobby, you played most of your career here in Cleveland. You won the batting crown in 1954. What happened that year? It appears that everything you did was right.

Well that was in 1954 when I hit 341; I led the league in hitting and that was one of those kind of years, you know, you just swing and get base hits.

You played with some of the great players. When you look back, who comes to mind here in Cleveland?

Well especially the pitchers we had like Lemon, Early Wynn, Garcia, Feller, and then Jim Hegan, he was the catcher, he was a great catcher. Then we had two first basemen, Luke Easter and Vic Wertz, we had Strickland at shortstop. Al Rosen you know he was a great ballplayer. Never had trouble in the outfield. Dale Mitchell, Dave Pope, Harry Simpson. We had a real good ball club.

When you won the batting title, you were the first Latin player to do so. That has to make you proud.

Oh sure, you know at that time there were not too many Latin ballplayers playing in the American League and National League. I believed there weren't more than ten Latin ballplayers in the American League; probably six were pitchers, so actually only four guys came and could lead the league in hitting, so that's almost impossible for a Latin ballplayer to win hitting. Right now you have so many Latin ballplayers, you have a pretty good chance of them leading the league in hitting.

Later on you were the mayor of a city in Mexico.

When I was through playing baseball, I went into politics, then I went to the Congress twice and then I was Mayor of the city of my home, Veracruz.

Also you were President or El Presidente of the Mexican League.
   Yes, I was the President of the Mexican league from 1980 to '81.

The most memorable year for you would be 1954.
   I'd say so. Well the first year, you always remember that, the first year is the first time you've been in the majors it was something. I was dreaming since I was a kid, you know. But '54 was a good year. I really remember it. I will admit I do say with the pennant we won, I won the title for hitting, I mean you know it's something you remember.

I wish you all the best. And thanks for spending some time.
   It's all right, it's a pleasure to do it.

◆ ◆ ◆

Ernie Banks

If ever there was a great player and goodwill ambassador for the game, it would be Ernie Banks. Banks began his career with Kansas City in the Negro Leagues and went on to become the signature player for the Chicago Cubs from 1953 through 1971. The man known as "Mr. Cub" won back-to-back MVP Awards in 1958 and 1959. Banks, who was known for the phrase "Let's play two," displayed uncommon power for a shortstop in his era, hitting 277 home runs while at the position. He moved to first base and finished his career with 512 home runs, while batting .274 with 1,636 RBI. He was a 14-time All-Star whose number 14 was retired by the Cubs in 1982, and he was elected to the Hall of Fame in 1977. In 1999 Ernie Banks was named to the Major League Baseball's All-Century Team, and in 2013 he received the Presidential Medal of Freedom.

This interview was conducted in Toronto, Canada, on July 8, 1991.

Ernie Banks.
   Nice to see you, Ron Gerrard. Is this a wonderful life or what?

Ernie, I wouldn't have known it if you didn't tell me, but it's been a pleasure hanging around you. I learned a lot about baseball listening to you speak. You were talking to Dave Parker about who taught him to hit. Who taught you to hit?
   Well I just, more or less went out to practice every day hitting the curve ball. That was something I was weak at hitting and that was it. I just worked on my weaknesses, and I was around players that would look at my swing and they would tell me about it, like Ralph Kiner and Monte Irvin, they'd give me a few tips on pulling the ball and I stayed with that. But basically I just worked on my own natural ability of being able to use my hands and wrists to become a better hitter.

You had so many great seasons, but the MVP back-to-back and it was for a club that didn't win which was even more extraordinary. You were a shortstop and you had tremendous power. You were one of the first. You know we see a little more pop in some of the shortstops now, but back in your day you were kind of unique.

"Mr. Cub," Ernie Banks, baseball's goodwill ambassador.

Yes, I had one slight edge that I identified right away, and I think the sooner you can identify your slight edge, it can help you in whatever you do in life. Sometimes it can be physical and sometimes a mental thing. Mine was my wrists. I could be fooled on a pitch and still hit it like Hank Aaron and a lot of the great hitters that had quick wrists, and that was my big advantage. I did a lot of exercises to develop my wrists, worked on my wrists, did a lot of pushups and strength exercises to build up my wrists and strengthen my wrists, so it helped me a lot when I became a major league baseball player.

You used to move your fingers on the bat while waiting for the ball.
Yes, I keep my hand relaxed at bat more or less, not try to have a lot of tension in my swing, and that's something you have to really work on. I mean tension can, you know, take away a lot of your fluidity, and you become tight and you just can't swing relaxed.

I don't want to bring up an unfortunate series of events, 1969 was a great year for you, but everyone always talks about how you are such a respected and deserving player and you never got a chance to play in a World Series, and '69 looked like it was almost meant to be.
Yeah, and that happens in life. It all comes by; I look at baseball as life. You know sometimes you have things in the bag and the bag breaks. There's no real guarantee of anything, and you just have to go on and move on and adjust your life to losses and disappointments, and that was a big disappointment in my life that not to have been in the World Series or in a playoff game, but it happened to many players in many different sports, so I consider myself very fortunate to have played in the major league for 19 years.

You're known for your signature phrase "Let's play two." Where did that come from?

That began in 1969 at about 120 degrees and I walked in the locker room and told everybody, hey this is a beautiful day, let's play two. And they all looked at me and thought I was crazy. One of the writers was there and he wrote about it, and it stayed with me forever and I really enjoy that. I hear that today, so it, it's something I really enjoy saying and being a part of my life.

Being referred to as Mr. Cub.

That too is a great joy. That came around the same time, around 1968. Jimmy Enright, a writer for the Chicago American, was telling me that you're Mr. Cub. Then he wrote a book about that, calling me Mr. Cub, and started writing about it more and more, and it became a part of my life and I enjoy it very much. It's a great honor to be a part of a team and then called Mr. Cub.

The high point, what meant the most to you, maybe not to the fans, but to you in baseball—what is the most meaningful moment?

Well the meaningful moment, it's been many of those. On the field, just an opportunity to play. I would say personally the 500 home runs was a very meaningful thing. On the personal side, on the other side, you know raising my children and getting them through and having them have a good happy life and not into drugs and all the different kinds of things that happen today, to me is a real lesson, a real pleasure in my life.

We were blessed and it was a pleasure to have a person like you to inspire many of us, and you're still doing it. We appreciate you taking some time out and even though you made me wait 40 minutes, I still love you and you take good care of yourself.

Thank you very much. All I'm doing is trying to be a better person, that's all. Ha Ha.

• • •

Dick Bartell

Shortstop Dick Bartell was a member of the first All-Star team that took the field in Chicago in 1933. The man known as "Rowdy Richard" spent 18 years in the major leagues, playing with Pittsburgh, Philadelphia, New York and Chicago in the National League and Detroit in the American League. He compiled a lifetime batting average of .284 with 79 home runs and 710 RBI, and batted over .300 six times, finishing with 2,165 hits. While playing in three World Series, he recorded a batting average of .294. When he broke into the big leagues, he was paid a compliment from none other than the legendary Babe Ruth. Understandably, it was something he would remember the rest of his life.

This interview was conducted in Pittsburgh, Pennsylvania, in 1989.

Everyone knows you as Rowdy Richard. Who gave you that name?

Well I got it as kind of a gag. They just came up with something like that, they said oh you're a rowdy so we're going to nickname you as a gag as Rowdy Richard, and that's become my trade name now, everything says Rowdy Richard. I played hard and played to win and gave a hundred percent or more, and they said we're going to call you Rowdy Richard and that really took hold.

You played on some great teams. I know you were here your first four years in Pittsburgh. Who were some of the great players you played with and what you remember about your years in Pittsburgh?

Well there was Pie Traynor, there was Earl Sheely, there was Paul Waner, Lloyd Waner, Adam Comorosky, Glenn Wright.

A great shortstop.

Yes, I took his job.

What do you remember about Big Poison and Little Poison, Paul and Lloyd Waner?

Well, I thought they were two great players. Lloyd legged out a lot of base hits. But I thought that Paul Waner was one of the best hitters I've seen. You could bet all kinds of money that he'd go to bat four times, and he would three times hit the ball hard. Well, to me that's an exemplification of a good hitter that makes good contact. He could hit to left field, he could hit to center field, he could hit to right field. He went up there and you could bet money that he would hit line drives three out of four times.

You also played with the New York Giants. I imagine you played in the World Series over there. Were those great memories for you?

Oh there's no doubt about it, because I started off with Barney Dreyfuss and my dad had been offered a bonus if I would sign with the New York Yankees. So he said no, because of Joe Devine he's going to sign with Pittsburgh, and I did.

What about the great Giants ball clubs that you played on? How was Bill Terry, for example?

Well he was sensational. He's the best first baseman that I ever threw to. When you come up with the ball just throw it, he'd catch it and you didn't have to worry if it was a bad throw. On a tough play. He wouldn't get off the bag, he'd get the ball, and I thought he was one of the greatest managers because at one time he took our club, and we had a bunch of just about through players, and he managed us and manipulated us that we darn near got the winner of our division at that time.

Did you ever have any contact with John McGraw at all?

No. The only contact I had with him was when I went to the first All-Star Game and he was the manager and he didn't talk to anybody or mingle of say anything. He told us what the lineup was and he'd change. He never said a word, and he didn't have much to say at all to me or anybody that I saw.

Tough guy "Rowdy Richard," Dick Bartell.

Babe Ruth. Did you ever have any contact with him?

Well, I can tell you a little story about Babe Ruth. I think it's one of the greatest stories, and this is true. As a shortstop, when we broke in they made it as tough as they could, the old timers, to keep [us] from making the team. They all worked together and made you look bad. We were going down through Dallas and Ft. Worth, and Babe Ruth turned around and went like that to me (motioned me over) and I looked around to see what's going on. So I looked around and he went like that to me (motioned me over), and I looked around and thought what's the matter with that man? So I turned around and I looked over there, and he says come here, and I says you mean me? I went (surprised) me? Me? And he says yes you! So I fixed my pants leg and I walk out and I said yes Mr. Ruth. He said, "I just want to tell you one thing. I've never seen anybody work hard, practice hard, have the attitude that you have. I know what they're doing to you in spring training [in] regards to making the club, keep it up and you're going to be a great major league baseball player." I was on cloud nine for about six weeks because Babe Ruth telling me that. What a pleasant surprise that was, and I never forgot it.

How do you like people to think of you as a player when they hear about Rowdy Dick Bartell?

Well that was kind of a gag name and there's some people who thought I was a little over violence [sic] and I was, and I got the same thing and everything transpired in the same way. I just gave a hundred percent, and my dad said if you can't give a hundred percent why give it up. I played hard and I played to win, and I wasn't a good loser and didn't want to be a good loser. With what Babe told me and I kept going it worked out. I made a few enemies and we went for tit for tat because I took a beating all the time at shortstop being a cover man, covering for second, tagging players and doing this and that, and it just worked out that way and I played hard to win. I gave not a hundred percent but a hundred and ten, and that's what my dad said when I left to join the club. He says you don't give a hundred percent, you give a hundred and ten percent. I've tried to do that, it was impossible but it worked out pretty good.

◆ ◆ ◆

Joe Black

Joe Black began his career pitching for the Baltimore Elite Giants of the Negro Leagues and was a part of two championships over a seven-year span. He also played in the Cuban Winter League and the Brooklyn minor league system before getting promoted at the age of 28 to the Dodgers in 1952 and rooming with Jackie Robinson. Joe Black established himself as a force coming out of the bullpen, winning 15 games with 15 saves and an ERA of 2.15, and was presented with the NL Rookie of the Year Award. He was a starter in the 1952 Fall Classic and became the first African American pitcher to win a World Series game, beating the Yankees 4 to 2. 1952 would prove to be Black's finest season as he finished his six-year career in the big leagues with a record of 30–12. He later became a board director for the Baseball Assistance Team, or BAT, and consulted with players about their careers and life after baseball.

Years ago the focus was to get more blacks in other positions, not just as position players on the field, but in the front office. Jobs like player personnel and GM's.

Well see, it's not like you just walk down the street and say give me a job. See you know being black doesn't make you a superman. We must be qualified to do some of these jobs. Just because you play baseball doesn't automatically mean that you can run the front office and become president. Now Hank Aaron is there, but you know the assistant general manager of the Boston Red Sox is a black female, Ann Wennington, and we're proud of her because I am on the Board of the Jackie Robinson Foundation and she is one of our scholars. She went through our program and now she is an assistant general manager. The Dodgers have many blacks working in their front office. The Yankees have blacks in their front office. I'm trying, 'cause I travel around the country and I've been to these ball clubs. Baltimore has several blacks. In fact the guy who played football for the Dallas Cowboys is vice president with the Baltimore Orioles, Calvin Hill.

But see, these things are being done quietly. And most ballplayers as soon as they finish on the field, the first thing they do is look for baseball to give them a job. See my thinking is saying, ask yourself what job can you perform? Like when I was a senior vice president of the Greyhound Corporation. You couldn't come to me and say give me a job. I had to ask you what can you do? If you say anything, there isn't any job called anything. See people aren't; it's not the companies or baseball's responsibility and says, okay I'm going to give you a job doing so and so, if they don't know what you can do. And so we have to be honest with ourselves. Like with me, I didn't want to be a coach, I didn't want to be a manager. I'd like to have been a broadcaster, but they didn't, but at that time they weren't ready to have a black guy in a booth, so I walked away from baseball. Baseball had paid me every penny they owed me; they didn't owe me a thing. God gave me a mind for thinking, he gave me a body for working, baseball gave me an identification and I used that to open doors; and that's what I am recommending to a lot of ballplayers. Use your identification to open doors.

I mean you think, like Maddox who played with the Phillies. One of our subsidiaries was going to tie in a business partnership with him because he not only had the money, but he had the intellect to form a company and he had the kind of company that would work with a Greyhound subsidiary. I'd seen Sarge Matthews after he left the Cubs, I was talking to him. He's pursuing different things. See these are some of the things that the ballplayers have to understand, black and white. Baseball doesn't owe them anything. They have to look at themselves and say hey, I want to live a good life and so they have to start using their mind, develop friendships and then say I think I can have a business like this. Because I'm on BAT, the Baseball Assistance Team, where we help indigent ballplayers and now we're beginning to help players who played in the '80s. See they're not like in my day when the highest salary on the Dodgers, Jackie Robinson, $42,000; Ted Williams first made $100,000, he thought the world was coming to an end. I mean these are guys who when they're playing have millions and millions of dollars and it's a terrible thing and it gives baseball a bad name, but baseball has paid the guy every penny on the thing. There isn't any job you take that gives you job preparation for life after you retire, and neither does baseball. Baseball hired you to perform on the field.

And so this year, I've accepted the position as special consultant to the commissioner of baseball. I visited every major league team and it's my job to talk to the players about planning for life after baseball. So I talk to them and I let them know that there are many roadblocks that can hit you. When you leave baseball, your wife may leave you. When you leave baseball, you may not have any money. When you leave baseball, you might like to live like you're living now, but if you don't make plans you can't. You just can't say, well I got ten more years to play and that's when I'll start saving. You can run into a wall, break your leg and your career is over in two years. And the players are beginning to realize now that the future of their life depends upon them, and many of them are beginning to think and make plans, and I'm glad to see that. I'm glad to see it.

The only thing that I see in baseball now that's different, they pay so much money and it seems to have taken away the comradery and the team concept of baseball. You go in locker rooms, players don't seem to have that, that knit of a team sitting around talking about this team we're playing today. They are all concerned about how much money you're making. If I'm making $20 more than you, now you're over there and saying, why does he make more than me, when I've done this and that. And the money seems to be, and it's a terrible thing, that they put money ahead of their personal pride and job performance on the field.

◆ ◆ ◆

Ewell Blackwell

From 1946 through 1951, Cincinnati Reds pitcher Ewell Blackwell, referred to as "The Whip" because of his unique sidearm delivery, was one of the most feared hurlers in baseball. The tall right-hander was named a National League All-Star for six consecutive seasons. His best year was 1947, when he led the NL in strikeouts and posted a record of 22–8. At one point in the season, he set a National League record for right-handed pitchers with 16 consecutive victories. During his victory march, he threw a no-hitter against the Boston Braves, and in his next start against Brooklyn, he lost his second bid for a no-hitter with one out in the ninth inning. This came nine years after Reds pitcher Johnny Vander Meer threw consecutive no-hitters against the same two clubs. Blackwell would later pitch for the New York Yankees and Kansas City Athletics, finishing with a record of 82–78, an ERA of 3.30 and 839 strikeouts.

You were one of the outstanding pitchers of your era. If you had to draw a parallel of pitchers today, has the style of pitching changed or is it pretty much the same?

I haven't seen too many games in the last 30 years, because where I live now there are just no games. But reading the paper, nobody ever finishes the game anymore. And when I was playing you had to finish. There's no bullpen pitchers [who] come on like they have now.

Who was the first to call you "The Whip"?

Oh, they had a contest in Cincinnati and everybody sent a name in, and then they had judges pick it out. I had nothing to do with it.

When you look back on a very illustrious career, are there one or two things that stand out to you?

Well, winning 16 in a row, finishing 23 games one year, start and finish every one of them, pitching a no-hitter, almost a second in a row. I had a lot of fun.

When you won the 16 in a row, in dealing with pressure, you must have had tremendous concentration. What did it take to have a run like that?

No, just regular everyday game, and I was going for the 17th against the Giants. It had to be 3–2 in the ninth inning with two outs and the right fielder, [Willard Marshall], came up; I had two strikes and no balls on him, and the catcher calls a knockdown pitch, we could throw one in those days. Instead of knocking him down, I threw it right down the middle of the plate, and he hit a home run and tied it, then beat me in the tenth inning.

You primarily think of yourself as a Cincinnati Red. Do you follow the team today in the standings?

Oh yeah. Sure, sure do.

Who were some of the hitters of your day that were tough on you and made you bear down?

Oh, Musial leads all the way. I don't know, everybody gave you trouble in those days. You didn't have an easy out.

Where do you reside today?

I live in a little town called Brevard, North Carolina, in the western Carolina Mountains. I retired the last five or six years.

Cincinnati's Ewell "The Whip" Blackwell, 16 wins in a row.

Lou Boudreau

In 1948, Lou Boudreau guided the Cleveland Indians to the World Series Championship as a player-manager and distinguished himself as the league's Most Valuable Player as well, hitting .355 with 18 home runs and 106 RBI. In a one-game playoff for the AL pennant vs. the Boston Red Sox at Fenway Park, the man for all seasons was perfect at the plate, going 4-for-4 with a pair of home runs. The eight-time All-Star won the AL batting title in 1944, when he hit .327. He finished his 15-year playing career with a .295 batting average and led American League shortstops in fielding percentage eight times. He was elected to the National Baseball Hall of Fame in 1970.

This interview was conducted in 1991.

In 1942, you were the youngest American League field manager at 24 years of age, and then in 1948 you led the team to a World Series Championship. How you were able to accomplish that being such a young man, playing and managing?

Well, the good Lord was with me. I had to bear down a little bit more even off the field with my thinking and the stats, looking at the stats and everything, but I had an incentive. If you recall in '47, Bill Veeck tried to trade me, and the fans of Cleveland backed me up and changed Bill Veeck's mind. I owed them a lot and I still owe them a lot, and I tried a little harder and perhaps bore down a little bit more with my ballplayers on the field and off the field. I knew that we were starting to gel. Gordon was having a good year, Lemon was having a good year. My pitching staff of Lemon, Feller and Bearden were doing a great job, [Ed] Klieman in the bullpen and then Satchel Paige joined us late, and the combination of Gordon at second, Keltner at third, Eddie Robinson at first gave us quite an infield. We drove

Lou Boudreau, 1948 player/manager, MVP and World Series champion.

in close to 400 runs. Each man drove in 100 except Robby, and I think he drove in around 90, you can look that up. [Second baseman Joe Gordon had 126 RBI, 3rd baseman Ken Keltner had 119, 1st baseman Eddie Robinson had 83, and Boudreau tallied 106 for a total of 432 RBI by the 1948 World Champions.] My outfield of Mitchell, Doby and Kennedy was great. And it just gelled all in one year, and that's what happened. It happened to the Cubs last year, it's happening to the White Sox this year, and I was hoping, and I still have hopes that it'll happen to the Indians, because there are a lot of games left in this season.

It was a great year for you personally as a player and of course the playoff vs. the Red Sox.
Well that was a dream year, one that everybody dreamed about when he puts on a Major League uniform, to have a year like that. Some of the moves I made, I had angels on my shoulder, and the thought came to me in doing it and I did it. I remember the game in Washington, where Kennedy was sitting on the bench. I took him off the bench, put him in right field in the ninth inning, and he threw out the man who was going to the tie the game, then he drove in the winning run in the 11th. Many games, the game I came off of the bench injured, got the base hit to beat the Yankees in the first game. We went on to give our team momentum; they went on to win the second game. The playoff was just tremendous and it's a memory that I will never forget as long as I live, but not only to my teammates, but also to the fans at Cleveland.

You had a basketball career in Hammond, Indiana, you played in the National Basketball League with John Wooden, one of the game's coaching immortals.
That's right, that was the start of the NBA actually. Pittsburgh was in it, Sheboygan, Oshkosh, the older teams were in the National Basketball League at that time and I played until the Cleveland Indians thought I better give up basketball, and I was more apt to get hurt. I liked basketball. In fact they told me I was a better basketball player than I was a baseball player.

◆ ◆ ◆

Ralph Branca

In 1947, at the age of 21, Brooklyn Dodgers pitcher Ralph Branca won 21 games, and the sky seemed to be the limit for the native of Mount Vernon, New York. Others to have won as many games at that tender age include Babe Ruth, Christy Mathewson, Lefty Gomez and Bob Feller. Four years later on October 3, 1951, the right-hander would be center stage in one of the single most dramatic moments in baseball history. It was the final game of a three-game playoff series between Brooklyn and New York for the National League pennant, with each team holding a victory. The Dodgers looked to be in control as they entered the bottom of the ninth inning holding a 4–1 lead. Dodgers starting pitcher Don Newcombe gave up a run, and the Giants had two men on base when Brooklyn skipper Charlie Dressen summoned Ralph Branca from the bullpen to face Bobby Thomson. Branca quickly got ahead in the count with a called first strike. His second offering, a fastball up and in, was a pitch he wanted to waste, however Bobby Thomson turned on the offering and wasted the baseball, sending a sinking liner into the lower deck in left field. The walk-off home run would become known as "The Shot Heard Round the World."

Ralph Branca pitched in the Major Leagues for a dozen years, primarily with the Brooklyn Dodgers, compiling a record of 88 wins and 68 losses and an ERA of 3.79 with 829 strikeouts.

This interview was conducted in Pittsburgh, Pennsylvania, in 1989.

Ralph Branca, hurler of a fateful pitch in the 1951 playoffs.

What is the mystique about the Brooklyn Dodgers?
I'd say the fans and the ballpark. I mean they were famous before I got there, they were beloved Bums when they were lousy, I mean that lovingly, when they weren't a good ball club. You know in the twenties they were not very good. In the thirties they were not very good. But, you know, starting in '39 they started to be a good ball club and then in '41 they were a good ball club but then the war came along. After the war of course they had a real good team, and you know for a dozen years they were terrific. But I think it was the fans and the ballpark, and it was a synergistic action where you know one plus one didn't equal two, one plus one equals seven with the Dodgers. I think that was the whole mystique about it.

You were an outstanding pitcher but unfortunately there was that one pitch, the one mistake and people kind of get branded. I know it was a tough thing to live with and you must get tired of hearing about it.
Oh yeah, I mean it's 38 years and it's not all the time you know. I've accepted it that I'm going to live with it till the day I die. But I do get tired of it once in awhile, especially when [they] act rude and crude. You know they will come up to me and I'll get introduced to them and they'll say, "Oh Bobby Thomson," and I'll say, "what am I supposed to do now, faint or shrink or what?" Because you know I was a good young pitcher. I'm not saying I was the greatest but I was one of the top pitchers in the league and people forget that. You know I just look at these people and say hey you know it's not very nice you know to bring it up without even saying hello Ralph how are you nice to see you, you had a great career or it's too bad you got hurt. You know just to say Bobby Thomson like I'm supposed to fall over and dead faint.

Well this happens, I mean it happened to Ralph Terry, it happens to a lot of pitchers. I understand you put it on the line out there and it's just unfortunate it happened in a playoff. Bobby seemed to have fairly good success. That year was a big year for him. That wasn't the only home run he hit. Do you think that it did affect you and maybe you weren't as effective the rest of your career?
That's all the writers' BS to be blunt about it. All the writers think they're psychiatrists or psychologists. It never bothered me. The only thing that bothered me [was] that the

next spring I hurt my back and I wasn't able to throw effectively. I pressed to make good and that's how it affected me, because I pressed to make good. But it never affected me psychologically, I mean I knew I was a good pitcher and I lost the game, he was the better man, and that was the end of it. It lasted one hour. And I knew that it was a game that we lost, we lost the pennant, but I didn't lose the pennant, Charlie Dressen lost the pennant, he's the guy who should be blamed. He mismanaged the club and that was the end of it. I mean I look back at it, then I was you know 25 years old. But when I look back at it in retrospect, Charlie Dressen lost the pennant for us because he mismanaged the club the last half of the year. My only regret about the whole incident is that as I said before I hurt my back in spring training of next year and it was never effective after that. I pressed to make good and that's the only effect it had upon me is that I pressed to make good. There were times when I pitched in later years that I should have said hey I can't make it, my arm hurts, my back hurts or whatever. But you know I wanted to make good so badly and I was a competitor, and I pitched when I shouldn't pitch.

I imagine people always think that you're going to lament that one pitch, it was the second pitch to Thomson. I've heard it said that you were trying to waste a pitch and you threw it inside.

That's true. I was really trying to throw a ball up and in and then make him hit a curveball, but I'm not going to second-guess myself. At that point in time that's the pitch I thought I should make, and I made it and he hit a home run. You know you just can't second-guess yourself, you do what you do at the time under the circumstances and what you think is correct. I'm not going to second-guess myself at all.

Do you remember the people that gave you the most encouragement after that particular game.

Well basically, it was my family. I got married two and a half weeks later. My brother John was very supportive, my mother, my brothers and sisters and of course my wife, who I married right after that. As I said I didn't need, I mean they helped me but I looked back, I didn't need it, the only thing I needed was not to get hurt the next year. If I'd have gotten hurt the following year, I would have no regrets at all because it would have proved to people that it had no effect upon me. But you know I got hurt in '52 in spring training and was affected, and if I had stayed healthy I know I would have a good year in 1952 because I was able to throw hard again and I was a good pitcher.

Finally Ralph, how would you like people to remember you outside of that one pitch. How would you like people to remember you as a competitor and as a pitcher?

Well, if you ask me how I'd like people to remember me, it's going to be conjecture on my part. I'd like people to remember that I was a very good young pitcher, that I was unlucky and that unfortunately I had what I consider Hall of Fame talent. I could throw very hard, I got the ball over. I had a good fastball, when I say one of the top fast balls around, I threw it 93, 94 miles an hour. And it was alive. I got the ball over, I got a change-up over, I had a good slider. A curve ball unfortunately which I didn't know how to control, but I had a hellish curve ball except in those days you know we didn't have a pitching coach to help me shorten it and help me get control of it. I'm making this a long answer but I think I would like people to remember me as a guy who had a lot of ability, who was a good young pitcher and unfortunately was unlucky.

Lou Brock

When the Chicago Cubs traded Lou Brock to the Cardinals in 1964 for pitcher Ernie Broglio, many called the deal a steal for Chicago, but the man who would help define base stealing during the 1960s and '70s ended up stealing the show. In 1974, Brock stole a record-setting 118 bases and in 1977 he broke Ty Cobb's all-time stolen base record of 892. Brock led the NL in stolen bases for eight seasons and played in three World Series with the Cardinals. In 1967 against Boston, he hit .414 and scored eight runs along with stealing seven bases as the Redbirds defeated the Red Sox in seven games. Brock finished his 19-year career with 938 stolen bases and a batting average of .293. In 1979, Lou Brock became only the 14th player to reach 3,000 hits in a career (finishing with 3,023), and he hit 149 home runs while driving in 900 runs. His number 20 jersey was retired by the Cardinals in 1979, and in 1985 he was elected to the Hall of Fame on the first ballot.

Lou, over 3,000 hits, but everybody knows you for the stolen base. You were the player that really established it, you and Maury Wills. In 1974, the year of 118 stolen bases still stands. What was that like for you that season, going for the record?

I don't know as much as going for the record inasmuch as the Cardinals had instituted what we know today as the stolen base-driven offensive team, and we started day one with that. Of course at the end of the season we were a half-game out of first place, so we sustained. But it came late in my career; I was 35 years old at the time, and I asked the question, why didn't you do this when I was 23 when you could withstand the beating and the high tension that goes with that.

Yes, that was the thing, it takes a tremendous toll on your body and yet you had a long career. Was it special conditioning that kept you in shape to put up with all that?

Well, I think in a sense it's misleading most of the time. People think a stolen base guy he'll just get beat up, but he really doesn't. I think in a sense it depends on that player's body. I think the fact that Maury Wills got beat up on the bases, not by the wear and tear of running, he got beat up based on big guys hitting on him, pouncing on him. We learned from Maury,

Lou Brock stole the show as baseball's eight-time stolen base leader, and he racked up 3,000 hits.

we went in feet first, slide hard, and get that infielder out of there so he doesn't tag you hard. Maury, on the other hand, everybody was out to get him, he was a little guy, 5'8" tall and weighed 145 pounds, and when you get beat up by the first baseman and second baseman who weighed 220, you're gonna hurt. So some of us who came along a little later were a little larger than Maury. We could withstand that pounding and we had a recourse, and that was a hard slide.

You must be as equally proud of 3,000 hits in your career.
   Well, all I know there's a guy that has gotten 3,000 hits certainly winds up in the Hall of Fame, so I got 3,000 hits and wind up in the Hall of Fame. People seemed to think I could have had credentials to be honored either way as a shot at the Hall of Fame; one with the stolen base area, one was a hit area, and the other one with a performance in the World Series. So I might have been three different type of player and people to this day do not know, they're approaching and saying, you're the guy who stole all the bases; oh here's the guy who got 3,000; oh here's the guy who holds all the records in the World Series. But the fact is they're still the same person, so that's one of those types of things.

You hit .391 in those three Series, in '64, '67 and '68. Was there a particular favorite one of those?
   I think all three in combination. You look at, I think the last two I had 25 hits in those 14 games, established all kinds of hit records, some still stand today, slugging percentages. I think if that was a utopia, the peak of your career, that things happen and happen well, it was in the last two World Series. The first World Series, certainly I left the Cubs in the middle of the season and in the fall I found myself in the World Series. I had a good Series, I batted .300. The Cards beat the Yankees, but 1967, nothing tops that.

◆ ◆ ◆

Gates Brown

   Gates Brown played his entire 13-year Major League career with the Detroit Tigers, where he quickly established himself as one of the game's premier pinch-hitters. In fact, his first hit was a pinch-hit home run. His signature season as a pinch-hitter was 1968, when he came to the plate 49 times, posting a batting average of .450, which helped propel the Tigers to the AL pennant and eventually a World Series Championship in seven games against the St. Louis Cardinals. Brown twice led the American League in pinch hits (1968, 1974), finishing his career with 106, 16 of them home runs. Overall the popular clutch hitter batted .257 with 84 home runs and 322 RBI.
   This interview was conducted in 1992.

What is the psychology you adhere to when pinch-hitting?
   Well, the first thing I'm telling myself is that I've got to be aggressive. And by that I mean if that first ball is in there, I'm prepared to swing at it. I'm not up there to walk. I very seldom went up there looking for a walk. All I want to do is get a good ball out over the plate and try to drive it as hard as I could.

Can you explain the mental aspect?

Well you know, there were a lot of times when you got to have little conversations with yourself, you know what I mean? And what I would do a lot of times is I'd be sitting on the bench and I'd put myself in certain situations, and this way when you're still a little nervous, you're always nervous, but at least I have went over it. I've seen the situation in my mind's eye and I can approach it a little better that way.

Other pinch-hitters you respect?

Well, I'll tell you—I liked Smokey Burgess and I'm gonna tell you why. Because here was a man, well when I seen him in the American League—he couldn't run, he couldn't run that good. And I never seen him, very rarely seldom seen him swing and hit a ground ball with a man on first base. And by this I mean that he always had the ball in the air some kind of way or was hitting a line drive. Now he knew he had to stay away from ground balls because nine out of ten it was gonna be a double play. I can't even remember him hitting a ground ball. And I liked his approach because here was another guy who came up there swingin' and he was a long ball threat.

How about pinch hits that stand out?

Well you know, of course, I always will remember the first time up in the major leagues. I pinch-hit a home run in Boston in 1963 my first time at bat. There is also the 1968 championship season when we were playing Boston, and at the time they were right on our heals. And they came into Detroit to play us a doubleheader. And the score was tied 5–5 in the bottom of the 14th with two outs, and I pinch-hit a home run to win the first game. And, I think those two really stand out. Although there was one pitcher that I faced him in the minor leagues numerous times by the name of Al Worthington. And he had a good slider, good hard slider or running fastball however, but I always knew I had trouble with him. And I faced him in the big leagues one time—it was also in the ninth inning and we were behind a couple of runs, and I pinch-hit a three-hit home run off him. And, I think, going around the bases—out of all the frustration that I've had against him, that was a most enjoyable moment.

Do you think the difficulty of pinch-hitting is appreciated?

I think more people take it for granted for the simple reason you've got to have some guys on the bench—right—and they're going to be pinch-hitters. They might not call it that—they may call it something else—but I know when I was playing—I took my job serious for the simple reason that most of the managers I played for seemed like they would always pinch-hit me in crucial situations. So I very rarely had time to relax when I went to bat. It was always more of those do or die times at bat and you got to approach it positively, and seriously and I took my job serious.

Do you think you suffered from a lack of notoriety?

Well, I don't know, maybe some of us think we [were] unsung but I know in myself that I won a lot of games coming off the bench. It wasn't a job that I wanted, don't get me wrong, I don't think anyone wants to come to the big leagues and be a pinch-hitter, that was just the job I had to do to survive in the big leagues. Because, you know, we had an abundance of good outfielders with Willie Horton and Al Kaline, Mickey Stanley, Jim Northrup and that was one of my primary reasons for surviving. I think that it's a job that you're put in a situation and either you do or you don't. And I look at my record after I got through playing, and I think I ended up with something like 107 or 108 pinch hits out of 400 and some at-bats. I drove in around 75 runs so I didn't waste a lot of hits if you know what I mean. Seems like I was getting almost an RBI for each hit. That's the way I look at the game.

Was it mentally tough to adapt to the role of pinch-hitting.

Well it was mentally tough for the simple reason I was 23 years old when I came up and nobody wants to be a 23-year-old pinch-hitter. I played one good year, that was 1964, my first full year in the big leagues. And then here I am, I'm 25 years old and I'm sitting on the bench, I'm pinch-hitting. There were a lot of times, believe me, I had to fight myself to keep from being angry because you know, I always figured that I could help a team more getting up two, three, four times a game than one time a game. A lot of people talk about pinch-hitting ability, which is true, but if you look at my record I also won a lot of games when they put me in the lineup. And being a ball player, I'm no different from anyone else. You always think you should be playing if you know what I mean.

Do you think being a long ball threat gave you an advantage.

Oh, definitely, because there were times when, number one you look at the situation, I mean sometimes I gotta try to get on but more than likely if the game was on the line I know that one swing and the ballgame is over, and not only the opposition knew that so they had to also be careful. And another thing I also had going for me was that I could run pretty good and I didn't hit into a lot of double plays. So that was two pluses in my favor being a pinch-hitter. I could hit the ball out of the ball park, I mean I could also get you an extra-base hit plus I could stay out of the double play.

When your name comes up, many remember hearing the story about you stuffing hot dogs in your shirt.

Well, I must admit that is a true story. It was one of those games where you know, they very rarely hit me in the middle innings—most times I'd hit in the eighth or ninth inning. But this particular day it was around the fifth or sixth inning and all of a sudden the manager, Mayo Smith at the time, looked down at the end of the bench. I was sitting there and he called for me to pinch-hit. And, I had a couple of hot dogs, didn't want to throw them away, I didn't want to leave them for Cash and Horton and those guys to eat them, so I put 'em in my jersey—grabbed a couple of bats and went up. And I think of all the times when I wanted to make an out, I hit one up the alley and I did—I hit a double, slid into second, and there was mustard and ketchup all over my uniform and I drove in the run. But Mayo was furious, he fined me $100 and my hotdog was all smashed to heck.

What about the difficulty in pinch-hitters stringing consistent seasons together?

Well I think that goes back to—you know, the old saying is "you're only as good as your last hit." Now if you can get off the season with a good record. Well, let's take '68 for a second, for instance, the second game of the season I pinch-hit a home run against Boston to beat them. And that really lifted me and it seemed to carry on the whole season. Now I can also remember one year, I think it was '65 or '66—I went about 0-for-15 pinch-hitting. I mean, you know, I didn't get my first hit until June. So it was a rough period for me and for the simple reason that you know the manager's gonna keep putting you up in a lot of tough situations. A lot of times your stroke isn't together. I know, I could tell when my hands were quick, my bat coming through the strike zone, and my mind was mentally sharp. Now this is beautiful whether you get a hit or not, you feel good mentally. I think one of the roughest times is when you know you're not swinging good, your coordination isn't together, you're struggling—and the manager doesn't have enough sense to put you in a ball game where you can get up two or three times where maybe you could work it out and get your swing back together. But instead they keep putting you up there and you just got one swing to try to work yourself back into a nice groove.

The great Detroit Tigers team of 1968, you must have great memories of winning the World Series.

Well, it was one of those, you know, you always pull for your teammates. You want them to do good, you also want to play but you don't want anyone to get hurt, right? I think '68, I felt very comfortable that year, because I really felt that I contributed to the team winning. And I know I came up off the bench quite a few games and kept a lot of rallies going with my pinch-hitting ability. And that being a championship season, I think, was the greatest feeling of all because I really thought that I was helping the team.

Is your birth name William James Brown?

My real name is William James. My mother called me Gates as a little kid—I had a lot of nicknames—Gates, Bill, William, Jimmy, but Gates stuck for some kind of reason. I feel pretty good about the name because number one there are not too many people named Gates. It is a unique name and I consider myself a unique person. So I think it goes together.

Why did she call you that? Did she ever tell you?

Well, maybe she said I was real bow-legged as a kid. So, you know, I guess it carried over from there. I really couldn't tell you, all I know is that that name stuck with me more than all of the other names I had.

How would you like to be remembered?

Well I'll tell you what. I didn't play as much as I would have liked to, but I did come to play. I would like for them to think of me as a man when the game was on the line, sometimes that was when I was at my best. And I don't think I could have did anything different other than wish I could have played a little more. But a lot of people say, well Gates don't want to play, he's satisfied sitting on the bench. That is one of the most untruths that I could ever think of because I wanted to play. I knew that I could play the game, I wanted to show people that I could, I guess the only way I did show them was mostly by pinch-hitting because when they say Gates Brown, that's what they think of. But I would also like to think I was a pretty decent ball player.

◆ ◆ ◆

Lew Burdette

Lew Burdette finished his 18-year career with a record of 203–144, an ERA of 3.66 and 1,074 strikeouts, primarily with the Boston and Milwaukee Braves. The right-hander, who twice won 20 games in a season, was named MVP of the 1957 World Series against the New York Yankees, which the Braves won to give Milwaukee its only championship while playing in the Midwest city. Burdette won three games in the Series, with two of them being shutouts. On May 26, 1959, Lew Burdette was the winning pitcher when

Pittsburgh's Harvey Haddix pitched a 12-inning perfect game only to lose in the 13th inning. Burdette stayed around and pitched 13 innings of shutout baseball for the victory.

We're talking about 1957 and 1958, the great teams from Milwaukee, and you were a member of one of the great pitching staffs, you and Buhl and Spahn; and you mentioned that you couldn't find a fourth starter that year?

That's right. We had Spahn and Buhl and myself and, well for the all the years we were in Milwaukee we never had the fourth starter, never did have a regular one. We had Joey Jay and Carlton Willey and quite a few guys that came and went. But we never did have the fourth, but that worked out pretty nice in case we had a rainy day, we didn't get put back in.

When you're on the great ball clubs that you played with, what stands out in your mind, what do you think about when you think about those clubs that you were with that won a National League pennant and then a World Series.

Well we had a very good ball club, good defensive ball club, and a very good offensive ball club. We scored a lot of runs most of the time. Sometime we'd get shut out, but good pitching stopped good hitting most of the time. But we did have a very good ball club and we were a very close-knit club and very loose. We had a good time together and enjoyed being together and we did; it's the best team I have ever been [on] as far as the morale, I think.

Select company. From left: Warren Spahn, Lew Burdette, Bobby Thomson, Mickey Owen.

You were known, you always seemed to come up big in the big games. Is there a reason for that, that you, you as a pressure pitcher, you seemed to win a lot of big games in your career?

Well, I think most of the time it was just my turn to pitch; except in the final game of the '57 series, I pitched with two days' rest, but the reason for that was Spahn came up with the Asiatic flu in New York … I'd been carrying that little vial of flu around with me for a long time and I finally got a chance to use it; that's what I tell Warren anyway.

You were roommates with Warren for years.

Yes, we'd been together about 13 years and the closest friend I've ever had, and we both liked the same things. Today is your day to order food when we were on the road; and today is your day and tomorrow is my day. We just alternated every other day.

If you had to pick out a few of the high spots, obviously the World Series, was there a game during your career that stood out that you can relate?

Well, I pitched a no-hitter against the Phillies, only faced 27 men. I hit Tony Gonzalez and then we got a double play after he got on first base, but that was [it]; and it's nice to pitch a no-hitter. I pitched a lot better ballgames, I thought, but you have to have a lot of luck involved with it. They had to hit a ball at somebody where they can catch it. Well, the no-hitter and the, I think, I got a big, I felt sorry for Harvey, but I was the one that won the greatest game that was ever pitched, but Harvey pitched it with 12 perfect innings. I really felt sorry for him not getting the win, but I went out there after the win and I got one, so I was happy about it, but I did feel sorry for Harvey. I had a lot of good things happen to me, I led the league in earned run average and of course back then you get to talk a half-hour longer and get the same money, it didn't mean anything, but it's an honor to have the lowest earned run average in the league and the least number of home runs a couple years, and I also tied Robin Roberts one year with about 37. I've had it both ways.

Looking back on your career, the great numbers you put up in the games that you pitched, why do you think there was a lack of notoriety for a winning pitcher of your stature?

I don't know. I guess I didn't get along with the press too well. I didn't mean to be the way I was, but I didn't like to blow my own horn. You know after a ballgame I didn't back up in my locker and go over the whole ballgame and tell them how I got everybody out and all because I would just play right there. Del Crandall, my catcher, I never shook him off, would pitch the whole game, so talk to him, but I just really didn't like to talk about a game that was over.

How would you like to be thought of and remembered as a professional pitcher?

Well, I don't know, I can't answer that. I would like to just be regarded as a peer of the best, because I think my record proves that I was just as good as a lot of them.

❖ ❖ ❖

Rod Carew

Rod Carew won the American League batting title seven times during his 19-year career on the diamond. As a member of the Minnesota Twins and California Angels, he was chosen for 18 All-Star teams and was the recipient of the league's Most Valuable Player Award in 1977 as a member of the Twins, when he batted .388 and drove in 100 runs. During his final season in 1985, he became just the 16th player to reach 3,000 hits, finishing with 3,053. The native of Panama was inducted into the Hispanic Heritage Baseball Museum in 2010. At the time of his election to the Baseball Hall of Fame in 1991, he became just the 22nd player to gain entrance in his first year of eligibility. His number 29 has been retired by both the Twins and the Angels.

When people mention Rod Carew, or hear the name, they think of hitting. I know you were proficient in all areas of the game, but the ability for you as a hitter was just extraordinary, and I know you are a man who had many stances depending on the pitcher. Did you always do that from the beginning?

No, you know when I was a young player playing on the sandlots in New York, I was more of a power hitter. I used to hit the ball quite a ways, and when I got into pro ball I started experimenting, doing different things as far as my hitting goes. Just trying to get comfortable in different positions. You know because I think you want to learn to study pitchers and see how pitchers are going to pitch you so that, and if I worked on a different stance it was for a particular reason guys get me out one way, I just felt that I needed to adjust and that at-bat, I could just go ahead and do it and be comfortable and not worry about where my hands are or where my feet are or anything like that.

Is there a philosophy that you can describe as the Rod Carew style of hitting?

I don't think there's any particular Rod Carew style. I think what I tried basically to do was just stay focused at all times when I was at the plate. You know I used the whole field to hit because I felt that that way, I could get base hits up the middle, left field, left field line, right field or right field line. I tried to basically center myself, hit the ball up the middle and then just let the whole field open up to me instead of trying to pull the ball in one small area, because you do that and sometimes you find yourself getting in the slumps, and now you have to battle your way out of those things.

Nineteen seventy-seven was the year that you were looking for the "magic" .400 mark. You ended up at .388, and with just a few hits here or there you could have been there. It's still an extraordinary run at .400. Was that year the high point in your career?

No, I think the high point for me was you know after my rookie year I had a pretty good year, and then my second year I started to try and do too much at the plate and I think I ended up hitting about .273 my second year. So when I went into spring training in 1969, I decided that I was going to stay within myself. You know, I learned about myself and what I could do as far as hitting goes, so I just stayed within myself and I ended up leading the league that year, so I think that was really the turning point. As far as 1977, it just seems that everything that I hit found a hole. You know sometimes I would see players moving and you know I'd hit the ball close to where the spot that they were standing, and the ball happened to go through. So that year was just an uncanny year for me.

The seven batting titles. When I spoke with Tony Gwynn, I mentioned to him about winning one, then two, you win three, you win four, and asked what it meant to him, and he told me not really that much after he won a few. How was it with you?

Well, I think every title I won was important because I think it shows that, you know, you've maintained a consistency over the years as far as your offensive play goes. You know, you're winning titles and not helping the ball club is a different thing. But you're winning battle titles and you're getting key hits in certain situations and we're getting base hits to keep rallies going or to start rallies, then it is important, but I think it shows the consistency of a person when they can go out there and hit .340 or .350 every year.

Another place you were outstanding was on the bases. People remember your seven steals of home one season. You see that very seldom any more. Is that a lost art, I mean the art of stealing home?

Eye on the prize. Rod Carew was the AL's batting champion seven times.

Well it's not so much a lost art, it's just that when guys that can run get on third base, pitchers are not going in for the full wind-up any more. They're going to go into the stretch and try and keep the guy close, and it's real hard to try and steal home plate if the pitcher is holding you on, because you can't get a good walk and lead in and there's no way that you can take off at the opportune time. If the pitcher goes through the wind-up, you can usually time his wind-up and I think it's one of the easiest bases to steal.

On defense, over 1,000 games at second and a 1,000 at first base, not many people played that many games at two different positions. Was that a tough adjustment because, I mean second base is probably more physically draining on you and you were younger.

Well, I think the reason the move was made, you know I had my knee torn up in 1970, I started off after a good year swinging the bat, then I got my knee torn up, and you know I had a couple more close calls. Then in 1975, the Twins decided they did not want me to take a chance and get hurt, so they moved me over to first base. It was an easy transition because you know it was still on the infield, so I was able to go to first base and learn about playing the position, I think the last two weeks of the '75 season, and ended up playing over there regularly until I retired.

With all of the great accomplishments you had on the field, is there any way that you would like to be remembered as a ballplayer?

Well, I think as a complete ballplayer I used to do a lot of things to help the team. I felt that I was a team player, I wasn't an individual when I went out there, you know, I used to move runners over, I used to bunt the ball, I used to hit and run, I used to steal bases and I played defense. I didn't want, I don't want to be remembered as a one-dimensional player. You know when people talk about me they always talk about batting titles, but I felt like that I did a lot more on the field to merit, you know, more recognition than just swinging the bat.

Gary Carter

Gary Carter was an 11-time All-Star catcher who broke in with the Montreal Expos and played for them his first 11 seasons, establishing himself as one of the best backstops in baseball. At one point, he earned three consecutive Gold Gloves (1980–1982) and was twice named the MVP in the All-Star Game. Carter was a major force in the New York Mets' 1986 run to the World Series championship. The player known as "Kid" caught 2,056 games and finished his 19 years in the big leagues with 324 home runs (298 as a catcher), and drove in 1,225 runs with a batting average of 262. His number 8 jersey was retired by the Expos, and he is a member of the New York Mets Hall of Fame. He was elected to the Baseball Hall of Fame in 2003.

This interview was conducted in Pittsburgh, Pennsylvania, 1993.

We're here to talk about your new book, The Gamer. *It's only been a year since you've been retired, but it's a recap of your life.*

Well basically the game plan on this book was that it was going to come out before the '92 season, and the publication was going to be from Thomas Nelson. Well, I said to them that I don't think it's really ready to come out on the bookshelves, because I feel like I have something else left to do before the remainder or the last chapter can be written. So because of that and the way that the book was being written, I guess they proclaimed it more as an autobiography and really kind of recapping the last few years more so than my whole career; but the opportunity was there to express my feeling about what had transpired the last few games, to give an insight to the fans and those kinds of things, and so then it turned out to be Word publishers that took over and we were not on as rushed of a time schedule, and I says well how about if we get it out there by the beginning of the '93 season, and that's the way that turned out. So this was really a two-year plan and it just ironically and coincidentally happened to land on the same time of the year that I retired, or the year before, and I just figured that you know it was a good opportunity for me to express some of the feelings that I've had to describe to the fans what it's like, you know, inside the game a little bit more than really just going with the glitz and glamour that everybody thinks that baseball is all made out to be.

Montreal's "Le Magnifique," Gary Carter, 11-time All-Star.

You've excelled behind the plate in probably the most demanding position and you've also played with many injuries throughout your career with over 2,000 games caught. What held you together?

Well, what held me together was my faith in Jesus Christ, number one; and then really I was blessed with a body that was capable of taking a lot of punishment. And I guess in that regard I look back and I say okay, well I used to play the game with a lot of aches and pains and that's how I got the tag as being known as "the gamer," and that's why they wanted to use the title as that. But primarily what it boiled down to was that you know I had six knee surgeries, two broken thumbs that required surgery, I had two torn ligaments in my ankles and did not have surgery on those. I had three broken ribs, I had over 30 cortisone shots, I had a number of other things, but my body seemed to have a way of holding up, primarily because of my love for the game and I guess if you were to make that analogy that's really what it boiled down to, that I would go out and play the game at all costs.

How did you get the nickname, "The Kid"?

That was really, just from my overzealous enthusiasm that happened when I first came to my first big league spring training camp in 1973 and some of the veterans, Ken Singleton, Mike Torrez, Mike Jorgensen, guys like that, saw the way I was. I mean I was just an over-enthusiastic guy that wanted to win every race and wanted to do everything first and all this and that, and you know, like when you go into the batting cage you say, just one more, one more; and they just says, look at this kid, I mean you know he's 18 years old and he's acting like he's 12, you know, I mean because he loves the game so much. So the nickname stayed with me and everybody after a while just called me "kid," and I mean I don't ever remember very often being called Gary or Carter or anything, they always called me "kid" so it just stuck.

People remember you as the greatest player in the history of the Expos, but when you got to New York you were finally on a team that won it all in '86.

My years in Montreal were wonderful and I will always have fond memories of my 11 years that I spent in Montreal, especially finishing off in '92 with the team I started with. Then to go to New York, there was a golden opportunity to finally be a part of a team that had a chance to win a world championship. I thought we had opportunities to win games or win World Series or league championships or whatever back when I was with the Expos, but it just never happened. So finally when I was traded to the Mets in 1985, our first year we came close, but then in 1986 we blew the whole division away. We won by 20½ games and then fortunately went on and won the World Series; but that wasn't an easy task either, trying to get by the Houston Astros and then ultimately getting by the Boston Red Sox and being down in Game 6 as we were and the deal was we were down 5–3 with two outs, and I was the batter, and you know fortunately I was a part of something that turned out to be really good. So there's a lot of great memories of that. There are great memories of my 18-year career, and I'm happy now to be a part of the Marlins' broadcasting and I get a chance to live at home and spend more time with the family.

◆ ◆ ◆

Rico Carty

Rico Carty was well-traveled during his career, playing for seven organizations, but he had his finest year in 1970 when he won the National League batting title as a member of the Atlanta Braves, batting .366. It was the highest average in the big leagues since Ted Williams' .388 in 1957. Carty was a product of Consuelo, a municipality in the San Pedro de Macoris area in the Dominican Republic. Although Carty was a converted catcher who played first and third base and outfield, San Pedro de Macoris is known as "The Cradle of Shortstops." Seventy-six players who appeared in the Major Leagues are reported to have been born there. Carty finished his 15-year Major League career with a batting average of .299, 204 home runs and 890 RBI. In 1996, he was inducted into the Caribbean Baseball Hall of Fame.

This interview was conducted in 1989.

Your hometown is San Pedro de Macoris in the Dominican Republic. Were you one of the first players to break into the Major Leagues from there?

Let me see. Manny Jimenez was the first one, him and Amado Samuel; but I became the first one who went on and had real success in the big leagues, I'd say I was the first one to do that.

In this country, we hear of that city and so many players come out of there. How do you explain that?

Well, I'll tell you what happened in our home, see jobs are very scarce and everybody is trying to get into baseball to have a better life. And once we saw Marichal, Felipe, and Mota and Matty Alou, well you know we find out that if we can be successful at being a baseball player, you know we have a chance to help our family better and have a better life I believe; and I think that's why too many ballplayers, even you have to be born with that and I guess God had blessed the talent of San Pedro de Marcoris with that talent, that given talent. That's all I can say about it.

While you were growing up, who inspired you? Were there leagues that you played in with players that we may not be familiar with that inspired you?

Yeah, I had lots of ballplayers. There are lots of ballplayers, really that inspired me of playing. For instance, my oldest brother, he was playing but you know he wasn't that good. He was a good hitter, but he wasn't a good outfielder. And I started out the same way. I was a good hitter, not a good fielder. It was late in my career that I started, you know, I started out as a catcher and ended up as an outfielder. I'd say mostly of the fellows that I saw play down there, they didn't have the chance to come into the big leagues, which today they would have been in the big leagues, and I was one of the lucky ones to come at the right time and get a chance to be in the big leagues and take advantage of it. It was, like you know I had become one of the two best two-strike hitters in baseball and I have to give credit to Dixie Walker, he work with me and he fight me and he argue with me and I just, I just used to tell him I can't do it. I said I can't do that. Ain't no way I gonna do that, and he said, "Rico I'm gonna make you a .300 hitter and I'm gonna take away some power from you." And that really did it because you know I was a heavy runner, hit and run and still I hit all my life over .300, and I'm very grateful to Dixie Walker that he really, you know, put it into my brains and I stuck with it and became what I became as a great hitter.

You played with a number of teams. You came up with the Milwaukee Braves, and to Atlanta, and of course Cleveland and a number of other teams. Which organization do you feel the closest to, would it be the Braves?

I say the Braves, I'll say the Braves, yeah. I played there for a longer time and my best years was with the Braves. I had to be grateful to one man, that is Phil Schaefer, when he brought me back from Mexico, the Mexican League and into the big leagues and I told him, I told him one day I say if you do you're not going to regret it and I really, you know, keep up with my word and I hit three consecutive years over .300. The following year they trade me, I ended up hitting .288 or .282, something like that. And I'm very satisfied, you know, the job I did in the big leagues. I'm very grateful to baseball and up to today, you see right now we're doing this old timers game and you know it's great to be with your ex-teammates and even the legs are not there you know is not dead, but you enjoy still being on the field, just like a fever, you can't keep away from the field and I'm very glad to be here.

"The Big Mon," Rico Carty, won the NL batting crown in 1970.

What would you look back on as the greatest accomplishment, the thing you're most proud of in your career? I know you led the league in hitting with .366. That year was just unbelievable.

Yeah that year was unbelievable in 1970, when I hit .366. It was something really though, when I look back today you know and I see all these hitters and I say gee I had to be a great hitter to hit .366 because I was not a fast runner, and to get an infield hit it wasn't that easy. In that year, I could remember Ted Williams said that the only man that he thinks that had the chance of hitting .400 was Rico Carty. And you know he says he's not a fast runner, the man just can hit. And I almost keep up with the word that he said really, but they took away that year from me more than 20 base hits. The ball was hit in the hole over second base and they were just giving me errors; and if I would have just had a little bit of speed, I would have hit .400 that year.

Finally Rico, the nickname "The Big Man"; where did this come from, who gave that to you?

That name game from Atlanta; but in Atlanta they used to call me the "Big Boy." When I came over here [Cleveland], John Lowenstein and Dennis Eckersley and Rick Manning say, "hey you the Big Man" and they changed everything around. It's, you know, just a nickname because of people used to call me smiley too, because I smile if I strike out, I smile if I made an error, you know, and it was something that you know just to keep my mind relaxed. I used to do these things, like I can remember my first year in the big leagues, first and second year, the umpire threw me out of the ballgame because I smiled when he struck me out. He threw me out of the ballfield. He told me you a rook, you can't be laughing up there at nobody. You know, really, you know. You don't see that in baseball and I was thrown out lots of time because I just would look at the umpire and smile. I had, you know I had no confidence in myself in two strikes and I used to wait until the last moment to make contact, and if I don't swing at that pitch to me, I wouldn't say that 100 percent of the time I was right, but I would say 95 percent of the time I was right, and I just would smile at the umpire or laugh at the umpire, and he threw me out of the ballgame just because of that.

The last thing. Everyone was always wondering how old you were. Did you ever really, did you ever tell your real age when you played?
No, I never did, I never did. I don't think no ballplayer ever told their real age. At the time I was always taking off three years off my age, but I'm 49 years old right now. And lots of people say I don't look it, but I'm 49.

• • •

Chris Chambliss

While playing for the New York Yankees, Chris Chambliss hit a dramatic, game-winning, walk-off home run off Kansas City pitcher Mark Littell in the fifth and deciding game of the 1976 American League Championship Series. Because of an overflowing crowd of Yankee Stadium fans swarming the field, Chambliss later had to be escorted back onto the field to touch the area where a stolen home plate had been. This action precipitated MLB to change the long-standing rule of touching a base and left the decision up to the umpires' discretion if a player was prevented from doing so. It is now known as the "Chris Chambliss Rule." Chambliss played with Cleveland and New York in the AL and Atlanta in the NL, hitting .279 for his career with 185 home runs and driving in 972 runs.

Chris, a very solid major league career beginning with Cleveland, and you had memorable seasons with the Yankees and finished your career with Atlanta; but everyone of course remembers you for the dramatic home run that you hit in 1976 in the League Championship Series. Do you ever think about it or look at it any differently as time goes by?
Not really, it's something that I'm proud of. You know I've played on some real good Yankees ball clubs and I was just happy to be a part of such a, you know, great team. For three years in a row we appeared in a World Series, and two of those years we were world champions. So you know to be part of the best team in baseball for a few years was, you know, that was a thrill. That home run was just something that really puts a highlight on it for me because that was the first year that we got into the World Series and it was just an exciting time.

It was Mark Littell, a fastball, were you looking for that?
Yeah, you know Mark Littell threw a lot of fastballs, he had some good fastballs. He threw hard and a hard slider, so there wasn't too much, he wasn't very tricky so it was, it was just pretty much a power pitcher. He's always been that way, and I just happened to get a hold of one and lucky enough that it went out for us.

I know you had trouble touching second base. You touched home plate later on, the team brought you out to make it official?
Well, you know in talking to the umpires afterwards, you know a few years after, it

was official when it happened because when fans go on the field like that that's just a circumstance that nobody can do anything about. They wouldn't have brought back any technicality about me touching the bases.

What about something you were very successful at in 1986 for Atlanta as a pinch-hitter. This is something that's an unappreciated art, I think you had 20 pinch hits that year. Is there a certain mental setup that you have to develop? Usually an older player accepts the role.

Yeah, there's a lot of truth to that and you just gotta understand what you're asked to do. It's hard because you know everybody wants to play and there are a lot of people in baseball that have to sit at the bench and only eight guys can play at a time, so there's a lot of guys who don't play. You know to do well off the bench you have to work hard and keep your skills going. You gotta run and stay in shape. So that's what I did. I took a lot of hitting and hit in the tunnel during the game and stuff, I just got as many swings as I could.

Chris, you were a very successful manager in the Braves' system; now it's unfortunate just the other day there was an opening in New York. Your aspirations are to become a manager in the major leagues; are you patiently waiting for an opportunity?

I think someday I will get an opportunity to manage. I have managed in the minors and I was successful down there. I was real happy with what I did and how I related to the players, so right now I'm coaching here with Joe Torre's group, and you know I'm going to be loyal to Joe Torre. It's just really been a good situation for me to be the hitting coach over here, and I'm learning a lot as we go along. So I'm really concentrating on the hitting part of the game right now and the managing thing, I'll just let that take care of itself.

Do you have any feelings on minorities moving into responsible positions? You know every year there seems to be an outcry and then it seems to get lost. Do you have any feelings on that?

Well, you know obviously there have been a shortage of black people in those kinds of positions, but things are changing a little bit. The managing situation has changed quite a bit. There have been some real good black and minority managers out there and we are real proud of those guys. Right now I just think that if anybody can point to anything is that people just want a chance that are qualified; and if they are qualified, they ought to be able to get a chance to do the job.

◆ ◆ ◆

Ed Charles

Ed "The Glider" Charles broke in as a member of the Kansas City Athletics in 1962, hitting .288 with 17 home runs and 20 stolen bases. He followed up an outstanding rookie season by hitting .267 with 15 home runs and 79 RBI; however, four years later he was traded to the National League, where he would wait for his moment in the sun with the

Miracle Mets of 1969. Charles, who was the oldest man on the team at age 36, was at third base in four of the five World Series games against the heavily favored Baltimore Orioles. The solid-fielding Charles, who was a steadying influence on many of the younger players, scored the winning run in Game 2 to even the series. Charles posted a career batting average of .263 over eight seasons with 86 home runs and 421 RBI.

This interview was conducted in 1989.

Hey Ed, you were a very prominent member of that championship club in '69 with the Mets and of course this is the 20th anniversary. Was there a turning point during the year that made you as a team believe that you could actually win?

You know, Ronny, that question has been asked a lot, numerous times, and I always give this answer to that question. I think somewhere around July, around the 1st of July I recall, we were playing a series in Chicago and prior to this series, about a week prior to this series, the Cubs had played us at Shea Stadium in New York and we beat them two out of three there in New York. I remember Ron Santo, the third baseman for the Cubs, saying in effect that, wait till we get you guys back out in Chicago. And Ronny had a way of clicking his heels, what we call like showboatin', putting us down, you know, every time the Cubs would beat us, he would jump up in the air and click his heels. So that's sort of teed the guys off and really we didn't take to that too well. So he made a statement, we get you guys out in Chicago, we're gonna get you, we are so and so. But we go out in Chicago about a week later and we beat him the series in Chicago and after that year as I recall, we were on our way to O'Hare Airport, getting ready to leave Chicago I think for Montreal, and there was never in my time with the Mets that I experienced the type of spirit, the jubilation, the enthusiasm, the elation of the team as a whole. It was like, hey Ronny Santo, take this and shove it. You know we just beat them and we were a happy bunch, and to me I could see that whole spirit, chemistry among the players when they began to believe in themselves. We had, say to the effect like Seaver was saying, "hey Glider, you're the poet on the team, let's come up with a poem for the occasion."

"The Glider," Ed Charles, provided stability on Miracle Mets.

And you know I started the east side, the west side, all around the town. When October come around, the Mets will wear the crown and everybody would just breakout and laugh and you know. The spirit, it really caught up in everything and I felt right then as a unit we felt like we could overcome.

You had a tremendous season, You were a veteran player on that Mets team, were you looking to be a stabilizing factor on the ball club?

Well you're right, Ronny, I was. I was exactly the way Hodges wanted me to fit in and I accept that. I mean I could have rebelled because I was coming off a fairly decent year in '68, but I accepted the role because I knew that well this is gonna be my last year. And I tried to help the guys, you know guys like Wayne Garrett, Kenny Boswell, and Harrelson, guys like that, so it didn't bother me because I knew that hey, I'm on the way out, let's try to get whatever I could to stabilize this ball club.

Ed, finally, what are you doing now and where are you located?
I'm in Manhattan and I work for the Department of Juvenile Justice in New York. I'm enjoying myself, trying to redirect some lives of young kids that really have gone astray, stuff like this, so I'm enjoying it very much.

I thank you for talking with me.
Thank you, Ronny.

◆ ◆ ◆

Jerry Coleman

Jerry Coleman was the regular second baseman on the New York Yankees when the team won three consecutive World Championships from 1949–1951. He played on a total of six pennant winners in New York and was a member of four World Series championship teams. While serving as a Marine Corps pilot, he flew 57 combat missions during the Second World War and another 63 during the Korean Conflict. After his nine-year playing career, he went into broadcasting and called games for the New York Yankees, California Angels and San Diego Padres, where he became a legend behind the microphone. In 2005, he was honored with the Ford C. Frick Award at the National Baseball Hall of Fame, and in 2012 The Padres unveiled a statue of his likeness at Petco Park.

A wonderful announcer, tremendous ballplayer for nine years. You played on three straight world championship clubs with the Yankees. Yet the first thing I want to bring up was that you were a Marine Corps pilot in Korea and in World War II. Like Ted Williams, it took a chunk out of your career.
Well, the difference with Williams and myself was I never really made it back the way he did, and I'm not sure that Ted ever came back 100 percent. I know that when I went into the service the second time, I was 28 or 29, and when I got back after not playing for a couple of years, it took a lot out. I didn't realize it at the time, but looking back I know that it did. Williams was always a great hitter, and what he couldn't do defensively with his legs, he made up for it with his bat. I always knew that I needed my legs and all my reflexes to work well all the time, and it simply never came back; but I don't regret it. I mean it was one of those things that happened to you in life, and I wasn't up there setting any home run records or World Series records or any kind of records, so it was something that just developed and it came off just beautifully. I wouldn't give up the five years I spent in the service during that [time].

I think about baseball, it's a great game, but it's a game. Did your combat experience make you look at things differently?

Well the only time that I, I really felt different was in 1953. I just returned from Korea and I joined the Yankee ball club in September. And people were running up and down the bench, frothing at the mouth and trying to win and so on and so forth; and I just left the situation, you know, where you're seeing people die, and it became very unimportant in the who won or lost the game compared to the life situation. That was the only time that I really had it hit me hard, but after an off-season, I came back in 1954 and you know you forget those things. The mind is a wonderful thing; it seemed to block out all of those memories that you don't want to be with.

You played on so many great ball clubs, the three straight championships. What do you remember the most about those clubs? Obviously you had a cast of characters around you who were a who's who.

Well, we started the first part of my Yankee experience in 1948 when I was called up to Newark, and there's Henrich, Keller and DiMaggio, and then it went from there, it went to Rizzuto, to Berra, and to Mize and to Skowron and the great pitching staff of Raschi, Reynolds, Lopat, Ford, Tommy Byrne was in there, Joe Page a couple of years. Mickey Mantle came on later along with McDougald and those kinds of things. I was very fortunate to be in New York at a time when the players were simply outstanding, and when you put yourself in with a group like that they don't notice your shortcomings as much. But actually I was in the big leagues nine years. We won eight American League championships and six world championships, and those are the kinds of things when you look back you say, boy I was lucky to be there when I was there.

The Yankee mystique. I think it was more evident back then when you were a player, or was there one?

Well, it's changed, I must tell you. I think to be a Yankee then it was the goal of every Major League ballplayer. Maybe not some that went to Brooklyn or some that went to St. Louis, they had great records too and great dynasties; but the Yankee dynasty from 1921 through 1964 was an incredible run. And to be a Yankee, you know it wasn't our job, it was our religion. It really literally meant more to be a Yankee and have a bad year then have a great year with the St. Louis Browns and anybody who had ever got on that ball club; I never heard a player in my life say I want to get outta here. Being a Yankee was the ultimate at that time in Major League baseball. It's changed dramatically now because of the ownership and the cast of characters. They're just different people. They don't come out of the box with the fact that this is where I want to be the rest of my life. Players now say, hey if I can have a good year, I want to go someplace else where I can make more money. And money has become a very, very dominant part of the game. Now I'm not saying we wouldn't have been the same way. If we're staring at $5 million, you know we might think differently too. But at that time the one thing that I think is lost in baseball today is that hometown effect, where once you're with a ball club you became part of that club. Williams with the Red Sox, Musial with the Cardinals, Feller with the Indians. Nobody ever wanted to leave. You wanted to establish yourself and be part of that team the rest of your life. And the Yankees of course just dominated that thought.

In 1980, when you were in the booth, you came down and you managed the ball club and then you went back to the booth. That's kind of a unique thing. I don't know how many people have ever done that. What was that like?

Well it helped me two ways. Number 1, it was a mistake in the first place. You should never take anybody out of the booth and bring him onto the field who has been out of uniform for 24 years that I was. The people on the field have no idea who you were. You were born on Mars as far as they're concerned. They don't know who you were, what you did or why. And consequently have this terrible credibility gap to overcome, and I suggested that to the man who hired me and I said I think we're going to have trouble here, and we did have trouble. There were some people who wouldn't accept you no matter what. What it also did for me from a positive standpoint was it brought me up-to-date with today's players. See, I'd lost touch with today's players. I thought they all thought the way I did back in 1940 and 1950. They didn't think the way I did. This was a totally different group of people, and it really helped me because they were different people. I understood them better and it made a much better broadcaster out of me because I understood what they're thinking now compared to what I thought they were thinking then. The worst mistake I made, I said well at least I know this team. You don't know a ball club until you sit on the bench and manage it; then you know the team, or the people on the team. Consequently it was a great thing for me from a broadcast standpoint. It wasn't a wise thing to do. I wouldn't recommend this for anybody.

Well, we do recommend that you stay behind the mike and keep doing what you're doing. You're one of the best in the business and one of the nicest people. I appreciate you spending some time.

Well, you know what we say about the broadcast profession, Jack Buck said don't tell anybody.

• • •

Babe Dahlgren

On May 2, 1939, in Detroit, Ellsworth "Babe" Dahlgren replaced the legendary Lou Gehrig after the Yankees first baseman took himself out of the lineup, thus ending his 14-year consecutive game streak at 2,130. Tragically, the man referred to affectionately as the "Iron Horse" because of his durability would never play again, as he suffered the ravages of amyotrophic lateral sclerosis, a progressive neurodegenerative disease that affects the nerve cells, more commonly known today as Lou Gehrig's Disease. For the record, Dahlgren hit a home run and a double that day as the Yankees defeated Detroit. He would play three seasons with the Yankees and 12 overall for his career, batting .261 with 82 home runs and 569 RBI.

This interview was conducted in 1990.

Babe Dahlgren. You took over for Lou Gehrig.
 I took over back in 1939.

If you can try to recreate that, what was that like, because the man was, an idol and still is, and it must have been difficult for you to step in that role.
 Well, in the first place I was very disappointed when the Red Sox sold me to the Yankees, because in other words when Connie Mack broke up his great Athletics team in 1934 and '35, he made it possible for the Red Sox to buy Jimmie Foxx, who was a home

run slugger, and you know when I had started my first year with the Red Sox in the majors and had received kindly acclaim as being one of the top fielding first baseman defensively in all of baseball over the years, and they farmed me out when they bought Jimmie Foxx. I wrote to Collins, the general manager of the ball club, and told him I wouldn't go out again. So they brought me in at the end of the season and Foxx went to catching the 16 remaining games I believe it was, and I played first and then I think Jimmie felt that he'd rather play first base than catch, so he made that known.

So they sold me to the Yankees, and at the time I lived in San Francisco, where I was born, and they called me, one of the newspapers called me, and said there's a deal going on. Come on down and you can read it off the teletype, and so I hurried downtown to see. When I read that the Yankees had bought me and having Gehrig, who hadn't missed a game, I was, I thought well what the heck, what's my future, you know? The thing was that I sat around a month in 1937 with the Yankees and they sent me over to Newark, feeling I was too young to be sitting the bench.

I had made the All-Star team of the International League in Syracuse in 1936, and in going to Newark they had that wonderful ball club that won by about 26½ games during the season, and I had a .340 year there and made the All-Star team as a third baseman. Then the Yankees brought me in and I just sat on the bench playing very little in 1938. And we just thought that at the time in spring training of 1939, that Lou didn't have a great year in '38, but the newspaper men felt it was age, and they just felt that as we progressed in spring training, got away from the hot Florida weather and started north towards the season, that he would come around. But evidently it looked like he had one good day in Norfolk where he hit two home runs and two doubles, but there was a little band box of a field, but it gave him a good feeling that well he's coming back now and after playing the first week of the season, I think he had four hits in 28 times at bat. He just got the feeling I guess that he wasn't contributing; and we opened in Washington I believe that year and played Washington in Yankee Stadium the following series, and then off to Detroit, and that's where Lou decided to let it be known that he was going to bench himself.

But it was a day for me that I'll never forget when I was told by Art Fletcher, the third base coach that I was going to play. I couldn't believe it. And as he told me and then walked away, he says "good luck, Babe." So I went down on the field and it wasn't a publicized event. There were about 10,000 people at the park, and Lou being the captain took the, at the time of the game, he took the lineup up there to the umpire, Basil, without his name in it for the first time in years and his consecutive games streak of 2,130 games. But I had a good day myself and we had a good ball club, we won 22–2, and I almost had four home runs that day. I hit a home run and it hit the top of the outfield fence and two were caught off the top of the left field fence, it might have even been out; but feeling the left [field] fence was low there, it could have been; I'd a had four home runs, which would have been quite a record in itself for a guy pinching in.

I could image that. Did Lou say anything to you prior to that or even afterward?

Oh yeah, we talked and I had told Lou you know, in other words there was a lot of camera action and little short interviews with Lou and myself and I told him, straighten up and come on, get in that lineup. What are you doing this to me for? Because I had been entirely forgotten, you know, for a few weeks and I said gee you're really putting me on the spot. And he said no, he said; and during the game I went to him and he told

Ellsworth Tenney "Babe" Dahlgren stepped in for Lou Gehrig on May 2, 1939.

me I was doing well and then the seventh inning and eighth inning and ninth inning, each time I went to him he was sitting right on the corner of bench. I said, "Lou you gotta get in there and keep your record going." He said "ah you're doing fine, Babe," and that was it. He just said, and when the ninth inning ended why it was history. The guy had successfully had his own feelings taken care of and he didn't make any, there was no, no sorry I did it or anything about it, he just.

Then we left Detroit and went to Cleveland, and that's when he announced that he was going to the Mayo Brothers Clinic in Minnesota and he left the ball club. Meanwhile we went on in the western tour, the White Sox and St. Louis Browns, and returned; and when we returned to the Yankee Stadium, it was announced that he had been to the Mayo Brothers Clinic in Rochester, Minnesota, and that he was going to rest. One cameraman asked Lou to pose with me down at first base, so we walked down to first base and Lou said, "now what do you want? What do you want us to do?" He said, "well, I'd like Babe to be stretching out for a ball and I would like you to cheering for him and." He said, "wait a minute, I'm not cheering for him," he said, "that's my job, I'm gonna be back there." And I'm stretched out there and holding the pose and I said, "geez I'm rooting for you, Lou." You know for a couple of years now and even as a young man all the while I admired him for records that were going on, and then I thought as I stretched out, I thought well, I guess this is what it takes to be a Lou Gehrig, a great ball player, and forget about what he said about not cheering you, he's a competitor. And so we straightened up and the guy took a picture of me, and Lou went back to the bench and he took a picture of Lou looking out from the dugout with one foot on the stairs, like a manager's position. So he felt at that time that he was going to be back in there.

Well on July 4th they had a day for Lou and they gave him a lot of presents and things; at 37 he was the luckiest man on the face of the earth. But before he got into his message over the public [address] system, I was right on the third base line and the Washington club was on the other side of the field on the first base side, and they had lined up, and McCarthy came off of the bench to get into the picture before the thing commenced and he said to me, he said, "watch Lou, and if it looks like he might fall down, try to grab him, don't let him fall if you can possibly help it." Well, they had been talking getting Greenberg, another first baseman, to take the place and I was just a temporary thing, and Lou would be back. There was just all kinds of rumors buzzing around. Anyhow it started and I looked at Lou and, having been warned by McCarthy about Lou hitting the ground, I had noticed that his rear-end was just vibrating like he was sitting on a vibrator and I thought oh my God, this man is really sick and so I watched real close and ready to hop in if anything happened to him, but he made it, and it was a telltale moment because, I mean right at that moment where they were speculating as to what his future, I knew damn well that that was the end for Lou.

Do you remember the famous photo of, Babe Ruth, the other Babe of the Yankees, Babe Ruth and [Gehrig?]

Yeah, that was on the sidelines, whether they made up, something going on, is that what you're speaking of?

Yes, the famous photograph.

Babe had a nice cream suit on, old Babe, and he had come out to the park and say hello and give his best regards to Lou, and they took a picture of them and they started hugging each other. There had been a little animosity I guess, I don't know what that was all about. There had been some ill feelings and they were taken care of that day, I'd say. That was just before the ceremony started.

I see. I guess to sum it up, Babe, you were an excellent ballplayer in your own right, but the fact that you had to step in for whom [sic] many people consider one of the greatest ballplayers of all time was a difficult thing to do. How do you view Lou Gehrig as a player?

Well, there's no doubt that he was outstanding. You know, when you say all-time, boy there's been a lot of good ballplayers down through the years. But I think in my own personal thoughts in 1935 when I was with the Red Sox and heard so much about Lou and his record and stuff, all in my growing up years. I was the kind of a guy who dove into the stands for everything, had a dirty uniform every day, the clubhouse men would say, you ever stay out of the dirt one day. We have to change your pants every day, they're full of dirt, and you're diving all over and diving into the stands.

So on this particular day the very time I had actually seen Lou, this was in 1935, he got a base hit to right field. I ran around into foul territory to watch him tag first base and then he'd go for two a double; and as he rounded the bag, it had rained that morning and they had pulled the tarp off and evidently there was a pocket of mud there on the first base side, and he hit that and went down. Normally all I had to do was get the ball and tag him. I called for the ball, but the umpire called time, which was, he protected Lou, and which I had never had an umpire do, you know, until he just called time because a runner fell down. But anyhow Lou seemed to be hurting pretty badly, and I'm looking at him and I walked up and see what's happened, and I'm thinking gee I could do this stuff every day, I'm sliding here and sliding there and belly diving and all that stuff. Here the guy has never missed a game and how can he be hurt so bad on that little fall he just had was just like he slid. His feet went out from under him, but just like he slid a normal slide on base; I have never forgotten that because he was groaning and moaning and saying oh my back, oh my back and the trainer, Doc Painter, came out and he finally got up and I forget whether he left the game or not, but the point is that I was impressed that something had happened, and I often think that possibly that disease had started on him in 1935; and in 1938 or '39 he already had this thing going and possibly didn't tell anybody about it, but I think when you see a guy just take a normal fall and not get up and just lay there and moan and groan, I think there was something wrong with him back in 1935.

Babe, I certainly appreciate you sharing those memories.

Well, I had done it so much in the past couple of weeks, but I think of it. There isn't a day that I don't in my memory relive some of those moments; a great bunch of guys that were on the Yankees at that time. It was a great ball club.

◆ ◆ ◆

Alvin Dark

Shortstop Alvin Dark was the National League Rookie of the Year in 1948, playing for the Boston Braves as they won the NL pennant but lost to the Cleveland Indians in the World Series. Traded to the New York Giants, he helped the Polo Grounders defeat the Brooklyn Dodgers in a three-game playoff to win the 1951 pennant and pulled his weight, hitting over .400 in a losing effort in the World Series against the Yankees. He also was a contributing factor in the Giants' sweep of Cleveland in the 1954 Fall Classic. All told, he hit .289 for his 14-year Major League career and collected 2,089 hits while driving in 757 runs. He later managed the San Francisco Giants, winning the pennant in 1962, the Cleveland Indians, Kansas City Athletics and Oakland A's, where he won a World Series in 1974, and finished his managerial career with the San Diego Padres.

When Willie Mays made the great catch on the Vic Wertz drive to center field in the '54 World Series, were you the cutoff man?

Well the shortstop always went out in the Polo Grounds, and so I went out and got the relay. But you know, I've seen Willie make many greater plays than that, oh yeah, but it happened in the World Series, so people look back at that play, but I've seen Willie Mays make better plays than that.

Did you think he would catch up to the ball?

When I saw him hit his glove, when he patted his glove, he always took off running and then right before he got the ball he hit his glove. He had a big glove and so he'd make sure the pocket was open and when I saw him hit his glove, I knew he was gonna get there, and chances are he was gonna catch it. But no one knew for sure. But I knew he was gonna get to the ball.

[In] 1951, where were you when Bobby Thomson hit the "Shot Heard Round the World"?

I had scored. I led off the inning and I hit a single, and I had already scored. Don Mueller hit a ball to right field, I went to third. Whitey Lockman doubled down the left field line, so I had already scored and Lockman was on third, well let's see, Lockman was on second and Hartung had run for Mueller. Mueller slid into third base and hurt himself. So anyhow, I already scored.

When did you guys believe, was there a point in that game where you thought, you know it looked like the game was dead. When did you start thinking, believing that [you] can come back?

You don't play baseball that way, you really don't. I know it sounds good in stories and it sounds good on television and it sounds good in books, but when you're playing a baseball game, we'd worked all year long to get where we was. We had played great, the Dodgers had played great, and now you're playing a two out of three playoff game and you go into it. You play each play one at a time. There isn't anything you can do about what happened to the play before, and that's the way you play the game. And once you start thinking back upon hey, I was pretty good last inning, that doesn't make a bit of difference what's going to happen now. You gotta get out there now. We never thought we were dead, and they knew we didn't think we were dead, and no reason that you should think you're dead as long as the game lasts. That's one great thing about the game of baseball. You know, you hear this only thing about the fat lady getting ready to sing? That fat lady doesn't sing until the last man is out, and that's what counts.

You had great success as a manager in '62 with the Giants, then interestingly enough, several years later you take over the Oakland A's in 1974.

Yeah, Dick Williams resigned. After the '73 season, Dick Williams resigned and I took over the ball club in 1974. A lot of those guys I'd managed before in Kansas City. I know a lot of those fellows. But it was like any other ball club, you're the manager and there are certain things you have to do as a manager to prepare yourself for the ballgame. The players prepare themselves for a ballgame, the manager prepares himself for a ballgame, and the coaches prepare themselves. And it was no different, it was just greater talent than I'd had since the '62 Giants.

They had...
Holtzman, Catfish Hunter, Vida Blue, Rollie Fingers, Lindblad. We had a great bunch of players on that ball club. You know, you got Bando, Campaneris, Green, Tenace, Fosse, Rudi, North, Jackson. I mean that's some great ballplayers.

How did you put your stamp on the team and make the team yours?
Oh no, you don't do that as a manager. You're the manager of that ball club. That's their ball club. It's a players ball club, and I think that too much hype is given to certain managers when they win, and then on the other side of the coin they blame the managers sometimes when actually it isn't the manager's fault. So I think a manager has to be very careful about putting himself in a position where he thinks he's a little bit better than he is.

❖ ❖ ❖

Tommy Davis

While playing with the Los Angeles Dodgers (1959–1966) Tommy Davis won back-to-back batting titles in 1962 and 1963. The three-time All-Star earned his only World Series ring when the Dodgers swept the New York Yankees in the 1963 Fall Classic. Davis would eventually play for nine other teams during his 18-year career in the big leagues (1959–1976). Through the years, the Brooklyn-born Davis established himself as one of the game's most dominant pinch-hitters, compiling a batting average of .307. In 1974, while a member of the Baltimore Orioles, he was presented with the American League's Outstanding Designated Hitter Award. Overall, Tommy Davis collected 2,121 hits and sported a batting average of .294 with 153 home runs and 1,052 RBI.

This interview was conducted in 1991.

You have the highest average for a pinch-hitter with over 150 at bats. You have two batting titles back to back '62, '63—how difficult was it to adjust?
Well, it wasn't that difficult if you're in the game from the start—let's say if you're not playing you almost have to feel that you had been playing. And by the time you get up there, you're not new anymore—you're watching the pitcher—watching how he's throwing. If it's a new pitcher that comes in, you're watching how he's throwing. You size up the situation and just act as if you've been in that situation prior to getting up there already. So by the time you get up there, all the newness is worn out so you just feel like you've been playing all day.

By not playing the whole game—how did you keep your concentration at a peak?
Well, just like I said, you're adapting to all the situations at hand. Every time somebody

else is up, you put yourself in that position and how did he throw him, what does he like to throw, you know, what am I gonna look for when I'm up there—especially, I don't want to be cheated when I get up there. Is he a fastball pitcher—I should get something to hit. You're always thinkin', you're just thinking about all the situations that will come up before it comes up, and by the time it does come up, you've thought about it already and it's easy to adjust to.

You were with ten different teams and played for a variety of managers. How important is the manager in terms of keeping you sharp?

He'll let you know situations and he'll tell you beforehand how he likes to use you. And you can almost know when you're going in. You know, he'll look at you—there is always a little something happens, some sort of trigger, you know, he'll give you a little nod, you know, you got to get ready, keep a bat in your hand, and he likes to see that—all pinch-hitters just keep bats in their hands. You go on in the tunnel, work your legs a little bit, and always keep your legs loose and stretch.

You had 62 pinch hits—any that stand out or won the game etc.?

No—I can't really recall, let's see, a pinch hit that stood out—but there were quite a few the year I played with Oakland. I was sort of a pinch-hitter and I played some games but I had about two or three good games in Oakland that came to be winning games with maybe a sacrifice fly or a base hit, and I remember some good days with the Oakland club.

Do you think regular players have an appreciation of pinch-hitting?

Well, I have to put myself in a different category because when I started playing early in my career—they talked about Smokey Burgess, and they talked about Jerry Lynch, and you more or less, you knew they were on the team we were playing, and you knew even though we were ahead by two or three runs—you knew they were going to be coming up, so you knew the importance of the pinch-hitter in those days, I thought, [more] than they do now. There were some great pinch-hitters then. I don't know if they keep an old timer on the bench like that around anymore. Because, I know, Graig Nettles has had a good year pinch-hitting. You need an old timer, a guy who can come up there and like I said feel like he's been in the game all day and it doesn't bother him. And I don't see enough of an old timer still staying around just to pinch-hit anymore.

Can you compare the DH and pinch-hitting?

Well, no, you can't compare the two. You're gonna get up three or four times. Ah, I thought DHing was great when I first started and I enjoyed it, knowing I was gonna get up three or four times a game and didn't have to go out and exert myself. A lot of old timers felt they were a half a ball player and didn't like it; but I was one of the few who did because I was an average outfielder but I wasn't really known for my glove, but it added three or four years to my career. But I enjoyed that but that's different, you know you're gonna get up and you can more or less redeem yourself if you don't get a hit the first time. But as a pinch hitter you're only gonna get one shot, and that's at any point of the game, and you have to show the manager you can do it. You have to help the club and if you're not doing that, then it's easy for them to say goodbye to you. But you know the importance of a pinch-hitter and you don't get that many times to show off or to redeem yourself. It's more important really to a ball player who is on the bubble that he has to show that he can do it. Where a designated hitter can prove himself every so often because he gets more times at bat.

I've heard you say "Hit to Stay rather than Hit to Play." Would you elaborate, please?

Well, when you're hitting to Stay—you know, you're not loose and you don't have enough security so when you get up there, you know, there are situations where maybe you could go for the long ball and you don't—you just try to get a base hit, you know, I mean, if you know you're gonna be there—you got a two-three-four-year contract—you take more chances. I mean, a man on first and third—you know, I'm gonna go for one and sometimes you get a home run, a three-run home run. Here I would think as much as getting, doing my job, and getting the man in from third and getting a base hit to continue the rally—there's the two differences. But when you're hitting to Play, you have that security and you can go for an extra-base hit or a long ball or maybe the first strike or second strike. But, when you're hitting to Stay, you're just cautious from the first strike on.

Tommy Davis, Dodgers legend, won back-to-back batting titles in 1962 and 1963.

You had 1,999 games played. Did you think about getting that 2,000th game?

Oh, the older I got, you naturally want it when I was out of the game. Never thought about it earlier, but I did as I got older and I was in my mid–40s, same way after seeing Minoso, Minnie Minoso, play and all these decades and McCovey playing all these decades—I thought about having just one more game to get 2,000. But what the heck, you know, I played a lot of exhibition games so I did get 2,000—didn't I?

You hit over .300 six different seasons and finished with a 294 average. You seemed to be a better hitter with men on base. How do you want to be remembered?

Well, when they needed a run, I just want them to know that I was the type of ball player who liked pressure, and when it came under pressure could do the job. You know, I wasn't a long ball hitter but did get the runs in, I mean I knew I wasn't a long ball hitter. I only had about 153 to 155 home runs and I got a little over 2,000 hits in my career. Then I look upon the fact that I got a little over 1,000 RBI in my career. So, it looks like every two hits I got, I was knocking in a run. And, I just felt that I was the type of ball player you could depend upon when there were men on base.

◆ ◆ ◆

Leon Day

Leon Day was generally recognized as one of the premier pitchers in the Negro Leagues. He has often been compared with legendary pitcher Satchel Paige; however, his quiet demeanor and workmanlike attitude prevented many from appreciating his great talent and may explain his long-overdue election to Baseball's Hall of Fame in 1995. During his career in the Negro Leagues, Day at one time or another played every position on the field except for catcher. While on the mound in 1937, he posted a perfect 13–0 record and an ERA of 3.02 for the Newark Eagles, and in 1942 he set a Negro League record by striking out 18 men while pitching a one-hitter. Mr. Day served during World War II and was in Normandy shortly after D-Day at Utah Beach. Because of poor record keeping, it is difficult to chronicle just how many games Leon Day won, but it has been estimated it could have been close to 300.

This interview was conducted in Baltimore, Maryland, in 1993.

You had tremendous physical prowess. You were out there almost every other day. What was that like for you?

Oh I loved it. I mean you know I loved to play. That's why I started. The only reason I started pitching was because I figured it was the easiest way to get to the Negro Leagues, you know as a pitcher. I see some of those guys out there playing second and I feel, I said geez, I can't take those guys' jobs. I can get in easier by pitching because I know all the teams need pitchers. And that's why I started pitching. I really liked second base. I played second base, third base, shortstop, played them all but catcher. I couldn't catch.

Some of the players on the great clubs around here, can you go through a few names for us that you played with or against.

Double Duty, Ted Radcliffe.

What do you remember about Double Duty?

Well he would catch and pitch. Double Duty would pitch one game and catch the next game. Or catch the first game and pitch the second game.

The pay wasn't real good and the traveling was very difficult for you.

Yeah, the accommodations after we got somewhere were real difficult. We couldn't eat, you know, we'd go somewhere and you couldn't get in a restaurant. They'd want you to go around to the back door and eat and all that stuff. So we used to, we used to eat in the grocery store. We'd go to the grocery store and get a quarter pound of bologna and a quarter pound of cheese, a loaf of bread and a bottle of milk and an onion, and go and ride.

Now how many games would you play in a season?

Who knows? You know we didn't play many league games but we played almost every day. If it didn't rain, we played, or unless we had too far to go to get to the next game. That's the only time we had off.

Did you ever pitch against Satchel Paige?

Oh yeah, I beat Satchel a couple of times. Yeah.

What was the pitch you relied on?

My best pitch was a fast ball. That was my strikeout pitch. A fast ball.

You're a great athlete but you aren't a tall man. Where did you get all your power from?

I don't know. I could run, I could throw. You know I don't know. I don't know where I got it from.

Now finally sir, many people are mentioning and believe that you should have already been enshrined in the Hall of Fame. You must be pleased that people feel that way.
Yeah, they said I missed it by one vote, you know, this year and I'm pleased. At least I was, you know, recognized to be there.

We certainly expect to see you there soon and thank you for your time.
Thank you. Thank you very much.

◆ ◆ ◆

Bucky Dent

With one swing of his bat in a 1978, tie-breaking American League Eastern Division game between the Boston Red Sox and the New York Yankees, Bucky Dent put his name in the annals of post-season baseball. He also assured himself of being referred to in a not so kind way in much of New England. Dent hit only 40 long balls in his 12-year career, but history will always remember him for his dramatic three-run homer off Bosox pitcher Mike Torrez that helped the Bronx Bombers defeat their rival, 5–4, and move on to the World Series against the Los Angeles Dodgers, whom they would beat four games to two. Dent, would ride his wave of success by hitting .417 in the Fall Classic and be named the MVP.

October 2, 1978, the historic home run that you hit in the playoffs against Boston. You've certainly had ample time to look back and reflect on that now. Does it mean more to you now than it did at first?
Well, sure it does. You know baseball and sports is a game of moments, and that was my big moment in my career. You know we went to a one-game playoff and I happen to, you know, get a big home run, and you know it's something that now I can reflect back on and say, "geez you know that, that's something very, very special." A lot of people asked me when I hit the home run did I know what was really going to take place, and I said no because everything happened so fast. We just took over the lead and we still had three innings to go, so anything could have happened. But after the game was over, you know after the World Series was over, I looked back and I really realized what happened.

You were using Mickey Rivers' bat?
What had happened was the last day of the season, we only took a couple bats, and I was out of bats, so when we went to Boston I borrowed a couple of Mickey's bats, and I broke one in batting practice, a hairline crack just under the cage. There was only two in the bat rack, so the one that I pulled out when I went up to hit with, I was fortunate that when I fouled a ball off my foot, Mickey came up and said you're using the wrong bat, that one is cracked; he gave me the one that was good, and the next pitch I hit the

ball into the net. A lot of people say now, you know, that they thought the bat was corked, which it wasn't because I started the rumor at the old timer's game a few years back, when baseballs were kind of souped up a little bit and everybody was kind of corking a bat and everything, you know. Mickey and I would joke around. I said, "Mickey, you know we can really blow some people's minds if I said that bat that you gave me was corked," and somebody heard it at that time, but the bat wasn't corked.

You're a guy that likes to get in there and play every day; you played 123 games that season and Bob Lemon would pinch-hit for you in certain situations. I guess it didn't sit well with you, and he didn't have much choice but to let you go up that particular day.

Well, I pulled a hamstring and I had missed 40 games, and usually in situations like that late in the ballgame, if the game was within one run, you know Bob or Billy would pinch-hit for me. But what had happened was Randolph was hurt, Randolph had pulled a hamstring and he wasn't available to play, so Bob had to make a decision on who he was going to pinch-hit for; was he going to pinch-hit for me or was he going to pinch-hit for Doyle? He wound up pinch-hitting for Brian Doyle, the batter before me. Spencer flew out, so I wound up having to bat, and you know I hit the home run. But like you said, you know in situations late in the game in the eighth or ninth inning, Bob would usually pinch-hit for me.

What were you looking for, I guess it was a fast ball?

I was looking for a fastball and he threw a fastball down and in, and that's a ball that I used to hit pretty good. The two times he threw me some fast balls just a little bit up, I just missed them. So when I came up after I fouled the ball off my foot, I was really just looking for something that I could hit hard someplace, because you had guys in scoring position.

Well, you went on to defeat the Dodgers and you were the Babe Ruth Award winner, outstanding player in the series. It would seem that that it could almost be anticlimactic after what you did, yet you went on to have a tremendous series in the Series in the field and at bat.

Well, it wasn't anticlimactic, it was, it was, you know we're playing for the World Series championship. We went from Boston right into Kansas City and nobody picked us to beat Kansas City because Guidry had pitched the playoff game. They felt that with him going in the playoff game, that it would hurt us in the playoffs with Kansas City, but we beat them and we went to play the Dodgers. And I think what happened was everybody had picked us to lose. We came from 14 games back, they picked Kansas City to beat us, and then we went into the World Series. Thurman said, "You know we're the world champions and we're the underdog." And I think it really kind of just sparked the guys. It kind of ticked everybody off to the point that they felt like we really had something to prove, and it seemed like everybody's intensity got a little bit stronger in their desire to win. We lost the first two games in Dodger Stadium, and on the plane flight back we knew we could beat the Dodgers Friday night. We would have a chance to come back and beat them, and Guidry pitched that great game and Nettles made some great plays over at third base. At that time it seems like it just picked our club up and the Series turned around.

Larry Doby

Larry Doby was the first African American to break the color line in the American League when, on July 5, 1947, he took the field for the Cleveland Indians. Almost three months earlier, on April 15, Jackie Robinson had become the first African American to play Major League Baseball in the modern era when he started at first base for the Brooklyn Dodgers. Although Mr. Robinson received the majority of the nation's attention, Mr. Doby was subject to the same indignities as Robinson was in the early stages. Doby, who played with Newark in the Negro Leagues, was a seven-time All-Star who helped lead the Indians to the 1948 World Series title and the AL Pennant in 1954. That same year, he led the American League in home runs and RBI and finished second in the MVP voting. Larry Doby batted .283 for his career with 253 home runs and drove in 970 runs. After his playing days, he became the second African American to manage in the major leagues (Frank Robinson was the first with Cleveland) when he skippered the White Sox in 1978. He was elected to the Hall of Fame in 1998, and in 2015 a statue honoring him was dedicated outside Progressive Field in Cleveland.

This interview was conducted in August 1987.

Larry, you mentioned you're back in baseball. What are you doing today?

I'm back in baseball. I work at the commissioner's office and I work for properties. What we are trying to do is to establish situations where there are some people out there who are not given the, the players who they are using in terms of their names, photographs, and what we are trying to do is get those people licensed so that some of the players' names and pictures and that, they're using that will get some revenue coming.

Of course you were the first black man in the American League to break the color barrier. You know, it seems that Jackie Robinson went through what you went through, or you went through whatever he went through here in the American League, but unfortunately there wasn't as much focus on you.

Well, I think that Mr. Robinson, who was the first to break into baseball, I guess they should focus on him. It doesn't bother me, I was fortunate enough to be involved in a historical event. I think that if you look back at history, you'll see where I was the first in the American League, second in baseball and I'm still a part of American history as far as baseball is concerned. That's all I'm concerned about, my family, my friends and those that if you're black and if you're involved in that type of situation in the early part of baseball, you'll get the same kind of treatment any other black would get.

You didn't play in the minor leagues, but you played in the Negro Leagues. I just wondered, in terms of preparation, obviously they did a heck of a job because you had an outstanding career.

Well, some people say well, you know, you never played minor league ball. I think that the Negro Leagues that I played in was a great brand of baseball. There were players in that league who could play in the major leagues; unfortunately they didn't get the opportunity to. So I couldn't think of any better place to start your baseball and learn the game and learn how to play the game, and of course get you an opportunity to play major league baseball, than the Negro Leagues.

Your feelings on the Hall of Fame. Do you have feelings on that?
No, not really. I just feel that it's very political. It's a personality thing to a certain degree. If you look at my statistics, you'll see statistics in there that are as good as some of those who were in and better than some of those who are in, so I don't concern myself about those kinds of things because I have no control over it; it's out of my hands, and my family, my friends, my closest friends and people in baseball knows what my background is, what my statistics are. I guess that maybe one of these days it will happen. If it doesn't happen, I'm not going to worry about it. I'm at that age now where I can't afford to worry about things like that.

The high point for you would have to be 1948, when this team went all the way?
Well yeah. I think any time you come into baseball your first year and then you're suddenly in the World Series, it can't be anything but good. I think those who have not had the opportunity recognized the fact that if the person who has been involved in baseball gets the opportunity to be in a World Series, it's got to be one of the greatest moments of your life.

When people think of you as a player and as a man, is there a certain way that you would like people to remember you?
I'm just another human being that got an opportunity to play athletics, got an opportunity to play major league baseball and was gifted by God above with the ability to play baseball. That's about it.

Larry Doby broke baseball's color line in the American League on July 5, 1947.

◆ ◆ ◆

Bobby Doerr

The Boston Red Sox have had many great players, and second baseman Bobby Doerr was certainly one of them. Doerr played his entire 14-year career with the Red Sox, and he never played anywhere but at second base. He finished his career posting a lifetime fielding mark of .980. He hit .409 in Boston's loss to the St. Louis Cardinals in the 1946 World Series. He was selected to nine All-Star teams and finished his career with a .288 batting average, 223 home runs and 1,247 RBI. He was elected to the Baseball Hall of

Fame in 1986, and appropriately, his number 1 jersey was retired by the Red Sox in 1988.

Bobby, you were associated with some of the great ball clubs in Red Sox history and you played with some of the great players—Dominic DiMaggio and, of course, you played with the great Ted Williams. If you had to pick a great year for you and that ball club, what would that be?

Well, I suppose stats-wise the 1950 season would have been my best, where I drove in 120 runs and hit 27 home runs. I did hit about .290 that year. '48 was a good year, I drove in over 100 runs, hit 27 home runs that year. Those three years, '48, '49 and '50, were big years. If we just had one more pitcher in there, we got a good chance of winning those pennants. Three of our best pitchers in '46 were all in their prime, got sore arms in '47. If we had Boo Ferriss or Tex Houston or Mickey Harris, or one of those guys in '48, '49, and '50, we had a good chance.

Bobby Doerr, baseball's gentleman player.

The Yankees and the Red Sox went head-to-head. You had such great respect for each other and your teams, but it always seemed that they edged you out.

Well that's right. When we won big in '46, we had those three guys that threw good too and then you had to come and almost rebuild your whole pitching staff. Mel Parnell came in '48, had a good year, and then they got Jack Kramer and Ellis Kinder from the Browns that helped us, but we had to just pretty much rebuild the pitching staff, which hurt us. But when we had the pitching, we won big.

What do you remember about who many consider the greatest hitter of all time, Ted Williams?

Ted was. My feeling is that theoretically if you can take ten of the best pitchers of all time and ten of the greatest hitters of all times and throw the good pitchers against the hitters, Ted would come out I think as the best hitter. He did not miss a percentage of any kind that was going to help him hitting. He was so sharp and so far ahead of everybody he just picked up. I always said that most hitters give probably 75 times at bat away if they go to bat 500 times in the major leagues, and Ted did not give ten away probably. That was the comparison in that way. But he was great. And it helps the ball club when you got a fellow like DiMaggio, you got a fellow like Williams on your club. It takes the pressure off the rest of the ball club and he was great; and he was good in the field. People say, he got the reputation about not being a good fielder, but he was good, he wasn't real great, but he had a good arm and he played the left field fence as good as anybody ever played it. If you know Ted Williams, he is not going to be mediocre in anything he does.

Finally, Dominic DiMaggio. He lost prime years to the war. Do you believe he should be elected to the Hall of Fame?

Dominic? Yes! Boy I played, he came up in '41, '40 I guess. And he could play that outfield as good as anybody. He was a good hitter. He was a tough hitter. Leading off, he didn't get a chance to drive in the runs that they would have been hitting fifth, sixth, in there he would have been driving in 100 runs; good ballplayer.

Appreciate you taking some time.
Well, thank you. I was fortunate I got to play in the era of the game when I did.

◆ ◆ ◆

Don Drysdale

In the 1960s, Don Drysdale and teammate Sandy Koufax were regarded as the most dominant pitching duo in the National League. The 6'6" right-hander was not afraid to back hitters off the plate, and it paid dividends as he compiled a lifetime record of 209–166 with an ERA of 2.95 and 2,486 strikeouts. He also recorded 167 complete games with 49 shutouts. In 1968, Drysdale established Major League records with six consecutive shutouts and 58 2/3 scoreless innings. When he retired in 1969, he was the last player on the Dodgers roster to have played in Brooklyn. Don Drysdale's number 53 was retired in 1984, the same year he was elected to the Baseball Hall of Fame.

Okay Don, here we are today, they're having a tribute to Roberto Clemente. You were a pretty tough competitor on the mound, and you were quite familiar with "The Great One." Clemente would never give in to anybody. What do you remember about him?
Well, I think Bob was really one of the best all-around players that I ever saw. I've said this all through my yesteryear careers and things like that, and my post-season play and things like that. I don't know of many better players, accumulation of players from the '50s and '60s that they ever put together in one class in those two decades, and I think that Bob Clemente, Henry Aaron, Willie Mays, you know, Willie Stargell. You take people like that and you hate to keep starting naming people because you don't want to leave anybody out, because you know you forget about the Mathews and the Spahns and the Musials and the Boyers and the Whites and people like that. So where are you gonna stop? But Roberto was a great player. He could do everything. He could run, he could hit, he could throw, he could hit with power; he was a great outfielder. Hey, you're right, he was a tough out.

A guy that was no easy touch was you on the mound. You had great stuff, but there was also an intimidation factor when batting against "Big D," Don Drysdale.
Well there might have been. I know that I was tall, 6'6"; there was one guy taller than me, Gene Conley over at Milwaukee, and I guess maybe that might be a little bit of an intimidation factor, but I learned I think from a master [a number of sources list Drysdale's height at 6 feet 5 inches]. If there's going to be any intimidation on the mound, it had better come from the pitcher and not the hitter. So when people say, did you ever fear this hitter? No, you never feared a hitter. The thing you knew they were tough outs, as Clemente was or the people that I just mentioned, but you know it's one of those

From left, Number 22, Donn Clendenon, Rollie Fingers, Johnny Mize, Enos Slaughter, Lou Brock, "Twin D" Don Drysdale and Bob Gibson.

things, you knew you were going to be in for a long day's work so you better bring your lunch; you're gonna be there a while.

You were a guy that was not afraid to come inside. I mean that's another thing. You think of Don Drysdale along with winning, but you were a guy that would go inside. We don't see as much of it today, but it was something that was part of your territory.

Well, I learned, as I mentioned, the fella that taught me a lot about that was Sal Maglie, when he came over to the Dodgers in Brooklyn in 1956. It's, hitters hit with balance and pitchers try and pitch in and out, and you try and keep hitters off-balance.

It's kind of a little bit of a ballet out there. If you really wanted to try and dissect it and things like that, you try and keep the hitters off-balance. Once you can try and keep them on their heels or something like that a little bit, at least keep them off-balance, why maybe there's a little bit of an edge swinging on your side. So that's basically all we're trying to do. You try and, most hitters hit in and out. There's not that many hitters that work up and down that well, and most pitchers pitch in and out, so that's just the way that I work.

You are associated with one of the greats, Sandy Koufax; you're both Hall of Famers. How did pitching in the same rotation with him help you, and how did you help him?
    Well, I don't think either of us really worried about that. We knew that we were on the same team and it wasn't just the two of us, the Dodgers always had great starting staffs. As I said many, many times, I said we've always had great relief pitching. Starting back in Brooklyn, when you think of guys like Labine when I first got there, and Roebuck and Bessent and those years in the middle '50s, there were always great relief pitchers. So Sandy was a teammate. We were friends, we were close, and we were in the Army together. People tried to make competition out of the two of us and things like that, but they really never knew us that well. Finally after a while that wore out and they said that well, isn't gonna work because we're barking up the wrong tree. But I was just happy to have him on my side. Every time that he went out there, I have told many people, I said you were, you were capable of seeing a no-hitter. He was that type of pitcher. He was the modern day Nolan Ryan. When they go out there, why you might see that.

You had the 58⅔ scoreless innings. At the time it was 45 years since Walton Johnson set the record. I guess that would be one of the high points of your career when you put that string together.
    Yeah, that would be one. I think team-wise, it certainly comes before the individual type accolades and things like that. I think the first year that I was with the Dodgers in Brooklyn in '56 and we won the National League championship. That was the year that I will always remember. I was in five World Series and we won three of them, and each one of those were great years. Whether you win or lose, we knew that there were other people sitting back watching us; we'd rather won more than we lost, but we won three and lost two while I was there. I was on ten All-Star teams, and it was a lot of fun and I enjoyed every bit of it.

Finally, Don, you were a pitcher that could swing the bat. I think you lead the league four times for pitchers in home runs. Was it something that just came naturally to you, you had great timing?
    Well, I wasn't really a pitcher until my senior year in high school. I played, and I wasn't as tall either. I grew five inches after I got out of school. I was an infielder and I played all around the infield, so the hitting part of it I enjoyed, and I tried to stay with that. That was one good part about being a pitcher and especially today in the National League, you get a chance to hit. That designated hitter I feel, I mean the game is so backwards in that respect I don't even want to get into it, but I feel sorry because that has backlashes all the way down, all the way down to high school ball. I mean you can come to possibly to the major leagues today and never get a chance to swing the bat, and to me that's not right.

Carl Erskine

Carl Erskine remains one of the faces of the beloved Brooklyn Dodgers of the 1950s. The Indiana native spent his entire 12-year career pitching for the team affectionately referred to as "Dem Bums," in good times and bad. Erskine threw a pair of no-hit games, with the first coming in 1952 and the latter in 1956. His outstanding season was 1953, when he compiled a ledger of 20–6, and later that season he turned in his most impressive performance in Game 3 of the World Series against the New York Yankees when he struck out a then-record 14 batters. Sandy Koufax would break the record a decade later when he fanned 15 Yankees in the 1963 Fall Classic. Erskine finished his career with a record of 122–78, 981 strikeouts and an ERA of 4.00.

This interview was conducted in Pittsburgh, Pennsylvania, in 1989.

Are you able to put into words the mystique of the Brooklyn Dodgers? What was it that made it a team that took hold of everybody?

Well, first of all we had a winning decade. The '50s were a new era for the Dodgers, who had been hard pressed to win in the '40s and the '30s, so we had a winning decade

Bobby Thomson (left) and Carl Erskine. Erskine had 14 K's in Game 3 of the 1953 World Series vs. the Yankees.

and that really made an impact. Plus we left the team in Brooklyn. The Brooklyn team left in '57 at the end of the season, very abruptly; so it was like somebody dying young. You know, they are, everybody's remembered the way we were more or less in our prime. And then Brooklyn had this great feeling toward the team, a very personal thing, and that hasn't diminished. I go back there to this day, and these people still get teary-eyed talking about the days that we were there playing.

You had a great year in 1953, and the World Series, you were a 20-game winner that season, and it carried over in the World Series. Of course everyone remembers the 14 strikeouts in the one ballgame, which was a record. What do you recall about that?
Well, what I really recall is how I got bombed in the first game in Yankee Stadium. I had a rough first inning, I didn't really get bombed, but I had a bad start in the ballgame and didn't pitch long, came out. Dressen talked to me after the game, "I'd like to start you in the third game," which meant one day in between, because there was no travel day in those New York games. So when I started the third game, my determination was the highest it ever was in my life not to have a bad first inning. So I pitched the ballgame with great intensity. It was a tough game because Raschi was pitching well against us. And when it was all over, I had 14 strikeouts, which at that time was a record against a great Yankee team, and of course that's probably my all-time thrill in baseball.

One of those players, was it Mantle, went down on strikes four times?
Mantle struck out four times and Joe Collins, a left-handed first baseman, struck out four times. I faced Mantle four times, but Collins I face a fifth time and almost got him a fifth time. He grounded back to me to end the game. But I had good stuff that day. Campy was very helpful catching and we just moved the ball around, had real good stuff—good fastball, good overhand curve. That's what Mantle chased mostly was an overhand curve. But it was a close ballgame, 3–2 final. Campy won it in the eighth with a home run off of Raschi, and it was a great ballgame.

◆ ◆ ◆

Elroy Face

During the 1959 season, Elroy Face had a record of 18–1 and a .947 winning percentage. At one point, Face won 17 games in a row. His dominance continued through the early 1960s as he dazzled hitters with his trademark forkball. The 5'8" dominator was more than a closer as he set himself up, pitching the final two or three innings on many occasions. In the stunning 1960 World Series upset of the New York Yankees, the man known as "The Baron" helped Pittsburgh win the seven-game classic by saving three games. The little right-hander with the big pitch completed his 16-year career with a record of 104–95, 191 saves, and an ERA of 3.48.

To begin with, could you talk about the World Series, the mystique of it, what it's like playing in one? Because we hear it's different for everyone.

Well yeah, it was a thrill for me in my first All-Star Game, but to be in the World Series, I mean that's a highlight of anyone's career. Take a fellow like Ernie Banks, he spent all those years with the Cubs and never got in one. It's really a thrill for us.

When, in that magical year in 1960, everyone remembers Mazeroski's home run and rightfully so; but what about Hal Smith, that shot that he hit was almost overshadowed, yet it was a monumental blow?

That's true, because if he hadn't hit that, we'd have probably lost because [with] Maz's home run we'd still been a couple of runs behind. That three-run homer that Hal hit put us two runs ahead, which made it when the Yankees got the two runs in the ninth, it was still only tied.

People speak about 1959, was it 18 wins in '59?

Right, I got 18 and 1; I won 17 and then lost one and then won another one. But I had five victories from the year before, so actually I had 22 consecutive victories.

Relief pitching today is more prominent than it was in your day; not any more important, but it seems that it's the way people look at it, you know, they're thought of as superstars and you were one of the first to really come to prominence.

Well that's true. Now even in the minor leagues they groom pitchers as relief pitchers, which they didn't do then. At that time, they figured if you couldn't go nine innings, well you're a relief pitcher. But I had spent four years in the minor leagues as strictly the starting pitcher, and I started 13 games my first year with the Pirates. But then Bobby Bragan,

From left, Frankie Gustine, Elroy Face, Hal Smith. Face was 18–1 in 1959, and a year later Smith went deep in Game 7 of the World Series vs. New York.

who managed me in 1952, knew that I did some relieving between starts for him, and he knew I had an arm that reacted quick, so as a result he more or less started me in relieving.

What does it take to become a good relief pitcher? What are the characteristics that you have to possess?

Eight good defensive ballplayers behind you. No, I think you just have to be able to throw strikes and make them hit the ball to get on, because if you walk them, there's no chance of getting them out. You have to make them hit the ball and then try to keep the ball down and have good control.

Your name comes up when they speak about the Hall of Fame. Do you ever give any thought to that?

Oh, I've given a lot of thought to it, but I haven't even come close yet, same as Mazeroski, he hasn't come close; to me he's probably the greatest second baseman to ever put a uniform on. Possibly after my length of time as being voted by the writers and that, we have I think it's a three-year wait after that, but the [Veterans] Committee might possibly vote me in.

Looking back, how would you like people to view you as a pitcher?

Well, in a way that a lot people walk up to me now and say you're the greatest relief pitcher they'd ever seen. And in fact Stan Musial had me as [the] best relief pitcher he ever faced in his book.

◆ ◆ ◆

Bob Feller

Bob Feller was one of the greatest pitchers in Major League Baseball history. He ended his 18-year career with a record of 266–162 and an ERA of 3.25 with 2,581 strikeouts. He also had 279 complete games, with 44 shutouts, and he threw three no-hitters, including the only Opening Day no-hitter in the history of MLB, in 1940. There is no telling how many more wins and strikeouts he could have recorded had it not been for his four years away from the game while serving in the Navy (USS *Alabama*) during World War II. Bob Feller was an eight-time All-Star and a member of the 1948 Cleveland Indians world championship team. He also was a member of the 1954 Indians team that won the AL pennant after winning 111 games. Bob Feller's number 19 was retired by the Indians in 1957, and a statue of the legendary pitcher stands outside Progressive Field. He was elected to the Hall of Fame on the first ballot in 1962.

This interview was conducted in Cleveland, Ohio, in 1990.

Mr. Feller, you were on some great pitching staffs. We know what a great pitcher you were, but a pitcher you're familiar with, the great Satchel Paige. What made him such an outstanding pitcher?

Well, Satchel was a tall fellow, about 6'5"; he's a stringy type guy, and he was very sneaky. He would throw the ball very easy, with very little obvious effort. He is fast, he had great control; he didn't have much of a curve ball, but he would come from the side, he'd come from around third. He had a hesitation pitch and by the time you see the ball coming out of his hand, why it would be by you. Then you'd make up your mind, I'm going to be ready for the next one, I'm gonna start swinging now and the first thing you knew, it was by you again; and he'd be one of the first five or ten or 15 best pitches in history if he pitched his career in the major leagues. But Satchel was a great friend of mine. We'd pitch against each other a great deal all around the country in the fall of the year in October, these barnstorming tours, and then he became my teammate the year we won the World Series in 1948. And by 1949 Satchel had lost it, even though he was in the big leagues for a few more years off and on, he still won some more ballgames. I think he won 12 games one year for Kansas City. But we thought he was all through by '49 and released him. He came back and pitched very well for Kansas City. I think he won a dozen ballgames.

What were one of the outstanding teams in the Negro Leagues that you played against, because you were one of the players that actually competed against them?

I didn't play against any other teams as a team. I played against their All-Star teams. When you played barnstorming, essentially the best players in the All-Stars, you meet up with the best players with the Negro National and American Leagues. We played all across the United States, in about 30 to 35 ballgames in 1946 and again in '47. The Kansas City Monarchs' owner and general manager got the team together, and their manager Frank Duncan and a catcher was their manager. So we won a game or two, they won a

Cleveland legend Bob Feller signing baseballs, one of the game's time-honored traditions.

game or two, we were kind of even-steven. Overall we won more games. I had great ballplayers on my team. I think we trained better probably and had better nourishment and so forth. We all made a lot of money and it was a racial rivalry affair. They won some very good ballgames and we won some very good ballgames. The fans enjoyed it, we all bore down and proved one thing; it proved to the American public that black ballplayers were just as good as the whites. No better, no worse and no different.

I know you had so many great moments in your career, however, you lost four years to World War II, so did a lot of other players. I've heard you say that you never lamented that fact, though, it was your duty to go out and serve the country.

Yes, I joined the Navy two days after Pearl Harbor, on December 9, and no I don't regret joining the Navy. I didn't have to go, my father was dying of brain cancer and died just after I went in. I was on a ship taking supplies to Russia at the time, convoy duty, and though we were losing the war pretty bad after Pearl Harbor and in Europe and in the Pacific, so it was my duty to get busy and do what I could. I mean, I'm no hero, 405,000 Americans were killed in World War II, and millions of Russians; but I'm proud of my military career and I did the thing I think should have been done and what any red-blooded American boy should do. You either fish or cut bait. I was the chief gunner's mate on the battleship *Alabama* for three years and we did win the war, with the help of the people at home and all of my shipmates and our military. So my baseball career; winning the World War, one win was more than a hundred wins I might have won if I stayed around, which I could have done because my dad was dying of brain cancer and you know, that's not the way Bob Feller works.

◆ ◆ ◆

Wilmer Fields

Wilmer Fields was primarily a pitcher but also played third base and the outfield in his 18-year career in the Negro Leagues, Canada, Mexico, and Latin America. He broke into professional ball with the famed Homestead Grays from 1940 through 1950 except for the three years he served in Europe with the Army during World War II. Fields posted a pitching record if 72–17 after returning from the war, helping pitch the Grays to victory over the Birmingham Black Barons in the Negro League World Series in 1948. After Homestead folded operations, Fields traveled to Latin America and Canada to ply his trade and won numerous MVP awards and recognition for his outstanding play.

This interview was conducted in Pittsburgh, Pennsylvania, in 1993.

You mentioned you played 11 years with the Grays. That team strung so many championships together. What made that team so outstanding?

Well, we had good pitching and we had good hitting and good defense. It was a complete baseball playing, at all times the whole time I was with them. That's really. In fact after we won those pennants in succession, we only dropped two and won the next one in 1948, the last year that we operated in the National League.

Can you describe the brand of ball in the Negro Leagues? You know we've heard so many stories about it. It was a running game and it wasn't necessarily looking for the long ball.

Oh no, not with the Homestead Grays, we had the path. We had pitchers that would pitch and play outfield that could hit as good as anybody, so that's what made our Homestead Grays as strong as they were. The pitching staff that it had, plus they could hit.

Who were some of the players that you played with that stand out that you remember the most?

Well, my teammates were Josh Gibson, who used to catch me, and Buck Leonard at first base and Sam Bankhead. They were the three main guys that helped me along. Because I was 17 when I joined the Grays, and they taught me everything I knew and they were my role models.

I heard so many stories about Josh Gibson, the home runs; you were there, you saw the raw power that this man possessed.

Oh yeah. He hit more home runs at Griffith Stadium in Washington than the whole Washington ball club in the left field stands. We only played there on Sundays and holidays when the Senators weren't there.

What about some of the opponents you played against?

Well, a couple of teams I have to remember is the Newark Eagles, who had Larry Doby and Monte Irvin and had a good pitching staff of Rupert Lewis, and Hill and Hobgood and Max Manning, one of my friends, they always had a good ball club. They won it in 1946 after we won eight straight pennants.

Did you play in Kansas City at all?

I played there one time against the Kansas City Monarchs. Sam Jethroe was with them at that time, and I kid Sam about it now, that he didn't hit nothing.

Now you served in World War II. How did the war affect or deplete the ranks of the Negro Leagues?

Well, that took it down to a point where they would pay such like a pitcher like a [Garnett] Blair, who used to pitch for the Grays, he used to be in the Army and pitch on weekends for the Grays in Major League parks. He was a good pitcher at the time and what it had done, it brought in the lower classification of ballplayers; but they continued to draw, I think it was during the war years that they were drawing the most to tell you the truth, because people would find some excitement somewhere, so they came to the major league ballparks.

Thinking that you guys faced discrimination not only in baseball, but even in the service.

There was discrimination everywhere we went. In the South we, there was so much discrimination when I was playing ball in the service, there was no black and white skin in the same barracks. Working beside each other that was done on duty that was done, we stayed segregated from the whites. So it never happened. Even after the war was over, it was still the same way.

Well, this has been a long time coming, it seems maybe in the last five years the players, the great players in the Negro Leagues that never got the notoriety or opportunity are suddenly being recognized. I spoke with many of them, and the thing that amazes me [is that] there is so little bitterness among the players.

Well, they didn't look for everything to happen in the past five years. In the past five years, we had progress still for it. We would believe things that want to be real. Take for instance like this year, 1993; I'm connected with getting benefits for black ballplayers. We have major league health insurance that came out in June which Joe Black was in charge of. We are in the process of getting money for the old black ballplayers; and we have moved more strongly this year than ever before in the past 45 years.

Is there an organization now that you're working with?

Oh yes, the organization was started in 1990 I think out of New York, a guy by the name of Richard Burke started it. He didn't make too big a success of it; so he turned it over to Reggie Jackson, Bubba James Jackson, he is out of California; he just called me this morning and asked me how things are going. See I'm connected, Max Manning and I are connected with James Jackson in trying to get something done. Now so far as our organization is concerned, it's a, well we go to different cities and promote card shows in which we turn over quite a bit of revenue from this. We're just getting started, but I see good things ahead.

We appreciate you doing the fine work you did today and for the fine work you did many years ago. It's been long overdue, it's a privilege to talk to you, and we wish you and your family all the best.

Oh I appreciate you interviewing me, and it's always a privilege for me to talk to someone concerning black baseball because I turned down five major league offers to play black baseball.

Wow, why did you do that?

Well the minimum salary at the time was $4,500 a year. I used to play ball in Latin American countries, in the Dominican Republic; I'd make that much in two months. I would make $2,200 a month playing three ballgames a week. In other countries I played, in all Latin American countries; Venezuela, Puerto Rico, Dominican, Colombia, Cuba, Mexico, Panama; all the Latin American countries I was involved with. This is where we made our money and saved money in the Latin American countries, not here in the states, because we didn't make anything.

What were the highest priced players making?

We had a couple of them like Buck Leonard and Josh Gibson. I was reading in a book not too long ago at home they were making like $1,000 or $1,100 a month. At the same time they were making that, in the Latin American countries I was making twice as much as they were making, but not with the Homestead Grays. I never asked for a raise or anything like that, but I used to pitch two and three games a week for them and I would never have turned them down because of the managers like Vic Harris and Sam Bankhead, you know they were so nice. And it wasn't just like a family team, but it was.

◆ ◆ ◆

Rollie Fingers

Rollie Fingers was responsible for bringing the art of relief pitching into prominence in the early 1970s. The workhorse of the legendary Oakland Athletics changed the way many viewed the role of a reliever. Fingers, with his famous handlebar mustache, which he grew to collect $300 from A's owner Charles O. Finley, was active from 1968 to 1985. He finished his career with 114 wins and 118 losses and an ERA of 2.90. More importantly, he retired with 341 saves, breaking Hoyt Wilhelm's record of 227. In 1974, he earned the World Series MVP Award while helping define the Oakland Athletics' dynasty. He was the Rolaids "Relief Man of the Year" in 1977, 1978, and 1980 while pitching for the San Diego Padres. In 1981, while a member of the Milwaukee Brewers, he won both the American League Cy Young and MVP Awards. When he was inducted into the Baseball Hall of Fame in 1992, he was only the second relief pitcher to be elected behind Hoyt Wilhelm. His excellence and popularity helped propel fellow relievers Dennis Eckersley, Bruce Sutter and Goose Gossage to gain entry to baseball's shrine in Cooperstown, New York.

People view you as one of the pioneers of relief pitching.
Relief pitching really came into prominence in the late 1960s. There were some relief pitchers before me but it wasn't really a glorified job because most of your starting pitchers went nine innings. Everybody was completing games, and there wasn't really much of a need for a closer then, but that's when it started back in the late '60s, '68, '69. Since then I think every organization realized how important it was to have a closer, and that's why all these closers are making pretty good money now. It's even changed since I was a relief pitcher. Today a closer is a one-inning pitcher. When I was playing, I was a three- or four-inning pitcher. Hell, I went seven innings in one game and I was the closer.

You were no doubt accepting of the role. Many who envision themselves as starters are unable to make the transition. Was it Dick Williams who thrust you in the role back in 1971?
[In] 1971 he put me in the bullpen. I was the starting pitcher and couldn't get out of the second inning, so he figured I was a two- or three-inning pitcher. He put me down in the bullpen and I kind of fell into the job. I was at the right place at the right time, and it turned my career around because I was on my way to the minor leagues and Dick Williams changed it around for me. I have to thank him for that.

He is another vital part of the Oakland Athletics' dynasty. Under his watch, Oakland won the World Series back-to-back in 1972 and 1973. He is one of only seven managers to win pennants in both leagues.
Dick Williams knew the game, and of all the managers I've had, he ran a pitching staff better than anybody I ever played for, and I played under 15 managers in 17 years. He knew when to make a change, he knew when to pinch-hit, he knew what right-handers got left-handers out and what left-handers got right-handers out, and he would manage accordingly. He was a fundamentalist. Everybody's going to make errors, but if you made a fundamental error without thinking he would let you know about it, and you would only do it once. One time I forgot to back up third base when I was so upset and got lazy and didn't run over and back up third base, and he met me at the top of the dugout steps and gave me "what for"!

Consistency was your M.O. Many relief pitchers have put together one or two outstanding seasons, but you performed at such a high level throughout your career.
That's the one thing you want to look for in a relief pitcher, consistency, and three or four guys in the Hall of Fame—Dennis Eckersley, Bruce Sutter, myself and Goose Gossage, we were all consistent over the years, and that's why we are in the Hall of Fame. There have been guys who have had one or two great years like Mike Marshall and Eric

Gagne more recently, but it's hard to go out there and do it year after year after year, 15, 16, 17 or 20 years. It's tough to do that and stay healthy because you are always warming up in the bullpen. Your starting pitcher warms up before a ball game and pitches the game and has four days off. It's not like that when you're a relief pitcher. You can be pitching four, five, six or seven ball games in a row.

You had the great fast ball and slider in your repertoire.

I probably got by more on control than anything else. If you're a closer, you need to have control. There are three things you need to pitch in the big leagues, and that's control, control, and control. If you don't have those three things, you're not going to be a closer. You have to know where you're throwing the ball because of the situation. You have to get ahead of the hitters. You have to throw strikes, and if you don't have control and know where you're throwing the ball, it's trouble. I mean you have to have command of at least two pitches, and in my case I had three. I threw a fastball, a slider, and I threw a forkball. It's a changeup that I developed about halfway through my career and that kept me around a little bit longer. If you don't have a good changeup, you're not going to get by either. That's another thing, any young pitcher, if he wants to advance, work on a changeup. The changeup is probably the best pitch you can have.

Elroy Face was the man who developed that forkball while with the Pittsburgh Pirates back in the late '50s and early '60s.

Yes, he threw the forkball.

You played from 1968 to 1976 in the American League and then took the hill for San Diego in the NL and never missed a beat as you dominated without a period of adjustment.

It all comes back to control. It wasn't that much of a difference, just a bunch of guys in different uniforms, that's all. Everybody bats from either the right side of the plate or the left side of the plate, and you pitch accordingly. I had to learn the hitters because I had never faced them, but I was able to learn them pretty quick. You face a guy a couple of times and you get them out and you remember. You have a mind like a computer when you're a relief pitcher. You have to remember everything that you've done.

You had great years with the dynasty in Oakland and with the Milwaukee Brewers in the early 1980s. If we studied your DNA, would we find the green and gold of the A's?

The Oakland A's, because I pitched there longer. I was there eight or nine years and I came through the organization for four years. I signed in 1964, my first year was in 1965, and I was with the A's organization from '65 to '76. I pitched for four years in San Diego and five in Milwaukee, but I think most people remember me as an Oakland A.

You were all Milwaukee in 1981, winning the American League Cy Young Award and the MVP.

That's just one of those years when nothing went wrong. It was like Disneyland. You just throw your glove out there and you get guys out. There was a lot of luck involved. There were times I came in and gave up three line drives and they'd be right at guys, so you get out of the inning even though you gave up three hard-hit balls. I had a great defense behind me with Paul Molitor and Robin Yount and Charlie Moore and Gorman Thomas and Ben Ogilvy and Cecil Cooper. We had a great defensive ball club and we scored runs, so if you make a mistake there was always a chance that we were going to score some runs later. It makes a big difference when you play with a good ball club because those guys can pick you up.

The Oakland Athletics of your tenure are one of the great ball clubs that I have had the privilege of watching. Your A's were a free-spirited bunch of guys.

We knew how to play the game. We had some talent on that team, and it's a shame that after the 1976 season, we had to split up. That's when free agency came into play, but if we could have all stayed together I think we could have continued to win. We were all in the middle of our prime when free agency hit, but Charlie Finley wasn't going to let that happen. He wasn't going to pay us. Charlie could have kept the team together back then but he just didn't want to cough up the money, and that's when we split. That's probably one of the saddest days of my career when we played our last game in 1976. We knew it was the last game we would all play together. The next year we were gone.

◆ ◆ ◆

Tito Francona

Tito Francona played in the Major Leagues for 15 seasons, with his career year coming with Cleveland in 1959 when he batted .363 with 20 home runs and 79 RBI. He would have won the AL batting title if not for coming up 34 at-bats short of qualifying. He was named "Man of The Year" by the Cleveland Baseball Writers Association. He was named one of the 100 Greatest Cleveland Indians in a poll taken in 2001 during the team's 100th Anniversary. The well-traveled outfielder played with six American League teams and three more in the Senior Circuit. Later in his career, he was an outstanding pinch-hitter for the Atlanta Braves. Tito finished his career with a batting average of .272, 125 home runs and 656 RBI.

This interview was conducted in Beaver County, Pennsylvania, in 1989.

Nineteen-fifty-nine was a watershed year for you. You came close to winning the batting title, hitting .363, but didn't have enough at-bats to qualify.

I almost made it. I went to bat, I think 399 official at-bats. You needed 477, but with sacrifice flies and walks and hit batsmen, like that, and then plus the last three games of the season I didn't play because there was not any way I could have made it, so if you would have totaled those up, I would have missed it by about 15 at bats.

That had to be the high point in a long career.

Yes, I think so, yea, you know when you go back and look at it. But I hit the ball just as well the next year and I only hit .292. But I was very lucky, you know, I'd get a couple of base hits with line drives and I'd bloop a couple in or something like that, where the next year I didn't get that lucky hit.

A big pinch-hit really got you started, correct?

Yes, yes. Well, the one in 1959 got me into the lineup to become a regular. We were in Cleveland and we had an outfield of Minoso, Colavito and Jimmy Piersall, and we were playing the Yankees. We were going into the tenth inning, in the top of the tenth the Yankees scored one run, and we were losing 1–0 and the tail end of the batting order was coming up. I can't remember who the pitcher was, and Joe Gordon looked out and said, "anybody bat against this guy?" and I said, "Yes, I batted against this guy." He said, "how about pinch hitting?" and I hit a two-run homer off him in the bottom of the tenth and we win. There were 70,000 people in the stands. It was a Friday night, and every Friday they used to give a car away, and I remember because they held me over to go out and draw the winning ticket. That was one of the bigger pinch-hits I got.

What was your thought process coming off the bench?
You know, we always had the theory when you're pinch-hitting, to come off the bench swinging, don't get cheated. Get three good swings up there. What I used to like when I came up to bat, I would hope that he would throw me a couple balls, you know, where I could see the ball. I would always hope that he would throw me a fastball and if it was a ball that I could gauge the speed of it. Then the next pitch I would like if it was a curveball so I could judge his curve. If I saw two or three pitches, then I really felt more comfortable than swinging at the first pitch. I always hit off the fastball. I don't care if a guy threw 100 curves that game out of 101 pitches, I would still look for that fast ball.

How would you like people to remember you?
Gee, I don't know. I'd like to think that I was a pretty good ball player. The thing I admire most about my career, you know, is that I had 15 years in the big leagues. So I must have done something right, you know, to spend that much time.

Tito Francona had a batting average of .363 for Cleveland in 1959.

◆ ◆ ◆

Steve Garvey

For many, Steve Garvey was the signature player for the Los Angeles Dodgers in the 1970s and early '80s. The ten-time All-Star also earned four Gold Glove Awards, had six seasons with 200 or more hits, and was the National League MVP in 1974. Garvey played 19 seasons in the big leagues, 14 of them with the Dodgers and the remainder with the

San Diego Padres. The Tampa, Florida, native, who collected 2,599 hits, played in the World Series in 1974, 1977, and 1978 and the world championship club of 1981. He also played in the Fall Classic with San Diego in 1984. The versatile first baseman, who once played in 1,207 consecutive NL games, completed his career with a .294 batting average, 272 home runs and 1,308 RBI.

This interview was conducted in Las Vegas, Nevada, in 2008.

The Dodgers will soon be celebrating 50 years in Los Angeles, and I understand you are the player representing the decade of the '70s.

I'll be the spokesman of the '70s, and it's quite an honor. 2008 will be the 50th anniversary of the LA Dodgers. The team and Los Angeles have been historic a la the Brooklyn Dodgers and their borough, so it ought to be a fun year.

You are closely associated with the Dodgers even though you later played in San Diego. If we checked your DNA, would it no doubt test positive for Dodger blue?

I'm quite sure as it oxygenizes, it turns blue. Tommy Lasorda's old philosophy of cutting his veins and Dodger blue coming out is indicative of the history of the Dodgers and the great charm and charisma of the players and the teams over the years. I was honored to be a part of it.

You played with an infield that stayed together for a long time.

Absolutely. It was a unique time when you could keep a team together. Starting on June 23 of 1973, our infield came together. I was the last piece of the puzzle at first base. Then we seemed to add a quality player every year like Jimmy Wynn, Dusty Baker, Reggie Smith, Rick Monday or Fernando Valenzuela. We continued to build over the next ten or 12 years, and that was a special time in Los Angeles. We went to four World Series during that time, culminating with a World Championship in 1981.

How do you remember the '81 team?

Well, you talk about destiny. After being frustrated in '77 and '78, having good teams and losing to the Yankees, 1981 seemed to have been a year when we easily could have gotten caught up in the strike and subsequently the six weeks off and barely missed our division and the playoffs, but everything fell into place. We were in first place when the strike and lockout happened, which put us into a special playoff at the end of the year. We beat Houston two out of three and ended up playing Montreal in a very close series. Playing the Yankees in the World Series, we lost the first two games in New York and everybody except us was probably thinking, "Here we go again," but then we rattled off four straight wins and a World Championship. As you look back, each one of these moments seems to fit the term destiny.

At the end of the '82 season, you signed with San Diego as a free agent. It wasn't far from LA mileage-wise but a far cry from what you had grown accustomed to.

You're correct, it wasn't far in terms of miles but was far away in terms of history. The Padres had come into the league in 1969. They had struggled and never really had an identity. Starting in 1983 with my joining the team and especially in 1984 with the addition of Goose Gossage, Graig Nettles, Tony Gwynn's emergence, McReynolds, Kennedy, Templeton, we put together quite a good team. Of course [we] won our division, won the National League and then faced an extremely talented Tigers team that beat us in the World Series. However, just getting to the Series started Padre history and it was great to be a part of that.

Outside of juicing the ball and some players, how has the game changed?

Yeah, remember when we used to talk about the juicing of just the baseball? The business has changed. It's a much larger business now. At the time I retired, the highest salary was around two and a half, three million, and the highest now is over 25. The economics have changed. It's very difficult to keep a team together for longer than two or three years with core players. Statistically things have changed, obviously through the adversity of steroids and drug enforcement. We've had problems not only individually but labor problems over the years. But year in and year out, regardless of the problems, the game still is our national pastime. It's still as charming as ever. The game is timeless; you need 27 outs and one more run.

You had the image of Jack Armstrong the All-American Boy. Is that how you want to be thought of?

Well, I think most importantly is that I was truly committed to the game of baseball, to my team and city, and to the fans. I realized it early, way back being a batboy for the Brooklyn Dodgers in spring training during the late '50s and having the boys of summer be the fellows that impressed me with their character and their style. You're out there to give 100 percent for the fans. They're the ones who pay your salary, and I played each game as hard as I possibly could, and I think people appreciated that. I did it with a certain dignity as a sportsman and did everything I could to help my team win.

◆ ◆ ◆

Bob Gibson

Bob Gibson has a career record of 251 wins against 174 losses with an ERA of 2.91. The Nebraska native finished with 3,117 strikeouts, which helped him capture a pair of Cy Young Awards in 1968 and 1970, and the Most Valuable Player Award. In 1968, Gibson put together one of the most incredible seasons on record, posting a record of 22–9 with a minuscule ERA of 1.12. After the season, a Major League Baseball rules panel voted to lower the pitching mound from 15 inches to ten. As dominant a pitcher as he was during the regular season, Bob Gibson elevated his game even higher in the fall. He won seven games and lost only two while pitching in three World Series (1964, 1967, 1968) with a 1.89 ERA. Against Detroit in the 1968 fall classic, he blew away 17 Tigers in one game and finished the Series with two wins, one loss, and 35 strikeouts. Gibson was awarded nine Gold Gloves and was elected to the Hall of Fame in 1981.

This interview was conducted in Pittsburgh, Pennsylvania, in 1990.

Everybody knows you as one of the fiercest competitors in any sport that you competed in, most notably baseball. When you look over the career of Bob Gibson, 255 complete games is something that you're never going to see again. You were the type of player that didn't pace yourself, you went out there and you went as hard as you could for as long as you could. Your era was a golden era. How did you manage the stamina?

Well you know, I don't know that the players today don't have the stamina, it's the way the game has changed. They don't expect a pitcher to complete a ball game. When I played, they expected you to complete ball games, and if you couldn't complete them that's when you got sent back to the minor leagues or they put this tag on you as a guy that couldn't finish ball games. But now they have a middle man, they have the setup man, they have the short man, they have the closer, they got all these things that they just didn't back in those days. But I would suspect that if the player or pitcher had to complete ball games today, they're big and strong enough, they could complete them.

Bob, along with the tremendous career from 1958 to 1975, the one thing everyone seems to focus in on is the "year of the pitcher," 1968, and [your ERA] was 1.12. It's like we went back to the Deadball era when you were out there with this ERA. No one has ever seen that since 1914, and no one has ever come that close again since 1968. You were always a stellar performer, but what happened that one particular season?

Yeah, but see, it wasn't that one particular season. If you look at my career, I went from winning six games to 12 or 13 games to 15 games to 18 games to 20 games. So I was getting progressively better each year, and actually the year before '68, which was '67, I broke my leg, but the year before that was my first 20-game season. In '67 I got into the World Series and I pitched as well as I did in '68, so it wasn't a thing that happened all of a sudden. It took several years.

That year, the focus in the American League was on Denny McLain also with the 31 wins. I guess the World Series had a little bit more of the limelight shown on it because you and Denny went up against each other in that Series, and of course it just carried through for you because you were so exceptional in the World Series as you were in '64. You always seemed to come through with a big performance.

I think one of the reasons I was effective in the World Series is because I hadn't seen these guys or they hadn't seen me. It was more difficult to pitch in your own league where [you] see these guys two or three times a year. But having faced [them] maybe in spring training, they get these scouting reports about you, and everybody knew that I threw the ball pretty hard but nobody ever talked about my breaking ball in the World Series. I always used that more than they expected it.

You had primarily the heat. You had two fast balls and you had a slider. You had a change-up; you didn't use that very often.

I didn't throw a changeup that often at all. I had a curveball and I threw the curveball to left-handers only. The reason for that was my curveball wasn't a biting curveball, and it had a tendency to hang. Well, it's ok for a right-hander to hang a curveball to a left-hander because he usually jams himself. But that same curveball, a right-hander will hit it 700 feet, so you just don't throw it to him.

Well, your fastball, one would sail, the other one would sink.

Yes. You hold it with the seams or across the seams. Today they call it a two-seamer or a four-seamer. I don't know, I don't have these terms down today.

When you first came up, it wasn't really that easy. You broke in with the Cardinals in '58. Solly Hemus was there, you were used as a spot starter, and then you were a reliever, and then Johnny Keane, he must have known something. He came in, he handed you the ball, and that was basically it. The man had a belief in you and you went on from there.

Well, Johnny Keane was my manager in Triple-A, and when I signed I signed with

Johnny Keane, so he had seen me a couple years. And actually it was '59, not '58. But when I came up with Solly, Solly was not really a patient person, and he didn't know that much about it, so he got fired in '61, hooray. And then that's when I took over as a regular starter. The day he got fired, Johnny Keane took over and told me I was pitching that day, and he said, "you're going to pitch every fifth day so don't worry about it." That's a pretty good ego and confidence builder.

Looking back at '68, with the spotlight on Denny McLain and yourself, did you have any kind of conversations with, now that I'm asking you I'm thinking there's probably no way that Bob Gibson's going to talk to the competition.

None whatsoever. Not only McLain but the hitters either. You know, I never felt like I was pitching against the pitcher. I always felt like I was pitching against the ball club because most pitchers can't hit anyway. So I just never felt all of this thing that the press gets all excited about, either me pitching against a McLain or Sandy Koufax. I always looked at that other ball club and if I had my good day, I'm going to win the game.

You mentioned [that] pitchers don't hit but that's not true really true because you were a guy that could, I think you hit 24 homers lifetime. One season you drove in 20 runs. You

Dick Williams (left) and Bob Gibson. Gibson was the NL MVP and had a 1.12 ERA in 1968.

won nine Gold Gloves; you were one of the finest fielding pitchers of all time. So you could do it all. You could have been a position player probably if you wanted to.

Well, the funny thing about that, before I signed with the Cardinal organization I hadn't pitched that much. I was [an] outfielder, infielder, or played most of the positions. In high school I was a catcher.

What was it that turned it around to make you go to the hill?

I didn't go. They put me there. When I signed, they signed me as an outfielder, possibly a pitcher, and I never got a chance to play any of the other positions because the Cardinals were looking for pitching at the time.

Here's a quote of yours, I think it sums up the competitor that you were and still are: "I've never come out of a game on my own. Never have I asked a manager to take me out. Never." That was kind of an attitude that you seemed to carry with you throughout your entire career.

Well, I don't know what the purpose of going out there if you're going to want to come out. You shouldn't go out there. Of course, the attitudes are a little different today. I'm not just talking about baseball, but our society is a little different. Things are more acceptable today than they were back in those days. You just were kind of a wimp if you wanted to come out of a ball game back in those days.

Another thing you're known for [was] the brushback, but you said a brushback is not to scare a hitter or to hit him. It's to make him think. That was just to get him off the plate I guess, but people had this intimidation thing going it seems.

Well, you know the intimidation, the word intimidation, was given to me by somebody else. I've never went about my job with the idea that I wanted to intimidate somebody. I had a good reason for just about everything that I did. And guy used to say that I threw at him a lot, and I said well no, I didn't throw at you because when I throw at you I hit you, and if I missed you I wasn't throwing at you. My idea was to make the guy think about the ball inside, and if you think about the ball inside, you can't hit the ball away. I don't know too many pitchers who are good enough where they can get guys out inside. You have to get them out away. So to keep them from going away, you have to come in.

One of the things we mentioned [was] your durability. From September 12, 1967, to July 4 in '69, you were never knocked out of a game, so that comes to something like 53 games.

That might be misleading. I was taken out of ball games; I wasn't taken out of the ball game in the middle of an inning while I was on the field. I was taken out for pinch-hitters inside when we were on the bench.

You weren't very healthy as a young man. Your mother was inspirational and of course your brothers.

You were reading a lot about me, huh?

Well yeah.

I had pneumonia and just about everything you could imagine when I was two years old. My oldest brother was pretty inspirational when it came to me being an athlete. I remember, vaguely remember when I was about five or six years old, I think it was five, I was in the hospital and I had pneumonia. I was a pretty sick baby and he told me if I would get well that he would get me a baseball and a bat, and so that's pretty much how that happened.

And then you got a basketball scholarship to Creighton. I believe and you were a tremendous basketball player but after that you went on to the Globetrotters, but that wasn't really to your liking.

No. I wanted to beat somebody. Playing with the Globetrotters was a lot of fun. Because I was 18 years or 21 years old I guess, I had just gotten out of school. And you go out and you kind of clown around. Well, I've never been one to clown around, but it was a thing that I always thought I wanted to do when I was a child. I wanted to play with the Globetrotters because it seemed to be so much fun. Then after I got a chance to play there, I found out it wasn't nearly as much fun. It was more clowning rather than to go and beat somebody, so that didn't last long.

You faced discrimination as a young man. I believe it started in college from what I read, when you went to Tulsa for a tournament or something, and then of course in St. Petersburg when you came up.

Well, our first point was it started when I was in college. No, it's always been there from the day I was born and even before that. It's just something that when you're young, you don't notice that much. As you get older, you understand what people are all about. And I would suspect that it's pretty much as prevalent right now as it was back then. People are a little more sophisticated but yes, it did affect me as far as living is concerned, but as far as baseball, no, it did not affect me. We had to go through some pretty tough things and perform when the circumstances weren't really easy for us, and I guess that's one of the reasons why black people are so strong. It's because of all the adversity that you have to face and still perform as well as somebody else. I can suspect that that's probably why we're feared. I don't know what any other reason would be.

Baseball says it's trying to bring minorities into the game. Do you think enough of that is really being done. Is there enough change?

You know we're talking baseball, you're talking baseball, I'm talking society. It's very easy to sit and point the finger at baseball. Baseball is antiquated as far as those things are concerned, but then so are most business in this country. So I'm not just talking about the baseball end of it. We're talking about the way America is today, and yes, there's room for a lot of improvement. There has been a little bit as far as baseball's concerned, there's been a little bit as far as our society is concerned. But overall, if you had to look at it, I don't know how much farther we are from 1950.

How have you changed as a man since you retired from baseball? People forget quickly. There is a difference I think when you step off the mound and you're no longer in uniform.

Oh, I've changed a lot. Now as far as the accolades are concerned, I could probably go the rest of my life and not even miss hearing people cheer and tell me what kind of job I did when I was playing, because I'm pretty much aware of that myself. But as an individual, you get a little older, some of the fight leaves you. Things that really used to aggravate me and I'd fight about 25, 30 years ago, I don't fight about anymore. And rather than to try sit and explain my point of view, a lot of times I will just walk away. If you didn't understand it 20 years ago, you're not going to understand it now, so why waste my time? I think I'm a little more laid back now then I used to be. I think age brings it on.

Is there anything on the horizon that you might want to bring out? That you're looking to get involved in other areas?

You're always looking to get involved in other areas, but those doors are pretty much closed too. So you keep on fighting till the day you die.

Well, I'm sure the type of person you are, if the doors don't open, you'll kick them open or get them open some way.
Well, I'll knock on there anyway.

◆ ◆ ◆

Al Gionfriddo

Al Gionfriddo played Major League Baseball for only four seasons, however, to those who love the game, more specifically the Brooklyn Dodgers, his name continues to carry with it the magic of the World Series and all that is possible. He broke in with Pittsburgh in 1944 and played for the Pirates for three seasons, having his best year in 1945 when he hit a respectable .284. The outfielder was acquired by Brooklyn during the 1947 season and saved his best for last in the World Series against the New York Yankees. Gionfriddo was brought in as a defensive replacement to play left field in the bottom of the sixth inning, and with two men on base, Joe DiMaggio drove a pitch near the 415-foot marker which the outfielder raced over and caught, robbing DiMaggio of an extra-base hit. The Dodgers went on to win the game, 8–6, but lost the Series in seven games.

You are known for making one of the great catches in World Series history, and it gets greater every year for Dodger fans.
Well, maybe it does, I guess. I get quite a few letters from different fans and even the younger fans, baseball fans, and they tell me how great the catch was. That their dad told them or their uncle told them, or their grandfather told them that they were at the ball game. Now of all the people at the ball game that day when I made that catch in the 1947 World Series against the Yankees, we would have had a million people in that ball park. But I do get quite a few fan mail letters.

Al Gionfriddo (left) with Lew Burdette (center) and Tommy Lasorda. Gionfriddo's catch left Joe DiMaggio kicking mad in the 1947 World Series.

Could you kind of retrace your steps these many years later? What happened?

Well, you know, that was the sixth game of the World Series, 1947 World Series with the Dodgers; I was with the Dodgers, the Dodgers against the Yankees. It was the sixth inning and we were leading the game against the Yankees at the time, 8 to 5. DiMaggio comes up to the plate, there are two men on and two outs and I am playing in left field, playing very close to the line to pull the ball. Instead, Joe DiMaggio hits the ball in the deep left-center field, which was 415 feet away into the Dodgers', toward the Dodgers' bullpen. At that time, I turned my back and ran towards the bullpen gate, looked over my left shoulder and saw that I still had quite a ways to go, so I put my head down and ran right toward the gate. As I reached the bullpen gate, I looked over my shoulder again and the ball was coming over my shoulder. I reached over and caught the ball, which saved the game, and we went on to win the game, 8 to 6.

Did it surprise you at all that you caught up with that ball?

Well, at that time you know as a young boy at that time, now I'm 66; at that time I was what, 22 years old, and I used to be able to run 100 yards in 10 flat, so I could run. It was somewhat of a surprise, but I knew I had a chance to catch the ball once I looked over my shoulder the first time.

How long was it until you spoke with DiMaggio after that, and what did he say to you?

Well, Joe and I are very, very good friends, and that winter after the World Series was over, Joe and I attended many banquets during the winter time. We enjoyed each other, and he talked about stats and I talked about his hitting, so we were good friends.

We always, always remembered the newsreel or film of Joe kicking second base; he was almost at second base, and his disappointment.

That's true, because I think Joe is disappointed a little that I made the catch, and if the ball would have gone over the fence, it would have tied up the game at 8–8. As you know, the score was 8 to 5 at the time; and they actually did get another run, which they would have beaten us 9 to 8 and the Series would have been over. That catch saved the sixth game, and we went in to play the seventh game of the World Series then.

Who was the first person to get to you when you came in from the outfield?

Well, Carl Furillo, who was playing center field, reached down and picked up my cap when I lost my cap as I was jumping, he was the first guy. When I got to the dugout, why they all mobbed me, so I really don't know who first greeted me. But I was mobbed by my own players as I entered the dugout.

• • •

Jim "Mudcat" Grant

Jim "Mudcat" Grant became the first African American pitcher to win 20 games in a season when he posted a 20–7 record for the Minnesota Twins in 1965. That same season, he established himself again by defeating the Los Angeles Dodgers twice with a pair of complete games in the World Series. In his second win, in Game Six, he belted a three-run homer to secure the 5–1 victory. Although the Twins would lose the Series, it was Mudcat Grant's signature season as a starting pitcher. Grant, who also pitched for Cleveland, the Dodgers, Montreal, St. Louis, Oakland, and Pittsburgh, would complete his 14-year career with a 145–119 record, an ERA of 3.63, and 1,267 strikeouts.

Jim "Mudcat" Grant had 21 wins in 1965.

This interview was conducted in Cleveland, Ohio, on August 22, 1987.

Jim "Mudcat" Grant. How did it come about, the nickname?

That's a long story. I went to camp my first year in 1954 to try to make a ball club. I walked in town with some WPA pants on, and 500 ball players thought that I was a welfare case from Mississippi. They started calling me Mississippi Mudcat. Later on they cut off the Mississippi and it was Mudcat. But I am from Lacoochee, Florida.

Lacoochee, okay. You played in 1965 with the Twins. You were in the World Series; I think you won two games in the Series? You were a fierce competitor from what I remember most; was the difference the atmosphere? How do you deal with the World Series pressure?

Well actually, there is no pressure. I mean the greatest thing in the world for an athlete is to play in a World Series or a basketball championship or a Super Bowl, and that's all that matters. I mean you get up for the game. The pressure is there, but it's a lot more fun than it is pressure. There is always pressure to win; there is always pressure to perform because so many people are watching you. But it gives you a chance to stick your chest out a little bit and give you a chance to compete.

When you look back now, those victories in the World Series have to mean a great deal to you.

There's no doubt about that. I became the first black pitcher to win a World Series game in the American League, so it means a little bit more than the victory itself. But winning two games in a World Series was something that a lot of baseball pitchers have not accomplished, so I cherish that and it was wonderful.

When you think about that ball club, what comes to your mind, that Minnesota ball club?

Well, just the fact that it was one hell of a ball club. I mean we had everything. We had speed, we had pitching, we had defense, we had home runs, Harmon Killebrew was awesome. Earl Battey is one of the baddest catchers that I've ever thrown to; Zoilo Versalles, Tony Oliva. It was a great team with a great bench. Jim Kaat, Camilo Pascual, Jim Perry. We had a wonderful ball club up there.

Tony Gwynn

Tony Gwynn played 20 seasons, all with the San Diego Padres, and won eight batting titles, tying him with Pittsburgh Pirates Hall of Famer Honus Wagner for most titles in National League history. The 15-time All-Star displayed his excellence at the plate by hitting above .300 in 19 of his 20 seasons. Gwynn, whose best year average-wise was 1994, when he batted .394, also stood out on defense, winning five Gold Glove Awards. He also collected seven Silver Slugger Awards and finished his career with 3,141 hits and a batting average of .338, 1138 RBI and 135 home runs. His number 19 jersey was retired by the Padres, and he was elected to the Baseball Hall of Fame on the first ballot in 2007.

This interview was conducted in Pittsburgh, Pennsylvania, in 1991.

In the past several weeks, you have been on fire as a hitter. It appears that you are in a groove and are seeing the ball really well.

Yeah, that's basically it. You get into a groove or whatever you like to call it. It's almost like things are happening a little bit slower than the norm for the rest of the guys. You know the ball comes out of his hand, and picking up the ball and picking up what it's doing, realizing what I have to do to put my bat on it; and most importantly, I find the ball. I don't feel like I've changed anything or prepared any differently than I have in the past. It's just this year I just find the hole. You hit the ball hard and there's a hole; I hit a ball soft and there's a hole; I bloop one, nobody's there. I have had runners on and just happen to hit the right hole. It's just like riding a wave, I call it. You're riding a wave and you don't know why or how long this wave is gonna last, if you can ride it out until the end. When it's over, you bounce back out and try to find another one. Now I've never surfed in my life, but I guess [it's] the only analogy I can come up with. When you're right in the middle of one, you can't, I mean I can't explain it. I just, you know, I just see the ball and basically put it in play, but this is the longest stretch I've ever had in my career. You know, I think I'm smart enough to realize that, you know sooner or later it's gonna come to an end and when it does, the quicker you can regroup and try to get back to where you were, the better off you're gonna be. You can't honestly go out there and expect to hit the ball like this the whole year. You know it's gonna end sometime, and when it does you prepare yourself for it, and then you regroup and you try to do it again.

Well, outside of the great talent you have, has it helped having a guy like Fred McGriff hitting behind you?

It's very hard to say. I would bet against right-handers I'd get better pitches to hit, you know, you get pitches to hit, you still gotta hit 'em. Last year with Jack Clark and Joe Carter and sometimes Benito Santiago, I felt like I was getting good pitches to hit, but I just didn't have a consistent swing to be able to go out there and put the bat on the ball consistently. Last year I hit .309; and for a lot of people, .309 is going to be a, you know, pretty good season. But the success I've had over my career, with .309, people look at it as if it were a bad year. So you take that and try and put things in perspective for yourself, which is what I did this winter. You know, like .309, [I] was not really satisfied with that and really worked hard this winter as far as finding a consistent swing. I changed some things that I had done in the past. I usually hit off pitching machines an awful lot during the winter, and I hit off live pitching all winter long, and when I came into the camp I had a solid swing and I had the kind of swing where I wanted it to be.

Just because you have it, you have to maintain it. There's little things that you have to do every day to get yourself in the right frame of mind to go out and play the game. So these

Tony Gwynn, "Mr. Padre." He won eight batting titles and was a 15-time All-Star.

days, just about every day off season I've taken batting practice for about three or four minutes and just worked on the swing and hope it's been good, you know. But that's nothing different than what I have done in the past, and you know, having guys like McGriff and Jack Clark and Benito and a different cast of characters that you've had batting behind you this year, I think really doesn't make that much of a difference. The type of hitter that I am, I'm going see a lot of different pitches anyway, and the key is to take those different pitches and somehow be able to put your bat on the ball and put the ball in play, because once a pitcher makes you look bad on a certain pitch, chances are they're gonna stay with it. But if you can put the bat on the ball on all the different variety of pitches you're gonna see, then that's gonna change every night from bat to bat. So you have to concern yourself with that and hopefully be able to make the adjustments.

You mentioned hitting .309 was looked at as an off-year for you. Now you had a string of three batting titles in a row and it was broken last year, and it looks like this year you would be favored to win another. After you win one, two, three, four batting titles. what does winning another mean to you?

Not very much, to be honest with you. I think a lot of people put a lot of stock in that. They talk about me because I won four, you know. Then you win one or two people appear to think that that's what you're shooting for every year, that's what you want to do. Batting titles are decided the last day of the season, and when it's over, the guy with the highest batting average wins and that's it. There's no ifs, ands or buts about it. So at this point of the season, you can't worry about whether you're leading or not. You just go out there and try to continue to help your ball club win, because at the end that's when things are gonna be decided. Now really, they're not going to dictate what kind of season you're having at the midway point, they dictate it by what you do at the end of 162 games, and that's basically the standpoint I take. I can't worry about things going real good for me right now. I have to wait until the end of the season for people to decide whether I'm having a good year. During the course of that season, you like to go about things the way that you normally would, and with me at this point I feel like I'm putting the bat on the ball; and that's all I want to do. I'm not going out there and trying to get home runs, I'm not trying to do things different than I've always done. You know, what I do best is put the bat on the ball, and that's all I'm going out there trying to do.

Did you ever consider going for the long ball more? Did you ever concern yourself with that?

I used to, I used to, because my goal in the big leagues has [been to] become the most complete player I could be and I was hoping I could add home runs and RBI to that by without messing up what I consider the best swing for me. I tried a whole bunch of different things by changing my bat, my stance, trying to do all those different things, and sooner or later you get to the point where you ask yourself this question: "am I doing the best that I can do for my ball club?" And you look at our ball club, sure we could use a couple other guys in here to hit the ball out of the ballpark, but what I do best is just put the bat on the ball and not necessarily hit it out of the ballpark. But put the bat on the ball. I get on base. I got an average of getting on bases about 250 times a year just doing what I do, and with a guy like McGriff and guys like Benito and Jerald Clark hitting behind me, you're giving them an opportunity to drive in runs. From my perspective and also from the Padres' perspective, they feel like that's the best thing for me to do. At some point sure, I'd like to go out there and hit 20 home runs, 25 home runs, but I think what I do right now is best for my ball club, and the people in charge feel the same way so that's all I concentrate on doing. Because the bottom line here is winning, it's not about putting great individual numbers on the board, it's about winning. Whatever you can do to help the ball club win, that's what you should be out there trying to do.

Tony, we talked about hitting and your name is certainly at the top of the "A list," but four out of the last five years you were a Gold Glove winner. Talk about being a complete player who can do it all, that must have great significance to you.

Yeah, to me it has more significance than the hitting aspect, because coming into this league, people generally thought I could swing the bat and typically they didn't think I could be, didn't think I'd turn out to be as good as I've been. You know I really had to work hard at every aspect of the game in baseball, but especially on the defensive end. What I've tried to do is not try to improve my deficiencies but improve on the areas [in] which I was strong. I felt like going back on a ball is pretty strong, charging the ball is pretty strong, and trying to improve those areas would help me in other areas that I didn't, that I wasn't real good at, mainly the throwing. I don't really have the kind of strength in my arm that a lot of other right fielders have, and what I try to do is charge the ball quick, then get rid of it and be accurate and then basically kind of brush off the fact that you don't have a strong arm. Winning four Gold Gloves to me is the biggest accomplishment in the big leagues as far as I'm concerned. Swinging a bat for some reason I've just always been able to do that, but the other areas of the game I feel like I've had to work really hard to try to improve on. The more years you play, it seems like the better I get. And defensively there is still a lot of room for improvement. You know I work hard on it every day, and I try to go out there and make the normal routine plays and every once in awhile come up with one, you know, out of the blue and make a play.

Harvey Haddix

On May 29, 1959, Pittsburgh Pirates left-hander Harvey Haddix pitched 12 perfect innings, 36 up and 36 down, against the Milwaukee Braves. Haddix, known as "The Kitten," was certainly purring that night, retiring 36 consecutive Braves at County Stadium. Ironically, he ended up losing the game, 1–0, in the 13th inning. Haddix finished his career (1952–1965) with a record of 136–113 and an ERA of 3.63. The following season, "The Kitten" was also the winning pitcher in relief in Game 7 of the 1960 World Series when Bill Mazeroski's ninth-inning walk-off home run propelled the Pirates to victory over the favored New York Yankees.

Harvey, today they are honoring you for your 12 perfect innings. It seems unbelievable, 12 perfect innings. Were there close calls in that game?

No, there were no really tough plays in the whole ballgame. Well, to start off with, I didn't even feel good to start with. I had kind of a summer-like flu, and I would get up early that morning here in Pittsburgh and we flew over there (Milwaukee), so I felt terrible.

Harvey Haddix, far right, pitched 12 perfect innings in 1959.

We get out to the ball park and start, and I warmed up the same as always, and as the game went on, of course I can remember a line drive at first. There were a couple of hard balls hit to short, and there were a couple of balls hit pretty good in center field. Outside of that, it was just routine plays the whole time. As I look back, the only time I really went for a no-hitter was the ninth inning, cause I'd been there before and never made it, so I said I'm going for it. And then after the ninth inning, I went back to pitching my normal way and it was just an unbelievable thing. The only thing I can say is I had outstanding control that night. I could pinpoint the ball where I wanted it.

Did the team stick to the ritual of not talking about it during the game?

They sure did. I was avoided like the plague. Nobody even came close to me. I'd go down and sit in the runway between innings, where I could look out and see; nobody messed with me. And after they'd turn around and leave, they would come down and start and see me sitting there, they'd turn around and walk back out, never say a word to me.

Is that the way you wanted them to react?

No, it doesn't matter to me. I laughed about it after they'd walk away. It didn't matter to me one way or the other.

How disappointing was it to go that far and not get the win?

It wasn't really disappointing in losing the ball game because of the 12 innings or the 13. The idea we didn't win, that's the toughest part. You're out there to win, that's your important thing. As far as losing the 12 perfect innings and stuff like that, that's immaterial. In fact that's what probably made it more popular today than it would have been if I'd of won.

Did you ever think, you know people say that that is the greatest single game ever pitched, you ever ponder that?

Well, I've heard that said. I never saw all the games pitched, so I can't say that. All I know is that I pitched the 12 perfect innings. Of course I didn't know I was doing it at the time, so it didn't really matter to me what I was doing. We were just trying to win the ballgame.

I spoke with Lew Burdette and he said he felt sorry for you after you pitched 12 perfect innings. We know that he was the winning pitcher that night. Have you ever thought about that particular game and discovered anything new?

No it always turns out the same as it did that very night. But it is fun to look back on it and to reminisce a little about what happened. But the strangest thing, and I mentioned it to Lew last night, during an Old Timers Game in Chicago about three or four years ago, Bob Buhl was a pitcher on that team (Milwaukee Braves), and he said they called every pitch against me that night. They knew every pitch that was coming with the binoculars in the bullpen. They got them off Smoky Burgess. They knew every pitch that was coming and it still didn't help. Now that's hard to believe.

That evening while pitching the no-hitter, when did you become aware of what was happening?

I was aware of the no-hitter all the way through but I didn't know that I did something that somebody else hadn't done. I never was a statistics man like that, but I did know I had a no-hitter all the way. The big scoreboard was in front of me, and every inning I'd go look up there and of course there were zeros up there. I was aware of it the whole time.

Did you have other games that you felt you were throwing just as well as the 12 perfect innings?

Oh, I had a lot of games I had better stuff and pitched just as good, but it didn't happen. It's an amazing thing to be able to do that, in fact there were no running or diving catches or no balls that were tough to catch. It was just one of those nights like you get in a trance and you just keep going.

Was it Adcock who broke it up?

It sure was, Joe Adcock. The second pitch to him in the 13th inning, and I got it up and over the plate a little. I wanted it down more. It wasn't a real bad pitch, it wasn't a good pitch but it wasn't a bad pitch, and he went with it and hit it over the right-center field fence.

Note—Adcock was not officially credited with a home run as Hank Aaron saw teammate Felix Mantilla score on the hit and walked to the dugout, thinking the ball hit by Adcock was a double and the game was over. As he rounded the bases, Adcock was called out for passing Aaron on the base path and credited with a double and an RBI, and the game went in the books as a 1–0 Milwaukee win.

◆ ◆ ◆

Bud Harrelson

Bud Harrelson is the only New York Met to be in uniform when the team picked up two World Series rings, first as a member of the 1969 Miracle Mets and the other as a coach in 1986. He was also at shortstop during the Mets' 1973 pennant-winning season. Harrelson was an outstanding fielder, compiling a .969 fielding percentage over his 16-year career winning a Gold Glove Award in 1971. Near the end of the 1969 regular season, he fielded a ground ball and started the double play that would assure the Mets of their first Eastern title in NL history. In the NLCS, he drove in three runs in the Miracle Mets' sweep of the Atlanta Braves. In the World Series vs. Baltimore, he had three singles and three walks for a .300 on-base percentage. During the 1990 season, Bud Harrelson was promoted from coach to manager of the team he had anchored at shortstop during many of its greatest moments.

This interview was conducted in Pittsburgh, Pennsylvania, in 1989.

This is the 20th anniversary of the Miracle Mets, probably one of the greatest upsets. People still talk about it today. Other World Series seem to fade, but this one stands out, and of course you were an integral part of that. You've had 20 years just to look back on this and reflect. How do you view it now?

Well, I think the reason why it is remembered so much, '69, is I think that the '69 results with what the team did is kind of the epitome of sports, that a team can go all the way from say last place, which we were mired in last place for so many years, and then all of a sudden you go from last place to being world champions. I think that is something that gives everyone hope that those things do happen and can happen. I think for the ones that were involved in, the players that were involved in, we'll soon be back together. Obviously this summer is the 20th anniversary of the '69 world champion Mets; it's that we kind of felt like we were a team of destiny, that things were really going well for us and they were going to continue to go well for us, almost as if we weren't in control, someone else was. I think there has been close similarities in the past; the Tampa Bay Bucs stick in my mind. You know they were moving along, a team that didn't do well, and all of a sudden they were doing well, and they just didn't quite come away with the same results that the '69 Mets team did.

At the time you were a young player, and of course you had some veteran players on the club. But as a younger player, how did that affect the rest of your career? Because in terms of emotion, where could you go from there?

Well, I think you matured through it. I don't think it can be duplicated. I've been on the '73 team which won our division, beat Cincinnati in the playoffs and then lost in seven games against the Oakland A's. The '86 Mets, who won 118 games total, and I was the third-base coach at that time. People were trying to make comparisons as to which was better, and I don't think there will ever be another '69 in the minds of those players. I don't think it is something that you can say, well this is the best thing I've ever done in my life. I still think the best things that I am going to do in my life are ahead of me, and I think most of the guys felt that way, that certainly we were disappointed in '70 when we didn't win, in '71 and '72. But there was always hope that we could, not duplicate it, but that we could do it again. And I think we matured as ballplayers, although we were for the most part the nucleus of the ball club, there's a very immature, inexperienced team. I think that was one of the reasons why it made it even more special, particularly to the public who thought naw, these guys don't know how to win. Naw, these guys will blow it in the end. And I thought it was just the opposite. I thought from the standpoint of a young player, we had everything to gain and nothing to lose. Everyone else had something to lose. Had we beat them, which we did, it makes it hurt more because you were expected to win. It will be a similar situation this year and every year since '86, when the Mets won the World Series in '86. We didn't win in '87 and in '88 didn't make it past LA. They almost were the team of destiny similar to the situation there, but not a lot of young players, more veteran players.

Finally, when you look back, the turning point for your club in '69, was there a moment, it may have not even been that dramatic, but you felt something?

Well, I think the turning point was '68 when we got Gil Hodges, I thought that was the turning point. Although he was a very popular player in New York, he did not know much about the ball club, and I think he sat back and let us play in '68. He had nothing to do but observe and see what we could do, and he really had a nice, refreshing attitude. I thought as a manager Gil Hodges was way ahead of his time, and as far as a psychologist, I thought he was one of the best psychologists; in fact he was the best psychologist that I had ever played under, and I think that's a lot in management now. You need to really be a good psychologist and learn to get the most out of all your players, not treat them all the same, but really get to know your players. And he did that, so getting him in '68 was the change, and in '69 I think he just set out to develop and strengthen our weaknesses and really get in our minds and make us play better and really supported us. We were a much better team in '68 than we showed, and we lost 36 one-run ballgames, and in '69 we won 42 one-run ballgames. So he was the reason, although we still needed to play well and do well, which we had good pitching and good defense. We didn't have big stars, big name players, but we had players that were really coming into their own all together with the Seavers and the Koosmans and the Ryans and the Grotes who had been traded for, and Clendenon certainly, and even a guy like Kranepool who was up and down, and then the Shamskys who we traded for, Eddie Charles. It was just a good mix of good pitching, good defense and key hitting.

• • •

Ernie Harwell

If ever a voice fit the national pastime, it was the soothing tones of Ernie Harwell. The son of the South called games for 55 seasons over radio and television, with 42 of them in Detroit. Mr. Harwell broke in broadcasting for the Atlanta Crackers in 1943, and after five seasons moved east to Brooklyn for two seasons and then to upper Manhattan and the New York Giants for three campaigns. It was at the Polo Grounds that he described one of the most dramatic moments in Major League Baseball, Bobby Thomson's "Shot Heard Round the World" to win the 1951 pennant for the Giants in their playoff against rival Brooklyn. Ernie Harwell would later call games for Baltimore and the California Angels after his first tenure (1960–1991) in Detroit. In 1981, the legendary announcer became the fifth broadcaster to receive the Ford C. Frick Award from the Baseball Hall of Fame.

So many people grew up with you and associate your voice not only with Tigers baseball but with major league baseball. The Atlanta Crackers originally, and Brooklyn and Baltimore, then the Giants and Detroit. You were working television the day Bobby Thomson hit "The Shot Heard Round the World."

Absolutely, it was probably the highlight of my career, Bobby Thomson's home run that beat the Brooklyn Dodgers in the third and final game in 1951, because it sort of climaxed that great rivalry between the Dodgers and the Giants. The pennant and everything else rode on that one swing of the bat by Bobby. I was on television; I was on NBC-TV that day. Russ Hodges, my partner and I, alternated on radio and TV, and it turned out to be Russ's time on the radio and somebody in Brooklyn recorded history. "The Giants win the pennant, the Giants win the pennant," and sent it to him. Russ sent him $10, they put it out as a record and it became the most famous sports broadcast of all time. And my television, nobody had replays or any kind of a recording at that time, so only Mrs. Harwell and I know I was on that day.

You're a Southerner, and it seems so many of the great announcers in baseball were from the South. Why does that lend itself so much to the game of baseball?

I really don't know; the facetious answer used to be we were too lazy to work for a living. But I think what it really gets back to is the rural atmosphere of the South, big families and sitting out on the porch and people talking about the relatives and the shopkeepers of the town that we grew up in and just telling stories. We became the storytellers in the process, I guess, and then when it developed into sports announcers, sports announcing was in its infancy at that time. Nobody had really developed a style. Red Barber, Mel [Allen] and those guys came along and they sort of set the style, and they happened to be Southerners. They were storytellers, and that's the way it happened.

You know Red does the Public Broadcasting Network on Fridays; did you speak with him at all? I know we're all saddened by the news about you, of course. (The Tigers had announced that they would not extend Mr. Harwell's contract.) Did you speak with Red or did you contact any of the veteran broadcasters?

I didn't speak to Red. I talked to Mel and Jack Buck and some of the guys; but Red and I do talk to each other once in awhile, and I always send him a birthday card and I hear from him, usually get a little note from him. And we were on the Hall of Fame committee, although he wasn't well enough to attend, and I talked to him about that from time to time. But he is down there in Tallahassee; he's having a great second career. I think it's marvelous that he can do that and he has such a popularity that extended beyond his baseball announcing.

Ernie, what has sustained you, because over the years, I know obviously you have a love of the game, but what keeps it so fresh for you? Because it's never, well this is just another game, you keep it fresh. How are you able to do that?

Every game is different to me, and there are nuances to see in every game that's interesting. I think we really owe it to the public to be enthusiastic and upbeat about the game, because the people that tune in evidently enjoy baseball or else they wouldn't be tuned in. I enjoy baseball, and we have sort of a bond because of that. I think our love for the game gets us together and I try to keep my energy up, I try not to get too tired, I try not to overextend myself, and then that way I can keep as fresh as I can physically and get the job done.

You no doubt like radio better than television in terms of being in the booth. Why is that?

I think it's because baseball and radio really belong to each other much better than baseball and television. To me, the analogy is like a book. When you broadcast a baseball game on the radio, it's like just reading a book. You can imagine what's happening, he can set the scene himself, he can determine what the hero or the heroine looks like. Whereas on television, it's like a movie and the director tells you what the hero looks like, what the setting is, what color the couch is in the living room, all those things, and you don't get to use your imagination. I think the best tool that anybody has is the imagination.

Ernie, we know what you gave to the game of baseball. Assuming that you're not going to announce any longer after this year, what has baseball given to you, what will you take from it?

Well, I've taken probably a lot more than I've given it. It's given me a livelihood for one thing. It's given me a job that I really enjoy, broadcasting a game that I love, and it's given me a lot of great association with people; managers, umpires, players, clubhouse men, media people, and I think most of all it's the people that I've met and the people that are in the game that have meant more to me than anybody.

Most of the public has a deep feeling for you; I'd say all of them, but you never know. But you are certainly one of the great announcers and like I said, I think we're going to see you surface because [of] your vitality, you have too much going for you. I hope to see you next season.

Thank you very much, thank you.

◆ ◆ ◆

Tommy Henrich

Tommy Henrich, who was referred to as "Old Reliable" during his 11-year playing career with the New York Yankees, was an integral part of four world championships for the fabled franchise from 1937 to 1950. Military service in World War II took away three seasons for Henrich, who hit for a lifetime average of .282 with 1,297 hits, 183 home runs and 795 RBI. In a now-famous at-bat in game 4 of the 1941 World Series, Henrich struck out to end the game, but Brooklyn catcher Mickey Owen dropped the third strike, allowing the ball to slide past him. Henrich ran to first base and was safe as the Yankees rallied to win the game and take a 3 to 1 advantage in the Series.

This interview was conducted in 1992.

What was it about those Yankees clubs you played on?
    When I got to that ball club in 1937, the day the season opened that year. I had just been declared a free agent. I got into New York a day before that and went out and met all the fellows, and I tell you it was very striking. I was cordially greeted by everybody, but the feeling in that clubhouse was professional, a bunch of pros, real pros getting ready to go to work. That was all created by Joe McCarthy; he's the greatest manager I think ever in baseball. Anyway that's, more than that, of course they had the talent, there's no doubt about that. But the Red Sox had talent too but they didn't win, and I think it was because the large dedication. Playing as a unit was as big factor as anything.

You know, Tommy, I think the important years along with you having a great career were the time you put into the military service. So many of the players in the major leagues served, but you guys didn't feel sorry for yourselves. However, it did hurt many careers, it hurt you and many of the people of your era, but you had to chalk it up to that's the way things were.
    That's exactly right. Everybody was hit the same way. It just so happened in our profession that our careers were, if we're lucky, we might go 15 years, and that this was right in the middle of it. Bob Feller and Ted Williams did the same thing, and that was a little more, I don't know, drastic as regards to our welfares then let's say a 22-year-old boy that doesn't have a career yet. But nevertheless you go to war and everybody's in the same boat.

The moment many remember about you is the time you struck out in the 1941 World Series against Brooklyn, and you ran to first base because catcher Mickey Owen had the ball get past him. It's been said the pitch that Hugh Casey threw was a spitball. I asked Mickey, and he said no it wasn't a spitball, it was a curveball. What's your side of that?

Absolutely, I agree with, I heard Mickey say that. The first time I ever saw Mickey after the incident was the old timers' game in Los Angeles. The Dodgers invited me out there of all things, and I told the Dodgers when I got an invitation, I said man, you've made my life to get invited to a Dodger old timers' game. Anyway I heard Mickey describe the thing, and I agree with him 100 percent and I told him that. It was the best curveball Casey ever threw in his life. It surprised me. I'm swinging at the ball, you remember the picture you're talking about. I'm in the paper every year in the World Series striking out. I swung at that ball. It just started to break and it was high and then I realized, man, that ball's disappearing, it went straight down. Anyway I'm trying to hold up and, if you look at the picture, you see me looking already at Mickey because I thought I had so much trouble, maybe he's having trouble too. Sure enough he did, and he's getting it out of the dirt and my bat is up in the air, so you know this was a real good curveball; it was not a spitter. A spitter is like a knuckleball, it just jumps; but a curveball has an arch to it and that's what it was, there's no doubt about that. All the wise guys, the guys that weren't at home plate says aw, it had to be a spitter, no it didn't. It was a curveball.

I was thinking we were going to have some controversy if you would have said something different. It's odd that Mickey, a guy that played 13 years and was known as a tremendous defensive catcher. I think he had a string of 100 games with the Dodgers that year where he didn't make an error.

That's right, absolutely true. Mickey points that out and he says that the guy that was doing the pitching has the best won and loss record of all relief pitchers and here we got, and I'm not a bad hitter, and the three of us got messed up on one play at the same time. Well, at least from my standpoint it worked out all right.

It certainly did. You know that, that's one of the things that we see every year in World Series time is your photo. But you know when we speak about you going into the service and such, a part of the book that really did stick with me was when you went up for your last at-bat and they made the announcement on the public address speakers. I think that was very poignant about how the people felt about you.

Well really, that has stayed with me all my life. And you know the pitcher was Dizzy Trout. I went up in the I think [the] seventh or eighth inning, and out of no place the public address announces that, "ladies and gentlemen, this will be Tommy's last appearance in the Yankee uniform for the duration of the war." And man did they explode and they really gave me a tremendous ovation. I don't know, it was, the Tigers always drew them in, so there were a lot of people there. The pitcher was Dizzy Trout; I know Dizzy Trout. He had a good fastball and he knew that I was a fastball hitter. So the people are applauding and I take this and I'm getting embarrassed and I stepped, I went up to home plate and I says, come on let's go; and he says, no Tom, he says you listen to this, he says this happens once in a lifetime. So that's what happened. In my mind then, I said well, now in appreciation for this I will now hit a ball to the moon. And the first pitch came in a fastball, and I swung and missed completely. I swung at another one and missed, and then I said to myself, never mind hitting to the moon, hit the ball some place. So at the count of three and two all fastballs, then comes another one, I hit a line drive, a beautiful line drive to center field for a base hit so, that pleased me quite a bit. That was my way of saying goodbye to wonderful people all right. I enjoyed the fans in New York. All over, Brooklyn, the Polo Grounds, they're smart fans there, boy. They can get pretty loud, but they're not mean. They can cut you up a little bit, but they are not dirty about it. I enjoyed it.

Something else that must have been enjoyable and something that would stay with you. You know you were very fortunate, and I'm sure the players you played which were fortunate to play with a guy like you, but you played with Lou Gehrig and Joe DiMaggio; it's almost like a who's who because the Yankees had so many outstanding ballplayers, and I know in the book you touch on so many of them. Lou Gehrig gave you a bit of advice.

Yeah, he was such a fine gentleman. He was, very early I found out that Lou would help me if there was anything that he could do for me. When I'd face a new pitcher, I'd say Lou, what do I look for from this guy, and in this instance it was Ted Lyons, he's in the Hall of Fame. He's a real tremendous pitcher with the White Sox. He says, "Tom, you hit the first good fastball he throws." I said why? He said, "because after that you're gonna have trouble." So I got up there, and the first pitch was a fastball low and on the outside corner for a strike. I said whoa, that's the one I should have swung at, and I says I'll get a better ball next time. Anyway, you can't make a living hitting low and outside. But the next pitch came in and it was shoulder high, as it got to home plate, it was a knuckleball, and it just drove right down through the middle of the plate, called strike two. I says well, that's a fluke, nobody can do that again. Next pitch came in, it was outside and it broke over the plate again, and I took a weak swing at it and got the heck out of there. That's why I say I disobeyed Gehrig's orders, but I would have had trouble with Lyons. I did have an awful lot of trouble with him, he's a great pitcher. Anyway I disobeyed Gehrig.

Well, but you learned from that.
Oh yeah, oh yeah.

You know, you talk a lot about Joe DiMaggio that you played in the outfield with him, and of course you touch on the outstanding, outstanding isn't the word for it, it's an incredible 56 consecutive games. I guess that's a record that you and a lot of other people feel will never be equaled.

It will be a tremendous feat. I tell you the way I analyze this thing. When DiMaggio broke a record, he broke a record at 44. He tied Sisler at 43, he broke it at 44, that's the modern that was recognized as the record at that time. Now what's facing a guy; and I'll tell you this, Joe DiMaggio was more nervous, if he got nervous at all in that whole streak, the most nervousness I saw in him were in the 43rd and the 44th game, 'cause he knew that's tying and breaking the record. Now what's gonna happen, you see Pete Rose hit in 44 and I think the pressure will build-up on him, and that is gonna make it very difficult to go beyond 56. That's what I think is gonna happen. A lot of guys, not too many are even going to go to 44, but if they do, the whole world will be watching them, I'll tell you that.

I'm sure. You know you hit the nail right on the head. In fact, each year it seems to get more and more coverage. Today once a guy gets past 15 or 20, you know they have a caravan that follows him around.

That's a good move.

But you have the nickname which is one of the great nicknames. You don't hear many nicknames any more, but "Old Reliable," and I believe it was Mel Allen that hung it on you or it could have been Russ Hodges.

They were teammates and they were a team with the Yankees at that time. Russ Hodges, I'm not sure, but I think from what I understand the first time they used it was in a ballgame in Philadelphia. We were one run ahead of the last of the ninth. Buddy Rosar hit a pop fly and our catcher, Ken Silvestri, didn't even touch the ball. It was a foul ball. Next pitch, Rosar hit it in the seats and ties the ballgame up. Now here we are going into extra innings, and I think it was Russ Hodges said my God, we might miss the train. Anyway, in the tenth inning, Rizzuto got a single, I put on a hit-and-run and punched it in the left field corner, and Rizzuto scored and out of no place, Russ Hodges I think says, "Old Reliable." He says he did it again. I think they were thankful that we're gonna get out of Philadelphia. Anyway, that's the first that I'd heard of it, and they use it and it stuck, very nice. I don't know whether it's true or not, but I enjoyed it, I still do.

Well I think it is true. I mean you can look at your record and see that you were the man. I think that many believe it because of a train, there was a train they called Old Reliable.

That's what, no, Allen said that. You know he came from, he went to Alabama and he was from Alabama, I think, and he said that it used to be well-known that this train was always on time and they got to calling it "Old Reliable" coming to, you know. Maybe that's where it started, I don't know, I can't prove that.

One last thing, Tommy, I forgot to ask you, which I think is kind of a milestone. In 1937 in the spring of '37, Judge Landis declared you a free agent. I think you were the first free agent. You were supposedly property of Cleveland.

You got that right, supposedly, yeah. See I was a softball player out of Massillon [Ohio]. I didn't start out till I was 19 and I played one year there and a Cleveland scout came along in the course of the year. I signed up with Cleveland and I went through three ball clubs in the minor leagues, Class D, C and D-1, whatever it was. And I was sold from New Orleans to presumably the Milwaukee Brewers, that was in the American Association, and during the course of the winter, I read in the paper where Milwaukee is gonna sell me to the Boston Braves and Cleveland is gonna trade me to the St. Louis Browns. And I said wait a minute here, who in the heck do I belong to. So I talked it over with my dad, and I said I'm gonna write to Judge Landis. He said why, and I said because he's the only guy I know who will be on the ballplayer's side and give me a fair decision on this. So I gave him all the facts that I could, and he dug into it and he found, which was true, that, what he found on me he could have found on hundreds of guys that ever went through the Cardinals. You know they kept Johnny Mize in the minor leagues for five years. He was a tremendous hitter, and that was Brian Schrieke, so he was breaking the rules too. Anyway Landis proved, declared that Cleveland was guilty of directing my progress through the minor leagues, and yet Landis had no record of Cleveland owning me, that's a violation. Based on that, I was declared a free agent, and I heard from eight ball clubs and one of them was the New York Yankees. I said, "hold the phone, boys, let's go." I told dad I was in favor of the Yankees. Now don't forget in '36 the Yankees were world champions and they got a great ball club there, so what's the chance on a rookie like me doing any good with the Yankees; and he said do you think you can make that. I said I don't know whether I can or not, dad, but I said one thing, if I go the Browns and turn out that I'm a good ballplayer, I'm stuck there forever. I'd rather take a chance on going to New York and if I can make it, man that's where I want to be, so that's what happened.

I appreciate you relaying those stories. It's an interesting book, "5 O'clock Lightning." There's only one criticism I have on this book, and that's on the cover it has Ruth, and Gehrig and DiMaggio and Mantle. You have to turn to the back to see Tommy Henrich; and Tommy, really you were an outstanding player and you're a great spokesman for baseball, and I think maybe we could have used a picture of you on the front.

You got to write to the publisher. I think they figured that Ruth and Gehrig and DiMaggio and Mantle will sell the book, but that's the publisher's side of it. They even made a mistake, they said I played with Babe Ruth. I called them up and I says, "hey, don't you say that, I did not play with Babe Ruth." They said, "well, you can blame it on us," and I said okay. Right now I'm blaming it on the publisher.

◆ ◆ ◆

Ralph Houk

Ralph Houk led what many consider the greatest team ever, the 1961 New York Yankees (109–53), with the likes of Mickey Mantle, Roger Maris, Yogi Berra, Elston Howard, Bobby Richardson and Whitey Ford. It was the year that Roger Maris and teammate Mickey Mantle battled it out to break Babe Ruth's home run record of 60. Maris would finish with 61 and Mantle with 54. Houk, generally referred to as "The Major," is the only manager to win World Series championships in his first two years at the helm. Houk succeeded Casey Stengel in 1961 and defeated the Cincinnati Reds that season and the San Francisco Giants in 1962. The Major finished his Yankees tenure with a record of 944–806. He later managed in Detroit for five seasons (363–443) and Boston for four seasons (312–282) for a 20-year managerial record of 1619–1531.

You had a tremendous career as a manager, and I'm sure people always bring up that great '61 Yankees ball club. You were one of the youngest managers; you were 41 years old.

Well, it's been quite a while ago, but I think that's about right, and that was a great ball club. I was very fortunate that Casey left me a team like he did, and then we added a few young ball players that year. I think it's the best ball club I think that I've ever been around because we had, you know, the fellows like Mickey and Roger Maris, and of course Yogi was still there and Howard, Boyer, Kubek, Richardson and Skowron. We had a good bench, a great relief pitcher in Arroyo. Of course Whitey had a great year, and it was kind of a ball club that could do everything. It had speed. They think of the power it had, but it also had good speed when we needed it in the close games, and a great defense.

To many people in the know, that team is mentioned as possibly one of the greatest teams of all time.

Well you know, it's really hard to compare one team against another when there is that much time between them, like probably saying whether Joe Louis was better than this guy or that guy, but it was a ball club that had power from both sides of the plate and did have all the things that you look for in a great ball club.

I understand that Mickey Mantle had a special relationship with you. I read where you were close with the bench players, you knew how to relate to them, yet here was a superstar like Mantle that you had a strong relationship with.

Well, when I took the job in '61, we needed a leader, and the Yankees never really had captains on their teams. With the ability that Mickey had and you know, being a kid from Oklahoma and from the Midwest, I related pretty good to him; and I told Mickey in spring training, I says, "Mickey, I'm going to tell the press that you are the leader of this ball club, which is about the same as saying a captain." And the thing was about Mickey, Mickey could hit two home runs and drive in four runs, and if we got beat you'd of thought that he had failed to do the job. Or if we won a ball game and he didn't do anything, he was as happy as any player on the ball club. That's the type of person he was, and of course as you well know he played injured all the time with both legs wrapped and with a lot of pain. He was just an unbelievable inspiration to a ball club because of those reasons, and those things kind of relate to the other players when they see a guy like that that all he thinks about is winning, it makes your other players do the same thing. It isn't like in a World Series, it's like every day he would do things to try to win, like bunt or get a guy over, and when he stole a base it was always a big one. I didn't let him run too much because I wanted to protect his legs. But those are the people that make, make great leaders on ball clubs.

The countdown to 61 for Roger Maris. We've heard so much about what the man went through that year and being in New York and the pressure. Were you able to relate to that or to help him at all?

I don't think anybody could. I mean people will never understand the pressure that Roger went through. Personally I think he should be in the Hall of Fame. He did something no one else has ever done, and people forget that he was a great defensive ball player and would break up double plays. He no more wanted really to hit 61 home runs than anybody. Right when he was up into the '50s, he would still bunt on his own to beat a ball out if he had a chance to win it by doing that, and he would do those little things. He would move a runner from second to third with nobody out, and a lot of people don't know that. And he would stand when he'd come to the ball park and sign autographs for an hour, and yet if the game was over and he didn't sign an autograph, people would get on him and things like that. When you get in the limelight that much, it's difficult to please everybody, and he finally got to the point where the press was so much following him that it really almost got to him, and at the end there he didn't ... well the game in Baltimore he came to me and said, "Skip, I just can't make it tonight," and of course the stadium was full. I think that's the night that he tied the record with 60, and I told him, I said, "Roger, you know why don't you just go ahead and play an inning and I'll get you out of there, you know, let people know you're not feeling well or something." But he did start the game and finish it, and that's the night he hit 60, and he actually, hair was coming out. I mean he was in bad shape at that particular time, and a lot of people don't understand that.

Your career as a manager had great teams after, '62, '63, and then of course everyone associates you with the Yankees. You went to Detroit and then Boston.

I went to Detroit for five years. Yeah well, I really thought I was going to retire and then Jim Campbell talked to me and said we need a manager that understands young players. We're going to have to get rid of all our old players here, and you're the guy we want. And of course Jim was a good friend of mine and I liked the owner, Mr. [John] Fetzer, at that time, so that's how that happened. And then when I retired from Detroit, I fully intended to not manage again, and after two years with the Red Sox, I knew Sullivan real well there and the Yawkey family, and they said well we're going to have to rejuvenate this ball club. That's when Fisk left and Lynn and Burleson and they talked me into coming up there, and I had four great years up there and left very happy. I'm lucky I've never been fired; maybe I left before anybody fired me.

"The Major," Ralph Houk, skipper of record-setting 1961 New York Yankees.

Finally, Ralph, I noticed you have a Twins ring on. I knew you worked with them in a capacity, but I'm just wondering that in terms of the Yankee tradition. I know you have Yankee rings.

I have the one where we won five World Series in a row, but I was Vice President of baseball in Minnesota for one year in 1987, and then I told Andy MacPhail hey, it's time for me to do some of the things my wife and I have always wanted to do. So I was sort of a consultant for a couple of years there after that. But right now I'm just doing these BAT, BAT stands for Baseball Assistance Team, and I do this for the simple reason that the money raised, over $1 million now in five years, goes to the ball players that are not as fortunate as the ones today. So I, I feel like this is something I can do and enjoy, and I get to see some of the players again, so I'm having fun doing that. And I thank Equitable for making all of this possible for all these old players.

◆ ◆ ◆

Monte Irvin

Monte Irvin was a standout player wherever he played, be it the Negro, Mexican or Major Leagues. While playing for Newark in the Negro Leagues, Irvin batted .422 in 1940 and .396 in 1941. The following season, while in the Mexican League, he won the batting title with an average of .397. He served in the Army during World War II and was present at the Battle of the Bulge. After the war, Monte Irvin rejoined the Newark Eagles, winning his second batting title and helping the team win the Negro League World Series. In 1949, he became one of the first African American players to sign with a Major League club when the New York Giants offered him a contract. He played in two World Series, 1951 when he went 11-for-24 at the plate, and 1954. He played the final year of his eight-year career in the Majors with the Chicago Cubs. He compiled a batting average of .293

with 99 home runs and 443 RBI, and in 1973 was elected to the Hall of Fame for his play and pioneering contributions to the game. In 2010, his number 20 was retired by the Giants.

Today we are honoring the 1948 Homestead Grays team of the Negro Leagues.

Well, the Grays won it, you know, some 40 years ago. They were the Negro Leagues World Champions back in 1948, and of course I never did play with them, but I played against them all those years, and I'm delighted that they would invite me back for this real celebration. I think the Pirates should be complimented for honoring this great club because most of these guys were real stars and could really play. It's just too bad that many major league fans never saw them play.

They have debated since Jackie Robinson broke the color barrier, the reasons why it took so long.

Well, it was a different era, Ron. You know you couldn't eat in a restaurant, you couldn't stay in a hotel, you couldn't travel first class on a train, so it was just a, you know, that's the way it was in yesteryear. I'm so delighted that the country has progressed far enough, you know, to do a thing like this. This is what I'm saying—the powers are certainly to be complemented. When Jackie broke the color barrier, everything opened up, and it's equal opportunity for the most part now, which is wonderful.

Many have said it could have been you, rather than Jackie, not that anyone was looking to compare or take any credit away from Jackie Robinson. Obviously you've heard that.

Oh yeah, but they picked the right man in Jackie, because he was very intelligent, he was [a] good speaker, he was a natural leader and he had great baseball talent. He was not the best player when they first brought him up, but he improved constantly every year and became the great pioneer and Hall of Famer that he became.

Were there other great players maybe that didn't get as much notoriety as some of the players in the Negro Leagues that you remember?

Oh yeah, there was of course Ray Dandridge, who just went in last year and was just a very outstanding third baseman. Leon Day [was] a great player, one of the great right-handed pitchers who pitched with the Grays just for a short time; he's one of the all-time greats. The Grays, the Homestead Grays had a pitcher by the name of Raymond Brown who was from Dayton, who was just an outstanding pitcher, pitcher, hitter, outfielder, play everyplace. He was a wonderful pitcher, one of the best in the Negro Leagues. Another pitcher by the name of Roy Partlow. He played in the minor leagues. You know, he was old when the opportunity came, but he was a star down there. And there were guys like Willie Wells, and Mule Suttles and Quincy Trouppe. These kind of fellows, I just wished you could have seen them play. They were simply outstanding.

What about the great Josh Gibson? Did you play against him?

He was the best. He's the best of all. Yeah Josh, you can then mention him and forget about all the players. He was twice as strong as the average man, he had a classic swing, he was big, he was handsome and he was boyish. He had charisma like Babe Ruth. Even though you played against him, you had to like his ability. He was just that great. He was about 6'2", run like a deer, had a rifle for an arm and was strong as two men; just perfect for baseball.

Carl Barger (left) presents an award to Monte Irvin.

What about the style of play? I think there was a term they used, the players called it trick baseball, the different style of making things happen as opposed to maybe in the major leagues where they're waiting for the one big shot from a guy like Ruth?

Well, they played more scientific, you know. For instance, the Grays might have had, if they had a pitcher who was not say a good fielder, well they might bunt on him for the first three or four innings. You know, lay the ball down the first base line, down the third base line, and then when they time out, you see, then they would start to swing away, and that's the way they would beat a good pitcher or a real fastball pitcher. And then we had all the, the hit behind the runner, they like to, you hit the ball where it was pitched and that kind of thing. You know you'd start a runner at first, and then had the hitter lay the ball down the third base line, and the runner would always wind up at third base. You know that kind of thing, play real scientific ball. Plus the guys played with intensity. They played for the love of the game. They had to because we certainly [were] not making that much money, so you had to love it in order to be out there.

How would you like people to look at Monte Irvin? When people think of you, how would you like them to think of you?

Well, when I got to the majors, I was almost finished. I wished they could have seen me when I, you know, from 1942, my really last great year in the Negro Leagues, and then of course I had to go into the Army and didn't play anymore until 1946. But I wish they could see me play before I got [to] the majors.

Ferguson Jenkins

Right-handed pitcher Ferguson Jenkins was a 20-game winner for seven seasons in his career, six with the Chicago Cubs consecutively from 1967–1972. He led the NL in complete games for three seasons and led the league in strikeouts in 1969. When he won the Cy Young Award in 1971, he became the first Canadian to receive the honor. A change of venue didn't faze him either, as he put up impressive numbers for Texas and Boston in the American League. In 1974, he led the Junior Circuit in wins with 25 and complete games with 29 with the Rangers and was named AL "Comeback Player of the Year." Jenkins completed his career with a record of 284–226, an ERA of 3.34 and 3,192 strikeouts. He was the first Canadian to be elected to Cooperstown, in 1991.

Ferguson, a Hall of Fame career. You played with a number of teams, but most associate you with the Cubs. Can you pick a high point for yourself in your time with the Cubs?

Well, the first year I won 20 games in Chicago in 1967 under Durocher as a manager, we had a good nucleus of players, Kessinger, Beckert for the double play combination, Ronny at third, Ernie at first and Randy Hundley catching. We had Williams and Adolfo Phillips and I think George Altman in the outfield, along with Ted Savage. So we had a pretty good ball club. Those were exciting years. I was 22 years old at the time, and you look back at those days that you know you were excited about going to the ballpark and playing, especially in Wrigley Field.

What about '69, it looked like the Cubs had it in hand.

Well, we played well. We played first division ball for well over three-quarters of the season, got caught at the tail end by the Mets, and the Mets proved to be the best team in baseball that year.

You went on to Texas. Many people would count you out at times, but you always seemed to bounce back.

Well, me personally, I knew what my capabilities were. I know that one year I was accused of having a bad arm, and that was the reason I got traded I think the second time from Chicago to Texas, I only won 14 games. I played at Texas and went down there and won 25, and I think I proved to the sports world I didn't have a bad arm. But I've never had a sore arm.

Ferguson Jenkins, a 20-game winner for seven seasons.

What about the American and National Leagues, we hear one is the breaking ball league, the other one the high strike. You didn't have a problem in either league.

The only problem I had was the one year with the umpiring system. They had the home plated chest protector when I went to Texas in '74, and I didn't think they called a low pitch. I was a pitcher that gets down in the strike zone, and I had a bit of a problem in a few games; but after they realized that I wasn't going to bring the ball up, they had to start calling a low new strike for me.

◆ ◆ ◆

Harmon Killebrew

Harmon Killebrew played for 22 seasons, stroking 573 home runs while batting .256 with 1,584 RBI. The power-hitting dynamo made his Major League debut with the Washington Senators in 1954 and remained with the organization after it relocated to Minnesota in 1961 and became the Twins. The man known as "Killer" led or tied the AL lead in home runs six times and won the MVP Award in 1969, when he led the Junior Circuit with 49 home runs and drove in a career-best 140 runs. He helped carry the Twins to the World Series in 1965 and was a 13-time All-Star. Harmon Killebrew played the last year of his career with Kansas City, primarily as a DH. He was elected to Baseball's Hall of Fame in 1984, and a statue commemorating his service to the Twins stands outside Target Field.

This interview was conducted in Baltimore, Maryland, in 1993.

Harmon, you were one of the most feared sluggers of your era. You played on some outstanding ball clubs with some great players. If you had to pick a particular year for you and the ball club, what would that be?

Of course, we won the pennant in 1965 and played in the World Series against the Dodgers, played against Koufax and Drysdale. But that was a great ball club in those days, but I really think that the 1969 ball club that we had that was the first year [of] the divisional set-up. We won the divisional race that year and then played against Baltimore in the playoffs and lost to them three straight. So I think that was the best year, the best year I ever had in baseball.

You played with some outstanding players—Bobby Allison, Zoilo Versalles, and Earl Battey. You guys really assembled a tremendous ball club.

We had a good hitting ball club in those days, and I was thinking about also in 1969 we also had Rod Carew with our club. He came to us in 1967. So we had guys like Tovar, Carew, Oliva, and then if I hit fourth, you know that's not a bad way to start off the inning.

Did you ever contemplate playing somewhere else? You were such a marquee player, but it seemed when you were an active player, you may not have gotten the notoriety.

Well, Minnesota was not the kind of place that you got a lot of media attention. I started out my career with the old Washington Senators; it was much the same way, and of course our entire ball club moved to Minnesota in 1961. I played my final year at Kansas City. Kansas City was much the same as Minnesota, but it was kind of a place that met my personality. I was from a small town in Idaho, so I wasn't really interested in all that attention playing in a place like New York or LA.

What was that like playing with such an established club like the Senators and then having the franchise relocate? That had to be mixed emotions.

Well, it was for me. I had real mixed emotions about it because I enjoyed playing in Washington. As we talk here in Baltimore at the All-Star Game, just down the road it was a warm, warm type of climate. Playing out here today reminds me of course playing in those days in Washington, and I enjoyed it.

What would be the most memorable moment to you as a hitter?

Gosh, when you play as long as I did, a lot of things come to mind. Hitting the first home runs in the big leagues and the last one I will remember, and quite a few in between. Hitting home runs in All-Star Games [was] a big thrill to me and hitting a home run in the World Series. The other day, Don Drysdale passed away, and it made me stop and think about the home run I hit off of him in the World Series in 1965. So a lot of things come to mind.

I appreciate you taking a few moments, Harmon, one of the great sluggers of your era. All the best.

Thanks, Ron, nice to see you.

Power in the heartland. Harmon Killebrew (number 3) speaks with George Will.

Ralph Kiner

For seven consecutive seasons, Ralph Kiner led or was tied for the lead in home runs, and he was the first National Leaguer to club 50 homers twice. Kiner played eight seasons of his of his ten-year career with the Pittsburgh Pirates, followed by seasons with the Chicago Cubs and the Cleveland Indians. He was selected to play in six consecutive All-Star Games from 1948 to 1953. The left fielder, upon his retirement, spent more than 40 years in the New York Mets broadcast booth. He finished his career with a batting average of .279 and produced 369 home runs and 1,015 RBI. He was elected to the Hall of Fame in 1975.

When you look back over your career, the big year for you was 1949 with the 54 home runs, and probably most outstanding year. You lead the league in RBI and slugging percentage. Would you think that's the most gratifying to you?

Well, it certainly was. Well, the 54 home runs of course was a lot of home runs. In 1947, I hit 51 home runs and that was extremely gratifying because I had gone from 23 to 51, and I became the second player in the National League to ever hit 50 home runs or more. But 54 was big, and I had a tremendous last month. In September, I hit 16 home runs in that month, and actually I hit 55 home runs that year, but one got rained out. I hit it off of Johnny Sain, and the game was called before it was an official ball game and I lost it. I'd say '49 was all-in-all my most satisfying year, because it sort of backed up the year I had in '47. You can do it once, but to do it two times I think is a real test and a real accomplishment, and that was really a fantastic year for me.

Leading the league for seven consecutive years, something that's never been done; when you look at that, it is an incredible accomplishment because of a consistency of power that you displayed?

It is a matter of consistency; also you gotta be able to play all of the games. Fortunately, in the early part of my career I was able to play all the time. There were many times, of course, in order to play a full season you had to play hurt; but I was never hurt that badly that I couldn't continue to produce and hit home runs, and I did have a pretty consistent margin. The one regret I have was the fact that we didn't have great teams, and it made it awfully hard to play because it's no fun even though you produce to lose ball game after ball game. I only wished the Pirates had been a little more outgoing with the acquisition of better ballplayers. Because if you have those kind of years and your team does win, then it's just, that's more icing on the cake.

Yesterday was the anniversary of, was it about 40 years, when you were traded from the Pirates to the Cubs. Was it on June 4?

I don't really remember the date. I knew it was coming because Branch Rickey was that type of general manager. He wasn't gonna pay me my salary, and he was the type of person that liked to have players he can manipulate and control, and I wasn't that type. I knew it was coming, I don't exactly remember the date. I do know it was June, just around the trading deadline. In fact the day I was traded, I took batting practice in a

Pirates uniform and then the trade was announced after batting practice, and I changed clubhouses and changed uniforms and went on to the other side of Forbes Field in the visiting dugout.

The home run that stands out, I guess people remember is associated with you, is [in] the 1950 All-Star Game off of Art Houtteman, I believe.

Art Houtteman, and that tied up the game in the ninth inning. We went on to win it in the 14th, and that was the first time that I had played a game that long. It was a very, very hot day in Chicago, and we were all looking forward to, of course in those days we went to the All-Star Game on trains and it was a little bit different. We had to get out right after that game and get back to the respective cities we were going to by train. But that was a very satisfying home run. Hit home runs in three consecutive All-Star Games, which was also a big thrill. Nobody has ever done that before. But that was a big one because it tied the game up, but then Schoendienst hit a home run in the 14th to win it.

Now the man that was an inspiration to you both on the field and off was the great Hank Greenberg. When you played with him one year in Pittsburgh, was it Billy Herman that wanted to send you down, and I think Hank kind of stepped in and explained something to him?

Well, it's kind of an interesting story. When Greenberg came over to the Pirates in spring training in '47, he sort of took a liking to me, and his first statement to me was, "you'll never hit a lot of home runs the way you're hitting." Of course that got my attention. But he had been a great home run hitter himself, and of course hit 58 home runs one season. And I said "what do you mean?" And so he proceeded to change my stance and my position in the batter's box, and totally kind of reconstructed the way I was going about hitting. The year before, I had led the league in home runs, but he had also led the American League in home runs. And so I believed him, I felt that he was really someone who knew what he was talking about, but the results didn't come right away. Going to the first of June, I had hit only three for the season. Billy Herman was our manager. He wanted to get rid of me. He wanted to send me back to the minors, and Hank went to the front office; Frank McKinney was the president of the ball club at the time, John Galbreath was also involved, but Frank McKinney was the main man then, and he said "don't send this kid out, he's gonna be all right." Well, from June 1 until the end of the season, I had 48 home runs. I ended up with 51 and everything fell in place right after that. I will never forget the day before, on the last day of May, I had faced Hank Borowy, outstanding pitcher and now pitching for the Cubs, and he had struck me out four times. That was the low point. I

Ralph Kiner led or shared the home run lead in the NL for seven consecutive seasons, 1946–1952.

thought I was going back to the minors, there was no question in my mind, 'cause I had heard the fact that Herman wanted to send me back. I didn't know Hank had interceded in my behalf until later, but it certainly worked out.

Ralph, on the announcing side, there are a number of people that I have spoken with, I'm surprised at how many people love your home run call; you know you're known for saying, "That ball is gone, good-bye." I mean how did that come about?

Well, you know you have to have an individual call. Everybody tries to work one out. I don't really remember how I came up with that. I know I must have done it subconsciously one time and I liked it, and I thought well that might be a good way to do it. So I've called just about every home run that has been hit in any game that I have been broadcasting that way. You have to come up with something that's different from somebody else, and that just worked it out.

Finally, Ralph, you were a dead pull hitter your whole career. You never changed. I know there were instances where they tried to shift on you, maybe Lou Boudreau did it, the way he did against Ted Williams, but you weren't gonna change your style.

Well, there were two reasons for it; one, you can't stop home runs by shifting the infielders, and the second one was that our ball club was so in need of runs and productivity that for me to get singles and get on base wouldn't have helped the team at all. So that was one of the basic reasons. I felt that okay, you lose a lot of base hits, it kept me from being a lifetime .300 hitter, there's no question about that, but at the same time you gotta stick with what got you there. I was the dead pull hitter and hit right on top of the plate, and of course that helped me in runs batted in and home runs.

Thank you for taking a few moments of your time. It's evident that everyone loves to listen to you call a game, and thanks for sharing your abilities with us.

Well, you're awfully nice to say that. I still enjoy doing it, I still like coming to the ball park. Baseball is still a great, great game, and as long as it stays this way, I'm gonna be around.

◆ ◆ ◆

Bob Lemon

Cleveland Indians right-handed pitcher Bob Lemon finished his mound career with a record of 207–128 and an earned run average of 3.23. He began his career as an outfielder-infielder, however manager Lou Boudreau penciled him in as a pitcher during his first full season in 1946 and it paid off. He was named to seven All-Star teams and led the American League in victories on three different occasions, complete games five times, and innings pitched four times. In 1948, he threw the first night game no-hitter in the American League. His 35 home runs rank second to Wes Ferrell's 37 for most as a pitcher. He later managed the Kansas City Royals, Chicago White Sox, and New York Yankees. He was enshrined in the Baseball Hall of Fame in 1976.

This interview was conducted in Cleveland, Ohio, in 1987.

Bob, when you started out you weren't a pitcher, you were an outfielder.
Well, I started out as an infielder and then they moved me to the outfield in 1946, when I came out of the service. I opened up in center field.

What was it or who was the person responsible for putting you on the mound?
Well, actually I signed as a pitcher/shortstop, but I never pitched until I got to the big leagues. I pitched some in the Navy, but my batting average as an outfielder had more to do with me becoming a pitcher than anything. I wasn't hitting my weight, and I didn't weigh very much either. So somebody had told Boudreau that if I couldn't make it as an outfielder, that you ought to try me pitching.

And I'm sure that they're glad that they did. When people talk about the great pitching staffs, of course the Indians are one of the premier teams, strong pitching. If you had to pick out a highlight in your career, there were many of them, but what stands out to you the most? What was the most meaningful to you?
Well, I think there's several. Every wonderful thing that can happen to a ballplayer has happened to me, and there have been real highs and real lows, but I just thank God the real highs are way ahead of the real lows. I mean I would probably think that pitching in your first World Series in 1948 and maybe your first All-Star Game that you participate in. Like I say, there's so many that happened to me, winning 20 games the first time.

You mentioned the '48 club. I mean you guys were unbelievable, and that again was a great staff, but you went all the way. Unfortunately it's the last time the Indians were world champions. Lou Boudreau was a young man as a player/manager leading the team. What stands out to you about that season?
Well, that was one of the great eras of baseball right after the war, and everybody was going great, everything was going good. There was a lot more camaraderie in the ball clubs then when you traveled by train, and maybe more day baseball, and maybe eight or nine of you would go out to dinner together on the road. There was just a team that all meshed together and we're all good friends and had a lot of fun, and when somebody did good, we all felt that. We were just one of the great teams. There weren't many real individuals, just a collection of good guys and good players.

Bob Lemon (left) and Tito Francona. Lemon was the 1948 Pitcher of the Year. Francona was Cleveland's Man of the Year in 1959.

Much joy after the war. It must have been a joy to be back playing.

Well, I think it was [for] everybody, the war was over and everybody was forgetting about it and things were trying to get back to normal. I think people were just baseball-starved, and the fellows that had been overseas and that and hadn't been able to get to a ballgame, and that goes for the fans, and then there was the same thing with the ballplayers. They were just glad to get back.

Who were some of the players that you pitched against that were the toughest for you?

All the ones you've read about, Williams, DiMaggio, Kell. In those days, you get quite a list because there were some pretty damn good ballplayers.

Finally Bob, you are living in California and retired?

No, I still work a little for the Yankees. I go to the Dodger games and the Angel games. You can see both leagues that way and keep up with them; but I'm not retired, I'm just tired, that's about all. But I was born in California and raised out there, so it's really home to me.

• • •

Al Lopez

During his 19-year playing career, Al Lopez caught 1,918 games and was known for his astute handling of pitchers and his overall defensive abilities. The Tampa, Florida, native, who played for Brooklyn, Boston and Pittsburgh in the NL and Cleveland in the AL, hit .261 with 51 home runs and 652 RBI. However, it was as a manager that he cemented his legacy, as he compiled a .584 career winning percentage over 17 seasons with the Cleveland Indians and the Chicago White Sox, where he won two pennants. He was elected to the National Baseball Hall of Fame in 1977 and the Cleveland Indians Hall of Fame in 2006.

This interview was conducted in Cleveland, Ohio, in 1993.

As a player, you caught an incredible amount of games. You played 19 years and almost 2,000 games behind the plate. How did you manage to do that physically?

Yeah, well again, I think it was easy for me. I always liked to play, and you know and I think the catcher is a position that you really like to play because you're playing every play in the game. It was easy for me. I was not a big heavyset guy; I weighed about 165 pounds, and I think the best part of my body was my legs, it didn't bother me at all. They still don't bother me.

Who are some of the most memorable pitchers that you caught?

I handled so many great pitchers. I handled a guy in Brooklyn by the name of Dazzy Vance, and if you look at the records he's one of the greats. He was a high-stakes pitcher at that time in baseball. I caught Dizzy Dean in the All-Star Game in New York, then I came to Cleveland I caught Feller and Lemon and Wynn and those guys. I caught Walton Johnson when I was a kid in Tampa. We played an exhibition game there, and I caught batting practice with the Washington club when they trained there, and I used to catch Walter Johnson. I caught a lot of great pitchers.

Was Johnson as fast as we hear?

Yeah. He was just as fast or faster than that.

Was that the All-Star Game when Dizzy was hit on the foot? Were you catching?

No, no that was at, this was the second All-Star Game. We played in the Polo Grounds. No, the day you are talking about he got hit in the foot by Earl Averill, a Cleveland player. He got hit on the foot with a line drive in Washington, D.C., that's where the game was.

Now you were not only a great player, but a great manager, and the signature event that stands out is the 111 wins in 1954 here in Cleveland; what a ball club.

Fantastic. It was a great club and we just had a great year. Too bad that we hit a slump when we went into the World Series. It would have been a beautiful year if we could have won the World Series.

And then of course you had success in Chicago with the White Sox in 1959.

I was fortunate again to come up with a good club in Chicago and we, again we had everything went right for us that year in '59. I think we beat the Cleveland club, I think they finished second. I think we clinched the pennant here in Cleveland that year.

What do you think made it possible for you to be so successful as a manager? What traits did you bring with you?

Having good players, that helped an awful lot. No, I think I just kind of had a theory about treating players the way I wanted to be treated myself. I think I got along pretty well with the players, which you have to, you know. You try to keep the players in a good frame of mind, keep them content, and sometimes they get mad at the front office because they don't get enough money, you know, the salary difference and stuff like that. And if you can keep the players in a good frame of mind and keep giving you 100 percent, most of the players I ever had, they would give me 110 percent, they really did. And I was fortunate, I had good teams, both here and in Chicago.

How would you like people to think of you or remember you as a player and manager?

As a friend. You know, I didn't want them to think I was a boss. I wanted them to think that well, he was one of us. And I've tried to be, I've tried to be one of the guys. I didn't try to boss anybody around. I was a player, that's the way I wanted to be treated. I wanted to be treated with respect, and I tried to treat the players with respect. I think for that reason, I think they kind of admired me and got along with me that way.

I appreciate you taking some time, Mr. Lopez. You were not only a great catcher and manager but one of the great people. And you look like you're about 55 years old. People can't see you, but they have to trust me. Best of luck.

Thank you very much Ron, I am 55.

◆ ◆ ◆

Juan Marichal

Juan Marichal was one of the dominant pitchers of the 1960s, winning more games (191) in that decade than anyone else. Known for his trademark high leg kick and great control, he struck out 2,303 batters and walked only 709 during his 16-year career. Marichal pitched for the San Francisco Giants for 14 of those seasons, recording 20 wins six times and 25 or more three times. The ten-time All-Star was named the game's MVP in 1965 and pitched a no-hitter against the then Houston Colt 45s on June 15, 1963. The Dominican great threw 244 complete games and ended his career with a record of 243–142 and an ERA of 2.89. The right-hander played the final two seasons of his career with the Red Sox and the Dodgers. His jersey number 27 was retired by the Giants in 1975, and he was elected to Baseball's Hall of Fame in 1983.

You were involved in a playoff with the Dodgers for the pennant in 1962.
We played three games in the playoff, I think it was two out of three, and we won, you know. There's no way you could forget those days and that playoff. That was a very wonderful year for the Giants. We get to play in the World Series against the Yankees, and we got beat in seven games of the Series and we played good ball, but you know we end up second.

Juan, the great thing about your career, 16 seasons, the durability, the complete games, phenomenal, 244 or thereabouts. What do you attribute that to?
The players, they, you know you have to condition yourself to be in top shape, and they want you to pitch nine innings every time you go to the mound. Today you don't have to do that, because you have so many good relievers, you know that [you] are supposed to go seven, eight or nine innings. I wish I could have had those type of relievers

Juan Marichal (left), "The Dominican Dandy," with Jose Rijo and an unidentified reporter.

in my career, because I think I could have pitched longer. I think I could have had better ERA, more wins, and I think I could have improved my win and loss in many games.

With all that you've done in your career, you had the 26 wins in '68 and you never won a Cy Young Award, it's just unbelievable.
   I think I was at the wrong place at the wrong time. Because of winning over 20 games six times, you know, you figured man, what happened that he never win that, the Cy Young, but somebody else come up with a better year. I remember the year I won 26 games, [Bob] Gibson come up with a phenomenal ERA record you know, 1.12 ERA, and then nobody can beat that.

Where did the leg kick, is that just as a young man you started doing it, because that's your signature, everyone knows you by that?
   No, I never pitched like that. My first two years in pro baseball, I used to throw natural sidearm, and late in '59 I started, I was learning how to throw overhand, and that's how I started kicking my leg. I fell in love with the style, and I think it gave me a plus, so I continued pitching that way, especially in the major league. I think that's why the people know Juan Marichal most, because of the high kick.

• • •

Eddie Mathews

Eddie Mathews holds the distinction of being the only Brave to play in Boston, Milwaukee and Atlanta. The 12-time All-Star put together an outstanding 17-year career, spent mostly with the Braves, that saw him hit 512 home runs and lead the league in 1953 and 1959. Between 1954 and 1966, Mathews and teammate Hank Aaron became the most feared power-hitting tandem in the National League, hitting a total of 863 home runs. The slick-fielding third baseman helped the Braves bring the only World Series championship to the city of Milwaukee in 1957. Matthews finished with a batting average of .271, collecting 2,315 hits and 1,453 RBI. His number 41 jersey was retired by the Braves in 1969, and he gained entrance to the Hall of Fame in 1978.

Eddie, you're the greatest power hitting third baseman of all time.
   Don't forget Mike Schmidt. I set the records, he broke them.

I grant you that, you and Mike. Now you and Henry Aaron in Milwaukee put up some great numbers. Looking back on those ball clubs, the '57, '58 ball clubs especially, what do you remember most about those years?
   I think what I remember most is the enjoyment we all had playing the game. We were like one big happy family. We all went out there and did the best could every day and enjoyed each other, and I liked every one of them.

You know your dominance as a power hitter, you did it year after year after year. Was there any formula, any secret that you had, 'cause you were so consistent?

From left, Johnny Logan, Eddie Mathews and Lew Burdette of the 1957 Braves, winners of the World Series.

No, there really isn't, because I [have] been a minor league hitting instructor for the Braves for the last three years, and I have watched; it's not something that you can teach. It's just there. You can polish it up a little bit and get it fundamentally a little more sound, but it's just there or it's not there.

Are there are any hitters that you watch today that you enjoy, power hitters, keeping your eye on them?

Well, obviously you gotta watch Canseco, and fortunately I met him as a young man when I was working with Oakland. But I really don't follow because the power hitter over a long period of time, you've gotta be consistent over a long period of time to establish yourself. This is what Hank Aaron did. He was a great hitter over a long period of time, and that's what I would say. Today if a guy hits 40 home runs in one year, it don't mean a thing to me. I want him to see him do it over a number of years, over a long period of time.

You're the only Brave who played in Boston, Milwaukee and Atlanta. What did that mean to you?

That can win you a beer any time you win a bet of trivia questions. Who's the only person in history that went to the same franchise in three different cities? Boston didn't mean a lot to me. I was very young and we were only there one year, and it was my induction into the major leagues. But Milwaukee, obviously the fans and the people in the Midwest were just something I will never forget. And then fortunately [we] went down to Atlanta. I had played in Atlanta in the minor league ball club in the 1950s, so I had a little relationship down there. But it's kind of unique.

When people look at your career and think of Eddie Matthews as a player, is there any certain way you'd like to be remembered?

Not particularly. I think what Stan Musial said when we were talking at the Hall of Fame dinner about Pete Rose, they call him Charlie Hustle. And Stan said, "geez I hustled all my life," and that's the way I played it. I gave it 100 percent all my life, and that's I guess the way I'd like to be remembered.

• • •

Bill Mazeroski

Bill Mazeroski is regarded as the greatest fielding second baseman of his era (1956–1972) or quite possibly any era. Maz holds the NL record for career double plays by a second baseman with 1,706. He played in seven All-Star Games and was awarded eight Gold Gloves. When his Pittsburgh Pirates defeated the powerful New York Yankees in the 1960 World Series in seven games, the defensive wizard proved that he was more than just a spectacular fielder by hitting the only walk-off home run to win a World Series Game 7. His offering to left field off pitcher Ralph Terry broke a 9–9 tie and sent the Steel City into a frenzy. Maz went deep, clubbing home runs in double figures six times in his 17-year career. He was a lifetime .260 hitter, collecting an impressive 2,016 hits and 138 home runs. He was elected by the Veterans Committee to the Baseball Hall of Fame in 2001, and a statue was dedicated in his honor outside the right field entrance to Pittsburgh's PNC Park in 2010.

This interview was conducted in Pittsburgh, Pennsylvania, in 1989.

You play in a number of Old Timers' games each year.

Well, I probably play five or six of them, but ah you know you're going to a new city, you're seeing new faces all the time and the people that you played against, and it's always fun to see these people and talk over old times. The hard part is going out and playing the game, not making a fool of yourself, and trying to get away safely without getting hurt.

You're known for the home run in 1960. You were also a great defensive player. Does it bother you that many remember you for only hitting that dramatic home run?

No, not really. I think it's great to be remembered, you know, be remembered for something you did good, especially for the Pittsburgh Pirates anyhow. I believe [if] it wasn't for that, they'd wouldn't even know I was alive, I don't think.

Do you ever think about the Hall of Fame? Perhaps the doors have now opened to more defensive-minded players. You certainly should be up for consideration. Do you ever think about getting elected?

Well, I think about it some, I think that the Hall of Fame is just offensively orientated and that's all they go by. If you hit 400 home runs, you're just about automatically in the Hall of Fame, and they disregard defense altogether. I think defense is the part that wins most games in most sports, and it's strictly on defense, not strictly on defense but defense plays a big part, and they ignore that in the Hall of Fame. I think that if a guy hits 400 home runs and didn't play the outfield very well, I don't see why he should be in the Hall of Fame if a guy who plays defense like I did and didn't hit that many home runs and I wasn't an out. I got over 2,000 hits, but ah they ignore that altogether. I think the Hall of Fame first of all is for people that did everything well, they could run well, they threw well, they hit, they played defense, and they did the whole thing.

On turning the double play. What was your secret? They called you "No Hands." No one in my estimation, I'm sure most people never turned it like you did.

Really, I got my footwork out of the way before I caught the ball. Most people catch the ball, take their step and throw and all that does is give the runner an extra step. I used to get my footwork out of the way, and I stayed right near the bag because you can't take a big step. It just takes time to get your foot, and you can't throw until your right foot [is] planted anyhow. So I planted my right foot before I caught the ball and had my left foot just slightly in the air ready to go, and it took just one motion to throw it. Everybody thought it was quick, but everybody could do that, and I just don't see many people doing it.

Outside of the home run, and we'll talk about that briefly, what are you most proud of in your career?

Well, just playing in the big leagues and realizing a dream, getting to the big leagues. It's something that very few people get to do, live out a dream and play a sport rather than

Painting of Pirates hero Bill Mazeroski used in film *Wonder Boys* (2000).

Bill Mazeroski, Pittsburgh's "Little Big Man."

work; you know it was enjoyable just playing the game. I think playing my first All-Star Game was a big thrill. I never expected to ever even make the big leagues, let alone play in an All-Star Game, and then just playing in the World Series, just playing those games, let alone hitting a home run. That's always a childhood dream too that every kid dreams of, but I've had a, I was very fortunate and very lucky to live out a career in baseball.

The home run. Bobby Thomson's and yours are probably two of the most notable home runs. After all of these years and going over and over and over again, talking about it, does anything else come up? Do you ever suddenly think one day, geez, I didn't realize this because it's probably been so dissected now? Do you ever find anything new about it?

Well, usually when anybody talks to me about it, they just tell me where they were. Everybody seems to know what they were doing and where they were at that time. Every baseball fan anyhow.

You have said you didn't think it was going to go out?

Right. I hit the ball, I hit it good and I knew that Berra wasn't going to catch it, so I started running hard. Going into second base, I looked up and it had gone over. I knew he wasn't going to catch it, and the reason I was running hard was I wanted to end up on third if he misplayed it off the wall, because I knew I hit it good enough that he wouldn't catch it. But I didn't know quite for sure if I hit it good enough to get it out of the park. It was what, 410 out there, and it's a long way. I wanted to end up on third if he misplayed it off the wall, but then when I looked up going into second and I saw the umpire giving it that little circular move, and the fans went crazy the whole stadium went goofy, and I went crazy right along with them, started to jumping around the bases. That's probably the first time I ever showed my emotions playing baseball because you know you can't get too high or too low in playing 162 ball games a year, and it would drive you goofy. So that time it was worth it.

Finally, Bill, how would you like people that have watched you play not only in Pittsburgh but around baseball to think of Bill Mazeroski when they think of him as a player?

Well, just a good, solid major league baseball player, and a team player, that just worked hard and did his job.

◆ ◆ ◆

Rick Monday

Rick Monday is remembered for two events as a player and as a citizen, and they both took place on the field. On April 25, 1976, during America's Bicentennial year, a pair of protesters ran onto the outfield at Dodger Stadium and attempted to set fire to an American flag. Monday, who was playing in the outfield for the Chicago Cubs, saw what was taking place, sprinted over, grabbed the flag, and sprinted away with it. It was a symbolic moment that has stayed with many to this day. Five years later, in a deciding Game 5 of the 1981 NLCS at Olympic Stadium in Montreal, Rick Monday poleaxed a two-out, ninth-inning home run off Expos ace Steve Rogers that proved to be the winning run and propelled the Los Angeles Dodgers to the World Series. Monday went on to play 19 seasons in the big leagues with the Athletics, Cubs and Dodgers (.264, 241 Home Runs, 775 RBI) but perhaps nothing he did as a player will ever surpass his one-handed grab of the American Flag in left-center field.

This interview was conducted in Pittsburgh, Pennsylvania, in 1992.

Rick, looking back on your career, one of the things that stands out [was] a really dramatic home run in the NLCS against Montreal, Steve Rogers pitching. We have seen since then Kirk Gibson; but I mean that had to be, that was a big one, that put the Dodgers in the World Series.

Well, I think because of the immediacy of the moment, and that moment was on a Monday afternoon, a very cold and rainy, had a little bit of snowy type of atmosphere, in the Olympic Stadium in Montreal. And I said, the immediacy of the moment, because the New York Yankees had already clinched the American League title; they were poised in New York. The World Series was going to start the following evening, and the game the preceding day on Sunday had been, well they called it rained out, but I guess if you call snow flurries being rained out, that was the situation. But to set the stage, whoever wins that ballgame between the Dodgers and Expos was going to go to New York and start the World Series the following night. Fernando Valenzuela was going to pitch for us, and I asked Fernando in the broken Spanish and the broken English that he spoke at the time if he'd ever seen snow before. He said yes, in Las Montanas, in the mountains. But Fernando pitched a terrific ballgame and knocked me in for the first run that we had [in] the ballgame. And did it set the stage?

Ray Burris was actually the starter for the Expos, they used Rogers out of the bullpen and then he came on in the ninth inning. Ron Cey hit a ball to start the inning off that I thought had a chance to be out of the park. Tim Raines caught it on the front edge of the warning track in left field. Garvey made the second out, and then Rogers fell behind to me, three balls and one strike. I don't know a hitter alive that does not like to hit three and one, especially if you need one blast. He threw a ball, not trying to walk me, he threw a ball out over the plate. I hit the ball, and strangely enough I lost sight of the ball. I knew it was hit hard, but it was hit very high and I lost sight of the ball. I saw Dawson in center field go over into right center. I thought well, it's hit too high and then he kept going, and I said well maybe it's got a chance to be off the wall. Then the ball disappeared behind the wall, and I got caught in the middle of a dance step celebrating between first and second. I almost fell on my fanny.

When you see guys now hit dramatic shots, do you relive that moment?

No, I don't relive that moment at the expense of other moments, and I say the expense of other moments. When Kirk Gibson limps from the dugout and he goes and he faces Dennis Eckersley and he hits a home run in the World Series, the Dodgers and Oakland A's, that's a moment in itself, and I respect those moments. What has happened in the past, you know, has been documented, it's over with and has no bearing at all on tonight's game. That's what I think is the enjoyable part about being with a ball club now. I broadcast with the Padres along with Jerry Coleman, and this is my fourth year doing that. Four years prior to that, I was doing the sports Monday through Friday [on] the station in Los Angeles. I did a Sunday night sports show and did a pregame show with the Dodgers, and did their cable as well. But one of the things that keeps me coming back is I feel very fortunate to have played for a long period of time. Really my fantasy as a child, as a young boy in Little League, I was able to live out my fantasy, and I'm still around it on a daily basis.

One thing that distinguishes you from many players, though, is the flag incident. Are you asked about that more than any aspect? It is special because you had a really solid career, but yet, when most people think of Rick Monday, that comes to mind.

You know, somebody asked me that a number of years ago. He said, "isn't it frustrating to have played for 19 different seasons on the major league level and be remembered for a flag that has nothing to do with baseball?" I said, "no, it has everything to do with baseball, because without the rights and freedoms of that flag for all of us, it's not a perfect world, it's not a perfect society, but we have the ability to change things if we don't like them. That flag, and to just set the scene, a couple of idiots ran on the field. I was with the Chicago Cubs, we were in Los Angeles on a Sunday afternoon in Los Angeles at Dodger Stadium, and two idiots ran on the field.

You never know, I mean, you see the guys go on the field and you don't know, you think of the past scripts where guys have either had a bet with somebody or they have had too much to drink or they just don't like you and they're going to come out and tell you [about] it. You don't know what's gonna [happen]. But these two guys came out and I saw that the first one had something under his arm, I couldn't tell what it was. They came out of shallow center field, they ran past Jose Cardenal, who was playing left field for us. Then they spread out almost like a picnic blanket, the flag, they started to douse it. I could see the reflection of the can, and they were dousing it with lighter fluid. So I started running at them, and the only thing that was going through my mind that I'm aware of at this time, years later, was the fact that what they were doing was grossly wrong. And the wind blew the first match out. The second match had been struck and was being put to the flag. I was there, scooped it up and went away from it. They threw the can of lighter fluid at me, and Tom Lasorda, that was the year before he took over the helm of the Dodgers, so he was the third base coach for LA, and he went past me going to these guys and yelling every expletive he's ever heard in this life because he was so infuriated. But I think the special moment in that ballpark [was when] these guys were led away. There's 20-some, 30-some thousand people in the stands, and without anything being put up on the scoreboard and without anyone saying anything on the PA system, everybody in the stands started singing "God Bless America." That was in 1976, and here we are in 1992 and I still get goose bumps; and by the way, that flag is in my home. Because after the court case and these two idiots were put on a two-year probation and fined individually, I had asked for that flag, and it sits very prominently in my house.

As well it should be. Did you ever meet or speak to the two people who attempted to burn the flag?

I didn't meet them. I didn't want to meet them then, I don't want to meet them now. What I do want to meet and continue to meet are the kids and the parents that continue to this day, on a weekly basis I still get letters that have some reference to the flag incident. Most of them as the encouraging thing, most of the letters are from youngsters, many of whom were not even alive at the time. So we wonder about where our society is going; our societies are in our hands, and they are going to be in the hands of our youngsters. I think they are in pretty good hands as long as we don't drop our end of the gauntlet.

I appreciate you spending a few moments of your time. I think it's a marvelous thing though. Baseball is numbers and this and that, and I hit this and I hit this average, but to be known for something like what took place, I think you should feel privileged and unique.

Well, let me tell you, first of all I truly have been, and to this day feel embarrassed by the attention that was focused upon me for doing something that you would have done had you been geographically where I was, the closest guy to these guys that happened to see them. And it's just the way that I was raised, and I am very proud of the fact that the way I was raised and proud of the fact too that I believe in what that flag represents. We're also reinforced and I mean greatly reinforced by the United States Marine Corp. When I was in the Marine Corp, obviously those are things that happen. We don't have people standing on our borders saying if you don't like things, that you're unable to leave. You can leave all you want, but why not stay and improve upon things rather than to constantly sit back and complain and do nothing?

• • •

Manny Mota

Although Manny Mota finished his 20-year career with a lifetime batting average of .304 he is best remembered as one of the premier pinch-hitters in Major League history. It was with the Los Angeles Dodgers that Manny began his magic off the bench. From 1974 to 1979, he averaged ten pinch-hits a year, and in 1979 he became the game's all-time leader in the record book. Upon his retirement in 1982, he would hold the record of 150 pinch-hits, with a pinch-hitting average of .297. The outfielder was born in the Dominican Republic, collected 1,149 hits in his career, and although his record has since been broken, he remains one of the best ever to come off the bench.

The game's greatest pinch-hitter; 150 pinch-hits. You have stated that to be successful you need three things—mental preparation, concentration and positive thinking. Can you go through that?

Well, you gotta have the mental preparation, the mental approach, to pinch-hit, 'cause you know you're going to be playing in the game. You have to prepare yourself. It's like basically you gotta be mentally prepared. You have to think positive, and you have to believe in yourself. Concentration gotta be the key. You have to concentrate. You have to concentrate a lot because you only gonna hit once. You got to be disciplined, you gotta be selective, and the same time you gotta be aggressive. You have to know the situation. The pitcher you're hitting, how you're going to be used, you gotta think ahead of time. You gotta prepare yourself. Don't let the manager surprise you. Check the scoreboard. Once you will be able to pinch, watching the pitch, you're watching the other team to see how they play everybody. You have to know the bullpen, you have to know the best reliever you might face. You have to know his best pitch.

The main thing is making contact. If you're making contact, you gotta chance. You have to be a different type of hitter. You got two strikes on you, you gotta try to make contact. If you got a man on third base and less than two outs, maybe the first pitch you swing to try to hit a fly ball. And after that, you want to make sure you get a piece of the ball. You put the ball in play. Because to me the worst thing to happen to a pinch-hitter is if you strike out; you gotta swing the bat. You gotta try to make contact with two strikes. But that is the difference of the game, if you gotta run on third base and you have no idea about what you're gonna do with the bat. You gotta adjust with the situation of hitting. Sometimes it's required for a long ball, some guys specialize in long ball, and some guys specialize in a single; starting a rally, getting on base; that's why they got two or three different guys as pinch-hitters. You got a guy to start a rally when they losing, they got a guy to hit the long ball. Some situations require and you have a guy, you can plan on it driving in a run when they got a man in scoring position.

In my situation, I used to love the pressure. I used to like to come on with men on base because I can play better that way, and I know the type of hitter I was. I know myself; you have to know yourself, that way you know what you are able to do. And I know I was going to try to make contact, I wasn't going to swing too hard, I wasn't going to try to lift the ball. My main purpose and the reason why they send me to the plate with men on base, I'm going to hit a line drive or hit the ball to the infield.

Manny Mota had 150 pinch-hits to his credit when he retired in 1982.

That's what I do most of the time. Most of the time, I can really make good contact and hopefully can find a hole. Hit a line drive, a ground ball, never swing too hard. I don't try to be a different type of hitter, I just try to get a piece of the ball.

But to me, anytime I go up to the plate, to me I'm the best hitter in the game. There's nobody better than me in that situation. There are no pinch[-hitters] better than me as a hitter. I know who's going to beat the guy at the mound. Because with me, I got enough confidence in myself. If you think that way, then that's how I do the positive thinking. Anytime I am up to the plate, in my mind I was going to get a base hit. I know that wasn't possible to get a base hit every time you're up to the plate, but I prepare myself that way.

Manny, you had excellent seasons as an everyday player. You played with Pittsburgh, then with the Dodgers. You were an excellent everyday player, too. But what about adapting to the role of a pinch-hitter after you're an everyday player. Is that more difficult for some players than others?

Well, I say some players adapt quicker or sooner than other guys. I do my work, I start getting any advice I can get. I have a book in my mind about every reliever and believe what I might face at that part of the game. Any time after the fourth inning, I went down to the runway and take some swings because I know any time after the fifth inning, it depends on the situation. Maybe the managers wanted to use me, and the last thing I wanted to happen to me was don't be ready when they call me. That is why I prepare myself that way, and I adjust from playing and going to pinch-hit. I know it's kind of difficult and it's kind of tough, but when you play you might hit four times; but if you don't get any hits, maybe you don't that day, you may redeem yourself the next time. But when you pinch-hit, there is not a second time. It's only one time at bat; and you gotta put everything in that at-bat; that's why it is so important, the concentration. You gotta have the desire to do it. If you don't want to be a pinch-hitter, it's difficult. If you want to do it, then you have to do the things to prepare yourself, the different approach to the game.

You had 150 pinch-hits. Are there certain ones that stick out to you?

Well, I hit one, I think in 1977, it was in the playoff against Philadelphia. Then we fell from behind in that game; after two outs, we beat Philadelphia. Then we get into the playoff and went to the World Series. That's one of my biggest pinch-hits in my career; besides the pinch-hit to tie the record or break the record. Another time I hit a pinch-hit home run in Santo Domingo. I'm not a power hitter, but that day, playing in front of my home people, I hit a home run. That was a big thrill for me, hitting in front of my home people.

Do players come up to you and want advice, the ones that find themselves in the role of pinch-hitting. Are you asked by a great many people to give advice?

Well, a lot of people ask me. I would be happy to give them some advice, but a lot of guys got a lot good, a lot of natural ability to be a really a good hitter, and they can be a good pinch-hitter. But they have to prepare themselves to do it and put everything together if they want to become a very good pinch-hitter.

When people mention pinch-hitting, you're the first name that comes up. I don't care who you ask, the people who follow baseball say Manny Mota—pinch hitting. That's the way you're going to be remembered, and is that the way you would like to be thought of? Do you take a great sense of pride of being the most prolific pinch-hitter in the history baseball?

That's a great honor to be the one who break the record, the all-time record of pinch-hitter, and somebody's gonna break mine, I don't deny it. I don't just want to be remembered as a pinch-hitter. I want to be remembered as a ballplayer, because as a pinch-hitter, if you take my record, I had a lifetime of .304 average and I don't do that just as a pinch-hitter.

◆ ◆ ◆

Ron Necciai

On May 13, 1952, right-handed pitcher Ron Necciai was a 19-year-old Pittsburgh Pirates prospect pitching for Bristol (TN) in the class D Appalachian League who accomplished something that had never been done in a nine-inning professional league game. Necciai struck out 27 batters on his way to a 7–0 no-hitter against a team from Welch, West Virginia. Four batters did reach base by way of a walk, an error, a hit batsman and a passed ball. Ron Necciai was called up by the Pirates in August of 1952 and finished out the season and his career with a 1–6 record in the big leagues. But he had his moment in time that lives on to this day.

This interview was conducted in Beaver County, Pennsylvania, in 1992.

At the age of 19, you pitched one of the most remarkable games in professional ball. You struck out 27 batters in a nine-inning game for Bristol in the Class D League. What was the atmosphere after the game?

Surprisingly, we didn't realize what had happened until the next day. You know, they'd been playing baseball for 100 years at the time, and we thought that surely someone had done this before, someone had struck out everybody. We just kind of went home that night and thought nothing about it. The next morning, the newspapers and television and radio started calling, and then we realized that no one in professional baseball, now you have to remember that this was a minor league game, not a major league game, so really we weren't that fascinated with it at that time.

Can you set it up as to what took place?

I hit one, walked one, catcher dropped a ball, and there was an error, so it wasn't like there were 27 men in a row that struck out. I think it was 13 or 14 in a row, and then we had some action so it wasn't like it was everybody up and down in order. But it was the only time in the history of professional baseball, that's the catch, it was the only time in the history of professional baseball that anyone ever struck out 27 in a nine-inning game.

When did you start to know you were doing something historic?

The first time we got wind of anything going down was late in the eighth inning. People started chanting in the stands, "one more" and "one two three, one two three," stuff like that. Prior to that, with the action we had with the walks, hit batsman, no one really realized, maybe someone did, I didn't.

How did you do in terms of strikeouts your next start?

I only pitched one game after that, and I struck out 24. I had 20 and 19 strikeouts prior to that. After that I only pitched one game and was sent to Burlington, which was another Pittsburgh farm club in the Carolina League.

Later you were called up to the Pirates but struggled at times.

Well, there's a big difference between the minor leagues and the Major Leagues. In the minor leagues, they chase a lot of bad balls, and [in] the big leagues they don't chase bad balls. I think my biggest problem when I came to Pittsburgh was bases on balls. You walk them, then you decide you better throw a strike, and those guys don't miss them. No matter how hard you throw, they can time the ball, so you walk a couple of guys and you want to make sure you throw a strike, and they wait on it and hit line drives. I think that was my problem, although I did have some good outings. I think the second day I was in the big leagues, after I got clobbered the first day against Chicago, I relieved the very next night against Cincinnati and I think I struck out five out of seven. I had good days and bad days, but when I could throw strikes I was all right. You throw the ball all over the place, you get what you deserve.

I imagine that after a 27-strikeout game, there are a lot of high expectations.

Yeah, it was, after this game where I struck out 27, I think I filled about every ballpark I ever pitched in. That's because if I was at home, everybody came to see if I could strike out everybody, and when I was on the road they wanted to see me get my brains beat out. But that's the nature of the business. The expectations were there for the strikeout. But that wasn't anything that ever fascinated me or what I was trying to do. It was just all part of the work.

Buck O'Neil

John Jordan "Buck" O'Neil played and managed in the Negro American League and later became the first African American coach in Major League Baseball with the Chicago Cubs in 1962. Previous to that, he served as a scout and signed a number of prominent players. Perhaps his most impressive accomplishment was his tireless work to help establish the Negro Leagues Baseball Museum in Kansas City, Missouri. He traveled and promoted the Negro Leagues across the country, helping to keep alive the memory of its brand of ball and many of its legendary players such as Satchel Paige, Willie Wells, Josh Gibson and Cool Papa Bell. In 2006, Buck O'Neil was posthumously awarded this country's highest civilian honor, the Presidential Medal of Freedom.

This interview was conducted in Baltimore, Maryland, in 1993.

The brand of ball in the Negro Leagues. You were speaking of it in the symposium earlier. How would you classify it in terms of major league ball at the time?

The only difference is it was just a quicker brand of baseball. We had quick fellas, and to actually capsule it for you, Rube Foster in 1920 has a ball club, he had eight ball players on that field, was like he had eight Rickey Hendersons on the field. Everybody on the field was capable of hitting 25 home runs. Everybody on the field was capable of stealing 20 bases. That was the kind of baseball that they were playing in that era. That was Negro League baseball. In that era, major league baseball now, you came up with Babe Ruth, that's the home run era. So you would hit the ball, wait for somebody else to hit it, wait for somebody else to hit it, so you might take three hits to get a run. Where in Negro League baseball the guy would probably drop a bunt, beat it out, steal second, steal third, and if you weren't careful would steal home. So actually, [with] one hit you just might have one run.

We hear of the outstanding players, Josh Gibson, Satchel Paige. You have a man here in Baltimore, Leon Day, that you're trying to get inducted into the Hall of Fame. What do you remember about him?

I remember he's one of the best pitchers I had ever seen. In the 1942 World Series, we had beaten the Grays three games in the World Series. Just one more ballgame to play, and the Grays needed another pitcher, so the Grays took Leon Day from Newark to pitch against us in Kansas City. He pitched against Satchel that day in Kansas City, and he beat Satchel 1–0. I think he struck out 14 Monarchs but actually it was against the rule because he wasn't eligible to play with that ball club against us, so that game didn't count. But that's what he did; he was just that type pitcher.

Satchel Paige, we knew he had great talent but what got him all the attention, was he a great showman also?

Actually what got Satchel all the attention, it started with, see the media didn't do much for our baseball. The Saturday Evening Post, when Satchel came to the Kansas City Monarchs, this got to be around "38, the Saturday Evening Post wrote a feature article on Satchel Paige and how he had pitched all over the country and what he did, now everybody started to knowing about Satchel Paige. I would see guys who were 70 years old and they would say, "My Daddy took me to see Satchel Paige." Satchel Paige at that time, Satchel Paige was 32 but now they are saying my Daddy took me to see Satchel Paige. He was 70 and Satchel was 32. But what they did, they equated that to every black pitcher that they had seen. They heard about Satchel, so this had to have been Satchel.

If my memory serves me correctly, did you sign Ernie Banks?
 I signed Ernie Banks, I signed Lou Brock. I signed Lou Johnson. I signed Joe Carter. I signed Smith over in St. Louis, the relief pitcher.

Lee.
 Yeah, Arthur Lee Smith, yeah.

Ozzie Smith, how does he compare with some of the greats you've seen?
 Ozzie Smith, I would put Ozzie Smith, Ozzie Smith was the closest thing defensively to Willie Wells, yeah, he's the closest thing to Willie Wells, but Willie Wells was a great hitter. Willie Wells was a great base runner too. Willie Wells was the type guy could steal 50 or 60 bases. Willie Wells was the type of guy could hit you 30 home runs. That was Willie Wells. Uh huh!

Who was the greatest player you ever saw?
 The greatest player I ever saw was Oscar Charleston. Oscar Charleston was the center fielder for the Indianapolis ABCs. I first saw him as a kid, I was a kid and I saw him. And the closest thing to Oscar Charleston, Willie Mays.

◆ ◆ ◆

Tony Oliva

In 1964, Tony Oliva won the American League batting title in his rookie year with a .323 batting average and walked away with "Rookie of the Year" honors. The Cuban-born star of the Minnesota Twins won another batting title the following season and finished second in the MVP voting after hitting .321 with 16 home runs and 98 RBI. In 1971, Oliva won his third batting crown, hitting .337. However, the eight-time All-Star suffered an injury to his right knee which would affect him for the rest of his career. In a 15-year career which saw him win a Gold Glove in 1966, Oliva hit .304, with 1,917 hits, 220 home runs and 947 RBI. His number 6 jersey was retired by the Twins in 1991, and he was elected to their Hall of Fame in 2000. In 2011, the Twins unveiled a statue of Tony Oliva at Target Field.

This interview was conducted in Cleveland, Ohio, on May 17, 1989.

You were successful at the plate, winning three batting titles. Can you explain your approach as a hitter, even with injury?
 I think the one thing was that I don't play that much baseball back at home because I'm from the country. We not play like you do here in America, where you have a Little League and all that stuff, but I play every week. I practice every time I have a chance to practice, like I hit any kind of baseball—I play every Sunday through the years. I think

they give me opportunity to play all year round plus in the meantime since I love this game—since I love baseball because I like to be hitting every time I have a chance. I used to hit baseballs with my brothers and friends. They helped me a lot. After I signed a contract to be a professional player, I practice, I practice a lot. I practice my hitting a lot. I learned how to hit the ball up the field and how to pull the ball. All of my career, I learned what I was able to do and catch different pitches. If I think I wasn't able to pull the ball and catch these pitches, this particular pitcher, I go there with the idea to pull the ball with this guy. I prefer myself to do that. If I face a guy like a Jim Palmer, who give me problem to pull the ball, but I was success to hit the ball to opposite field against him, is exactly what I was doing, and that territory was success for me. I thought to pass that along to my hitting here now in Minnesota, I try to give those guys some advice. But to be able to do that—to achieve that you have to practice in the right way. You no can go over there and play around while you're hitting batting practice. You have to go and work hard and put in your mind what you want to do. This is one of the reasons this was successful for me. I work hard on my hitting.

You led the league pinch-hitting one year after playing every day. What adjustments did you make, and did the game dictate what you would do?

Yes, the game dictate to me what I supposed to do in a particular time. Plus I was look, I don't look at too many times. I went over there with the idea—hey, when you're a pinch-hitter you're not gonna go over there and give one strike to the pitcher. Sometimes guys go to the home plate and the pitcher throw the first pitch right there because they want to get ahead of you, and you give that pitch to the pitcher—now you're behind. It is better to go over there and swing if it's a strike, and swing the first good pitch you see.

Tony Oliva, three-time AL batting champion, in 1964, 1965, 1971, instructs a Twins player.

At least if you hit a foul, at least you get loose. You ready for the next pitch. But if you give him the first pitch, now the second pitch he make a good pitch on you and two strikes and no ball—now you way in the hole. I think one of the approaches you have to do as a pinch-hitter is go over there, and the first pitch if it is around the plate, you should be ready to swing, not give it to the pitcher.

Why do some hitters have trouble adapting?
Well, especially the young players, it is very hard for a young player just to sit and be a pinch-hitter. But for the old players, I think it's easy because in his mind he says, hey my job gonna be a pinch-hitter, I have to be a success.

How would you like to be remembered as a professional player?
You're right. A lot a people think I was a great hitter but they forgot too I was a great outfielder. I work very hard. I take a lot of pride in my profession. I don't think I was only a hitter, I think I was a all-around ball player. I used to be able to hit the ball out of the ball park. I developed myself to be the best right fielder in the American League. I win the Gold Glove, all that stuff, but gee how to say how I want people to remembered. I hope people remember me that somebody that their own kid could look around and say this is a guy over here that come over from Cuba and play baseball here for many years and put a good example here for everybody. All the young players. I think all my career I never have any problem with nobody and play the game hard all the time. I hope they remember me like that kind of attitude, somebody who come to play ball with the idea to play the game and play hard.

◆ ◆ ◆

Mickey Owen

Brooklyn Dodgers catcher Mickey Owen was an outstanding defensive backstop with an excellent throwing arm, but has long been remembered for the mishandling of a single pitch in the 1941 World Series. It was Game 4, and the visiting New York Yankees were down to their final out, trailing 4–3 as Brooklyn looked to even the Series up at two games apiece. The bases were empty, and Tommy Henrich was the batter facing Brooklyn's Hugh Casey with a full count. The payoff pitch broke sharply, and Henrich swung and missed. However, the pitch hit off the heel of Owen's catcher's mitt and rolled by him for a passed ball. Tommy Henrich reached first base, and when the inning ended, the Yankees held a 7–4 lead. They closed out the win to gain a 3-to-1 advantage. In addition to Brooklyn, 13-year veteran and four-time All-Star Mickey Owen played for the St. Louis Cardinals, where he broke in, the Chicago Cubs, and the Boston Red Sox, compiling a career batting average of .255.

You are certainly one of baseball's goodwill ambassadors. An outstanding catcher but unfortunately many remember the passed ball in the 1941 World Series. It has been said that Hugh Casey threw you a spitball. Is that true?

No, it was a curveball, a big curveball, and with Casey he had two kinds of curveballs and two kinds of fastballs and could throw either one on the curveball or fastball sign, you see. So in the instance of Casey, when he came in, I gave the curveball sign, the first curveball, and it hung outside, the big curve, and I gave it again later on and it hung again. From that point on, he started throwing a hard, quick curve and they couldn't hit it. When it got to the ninth inning, with two men out and two strikes on Henrich, nobody on base, why I give the curveball sign and just kind of got caught in a rut myself mentally. I was expecting the quick curve, and he rolled off the big curve and it really broke. So he struck and missed it, and I missed it too.

You were an outstanding defensive catcher during your career, but everyone seems to only remember you for that one mishap.
Well, it isn't bad. Like I was telling Branca, they remember him for the home run that Bobby Thomson hit off him. And if he'd a struck Bobby Thomson out, they would never remember. They know about Ralph Branca pitching the game, but now he's famous for the rest of his life. And in my case, my name's Mickey and the greatest catcher to ever live was Mickey Cochrane, and they are more people when you ask them "did you ever hear of a catcher named Mickey?" they say, "Yeah, Mickey Owen," where they don't mention Mickey Cochrane. He was too good and didn't make any mistakes.

I was reading in Durocher's book about you. Someone asked you what are you going to hit here and you answered, "It's not how high I hit but who I hit."
Well, I don't remember but I probably said it. If Durocher said I said it, then I said it. I didn't hit too many of them. My job was to catch and to field the position and throw out runners, and I could always do that as long as I played. I didn't do too much hitting. If I had, I sure would have been happier.

One last thing. Freddie Fitzsimmons was said to have hated Johnny Mize, and he would always throw at him, and you were the catcher. Do you remember some of those confrontations?

Heartbreak in Brooklyn. Mickey Owen is remembered for mishandling a pitch in the 1941 World Series.

I remember him, and he hated Johnny Mize because Johnny Mize hit so many hard shots through the box at him. And sure he threw at him a few times because he was tired of Mize hitting line drives back through the box and about to kill him. One time he hit him on the bare hand, and of course he'd try to catch any ball hit back barehanded or with the glove. He stuck his bare hand out and like to tore his hand off, and it went through to center field. He should have been taken out of the game but he wouldn't leave, and if he didn't end up winning it. His hand was numb and he got a little bit better as he went along, got a little feeling, but he went on and beat the Cardinals.

Gaylord Perry

Right-hander Gaylord Perry pitched for eight different teams over 22 years and compiled a record of 314–265 with an ERA of 3.11 and 3,534 strikeouts. The two-time Cy Young Award winner was the first pitcher to win the award in both the American (1972 Cleveland) and National Leagues (1978 San Diego). Perry pitched a 1–0 no-hitter against Bob Gibson's St. Louis Cardinals in 1968 and led the league in wins three times with San Francisco, Cleveland and San Diego. The five-time All-Star was elected to the Hall of Fame in 1991, and the San Francisco Giants retired his number 36 jersey in 2005.

This interview was conducted in Pittsburgh, Pennsylvania, in 1994.

Gaylord, [it's] 20 years since you started a game here in Pittsburgh in All-Star competition.

You know you're the first press guy to realize that. I did. That was in 1974. I was with Cleveland, and it was a great honor to start that one, so that's quite something for myself.

What's your number one All-Star memory, or one of the many great moments in your career in an All-Star Game, whether it happened to you or maybe you witnessed it?

I have a couple of them. My first All-Star Game in 1966, I was just there and I just finally got in to pitch because it went extra innings. I got the win, and then in 1974 I got to start the game here in Pittsburgh. In 1979, I was pitching in San Diego and the right fielder for Pittsburgh, Parker, threw out a guy at home so I wouldn't lose the game, so I got a few breaks there.

You've been with so many clubs, a great career, but you have them all across your chest here. What team remains closer to your heart?

San Francisco. I started with the organization, I spent 14 years in the organization and got to play with so many great players. It was kind of like home.

Winning the 300 games, I mean it's phenomenal; it's hard to believe. What did it mean to you, what does it mean to you today?

Well, it means a great deal. To get there, you gotta stay healthy, you got to have some good teams behind you, and you gotta push yourself, plus push your teammates. If you're able to play 20 years, you got a chance. You got to average 15 wins a year, and sometimes it's hard to do that.

Gaylord Perry had 314 Major League victories.

Finally, Gaylord, what gave you the edge that you could go so long and be effective for so many years?

I think just staying healthy, conditioning.

• • •

Johnny Podres

The Brooklyn Dodgers finally won a World Series, defeating the New York Yankees in 1955, and southpaw Johnny Podres, who was just 9–10 during the regular season, stood head and shoulders above everyone, besting the Bronx Bombers 8–3 in Game 3 and shutting them out 2–0 in Game 7 to win the Series. Podres was voted the Series MVP and was the toast of the town. In 1957, the Dodgers' final season in Brooklyn, Podres led the NL in shutouts with six and ERA at 2.66. After moving with the Dodgers to Los Angeles, the big-game pitcher possessing one of the game's best circle change-ups helped the Dodgers win the World Series in 1959 and 1963. The four-time All-Star finished his 15-year career with a won-lost record of 148–116, with 1,435 strikeouts and an ERA of 3.68.

This interview was conducted in Pittsburgh, Pennsylvania, in 1993.

Johnny, I guess when people hear the name Johnny Podres, they associate you with, although you were with some pennant winners in LA, but with the great Brooklyn Dodgers team of 1955. You're 23 years old, you had a fairly good season, what were you, 10–9, or 9–10 during the regular season?

Well, you're talking about me having a good season. I really didn't have a good season. You know the Dodgers that year won over 100 ballgames, and I was 9–10 that year. In fact the only thing that saved my season was the World Series games. I won the third game, 8–3 and the seventh game, 2–0, and it was one of those things. You know in the last game of the World Series, the Dodgers had Newcombe ready to pitch, Erskine could have pitched, and Walter Alston after I beat the Yankees in the third game told me that if there was going to be a seventh game, I was going to be the pitcher in the seventh game in Yankee Stadium. That really boosted up my confidence because of the year I had. Although that year I got hurt in June, I hurt my shoulder, and I was on the disabled list for about a month, and I really didn't get it going until September. I started throwing the ball good again.

I know you had the great change-up, but what happens to a pitcher, I mean here you are in probably the most pressure-packed situation, the World Series, and you were unbeatable?

Well actually, when you're talking about a pressure-packed situation, which it was, but for me, coming off of a year that I had being a losing pitcher, actually there wasn't any pressure on me. Probably if I'd had a season where I was 18–7 or 18–9 where I was expected to do something against the Yankees in the World Series, then maybe I would have probably felt the pressure. I felt the pressure, yeah, but I just went out there, and it was one of those days that Campanella called a great ballgame. The shadows got there about the fifth inning, and I had a good fastball that day. First of all, I established my change-up in the third game, I used it a whole lot. But in the seventh game, I probably threw mostly fastballs and hard curves and maybe threw six or seven change-ups. In fact, I think I shook Campanella off one time the whole game, which is what I did, one time in the whole game, and it was the last pitch to Elston Howard for the final out of the '55 World Series. I tried to strike Howard out; I had him two strikes and I couldn't put him away with my fastball, and then I knew he was starting to get to my fastball. I said, I gotta do something different now. It was the only pitch that I shook Roy off the whole game.

I guess people remember in that seventh game, Yogi Berra hitting the ball and of course Sandy Amoros making that outstanding catch. What do you remember about it?

Well, the thing I remember is Walter Alston making a move in that inning. You know how things go. All of a sudden, you're playing in the Series, Walton Alston making a move in the sixth inning. He takes Don Zimmer out of the game who started at second base, brought Jim Gilliam in to play second, and brought in Sandy Amoros for defense. All of a sudden, the Yankees got men on first and second, nobody out, and here comes a play that Amoros makes after Alston just made the move. Maybe the Dodgers were supposed to win that World Series. I don't know.

They were due to win, because you know you mentioned Campanella and it makes one remember the great Snider and Hodges and Reese. These guys are legendary, and you were an integral part of that Brooklyn Dodgers team. There's a mystique about the Brooklyn Dodgers. Can you put it into words? What is it that makes them stand out so much?

Well, just the guys you mentioned is what made them stand out so much, were the Jackie Robinsons, the Pee Wee Reeses, the Duke Sniders, Roy Campanella, Gil Hodges, Carl Furillo. Those people played for so many years together in Brooklyn. I mean they couldn't do anything wrong in Brooklyn, and big Newk and Erskine. You know those kind of guys, you know that were the Dodgers, the real true Dodgers, and Clem Labine, one of the great relief pitchers in Dodger history back in the Brooklyn days, he was outstanding with a hard sinker and a great curveball. All of a sudden I came up in '53, and I end up two years later being a World Series hero for the Brooklyn Dodgers. You know, Duke Snider hit four home runs in that World Series and drove in about ten or 11 runs, and without a doubt he was very valuable to the Dodgers in that World Series.

In '59 and '63, you were also involved in World Series play. I guess nothing probably could top the '55 Series though, but what do you remember about the other two years?

Oh, the other two series, we played the "Go Go White Sox," they called them that year in '59, and I think John Roseboro threw out three or four of their guys in that Series. Of course, in 1959 Charlie Neal got some very important hits for us in that Series. Larry Sherry, who was the Most Valuable Player in that series, he was just outstanding. Wally Moon, you know. Then in '63, we beat the Yankees four straight games with Koufax winning two games and pitching. You know Ron Perranoski relieved me in the second game of the World Series that year, and he was the only guy that got into the ballgame as a [relief] pitcher. It was an amazing feat by the Dodger pitching staff. Drysdale beat him 1–0, Koufax struck out 15 the first game he pitched, and then beat the Yankees 2–1 in the fourth game of the Series.

You have taught the change-up, and many bring up the name of Frank Viola when you were with Minnesota. What is it about that change-up, especially the way you threw it, that made it so effective?

Well, I have good backspin on my change-up. Frank Viola throws his a little different, but the thing that Frank Viola does is he's got good arm speed, he gets good extension. He throws it anytime in the count, and he knows it's one of his best pitches. It may be his best pitch right now, and he's not afraid to throw it with 3–2 and the bases loaded. That's where you get confidence in a pitch, and he's got hitters out front, unbelievable with that pitch, and he just keeps throwing it low outside all day to the right-handed hitters.

• • •

Dick Radatz

Boston Red Sox reliever Dick Radatz was an imposing figure on the mound, standing 6 foot 6 inches tall. The right-hander known as "The Monster" usually dominated when he entered the game. In his rookie season, 1962, he led the AL in saves with 24 and posted an ERA of 2.24. In 1964, Radatz established the major league record for strikeouts in a season by a relief pitcher with 181. He was an All-Star in 1964 and played the majority of his seven seasons in Boston with the Red Sox. He completed his career with a record of 52–43, an ERA of 3.13, and 122 saves, while striking out 745.

Dick, you seem to me one of the first premier relief pitchers, at least in my consciousness. You had a string of years from '62 to '64 that were just incredible for you.

Yeah, '62, '63. '62 is my rookie year and '62, '63, '64 and '65 were all good years for me. I was, I think if I wasn't the first, I was one of the first relief pitchers to be groomed in the minor leagues to pitch relief in the big leagues. You know, back in those days, late '50s, early '60s, if you weren't good enough to get into the starting rotation, you simply went to the bullpen. So I think I was one of the first. I know I was the first relief pitcher ever chosen to an All-Star game in '63, in the American League anyway. But you know, before we had first Elroy (Face) and Hoyt (Wilhelm) had already done some great jobs before I came up. But I think our era of the early '60s was when the relief pitcher really came in the zone with John Wyatt, Bill Daily and just a number of people, Ron Perranoski over in the National League. But I think from then on, it just got bigger and bigger and it became a; as opposed to a throw-in or an extra pitcher, a very integral part of the ball club.

You know there is a psychology that goes with being a relief pitcher also, and you were just an awesome sight to look at when you were out there.

Yeah, it's a different mindset. I've always said the mindset of a relief pitcher and a starting pitcher is almost like a halfback and an offensive lineman. The end results obviously are the same, but you look at the game a whole lot different. The analogy would be the great Luis Tiant, 229 games won as a starter, but don't bring Luis into the short end of the ballgame. He didn't like it. Now if he loaded the bases himself in the ninth inning, he could get out of it, but don't bring him into somebody else's. It was a different mindset. I guess something you're born with. You know, you don't work on having that positive attitude. I needed it like three square meals a day. I loved the challenge of it. I also liked the idea of being able to help somebody else out, that being the starting pitcher usually.

Well, everyone called you "The Monster." How did that come about?

I struck Mickey Mantle out in Yankee Stadium in 1962 with the bases loaded to end the ballgame. When he left home plate, he called me "monster" with about ten other four-letter adjectives wrapped around it. But he said it loud enough that the people in the press deck heard him. They picked up on the name, and it stuck.

"The Monster," Dick Radatz, was a relief pitching standout.

You think today when you look at relief pitching, you just went through the evolution of it, better or just as the same, just as effective?

Oh, I think relief pitching is good as it's ever been. The numbers are a little misleading. A save, I don't know what a save is anymore; I guess you finish a game and you win, you get a save, it at least appears that way. But I think the Lee Smiths and the Jeff Reardons and the Eckersleys of this world could have finished any year and done very, very well. Of course there's others too, but we are blessed today with Elroy Face, and Kent Tekulve and everybody knows what Rollie (Fingers) did and what he was capable of, and very deserving to go into the Hall of Fame. I think you're gonna see more of that and I think rightly so. But I think today's present relief pitchers are just as good, if not better than we were.

Listen, we appreciate you taking a few moments of your time. You're one of the best. You're a nice guy, but you still scare me. Best of luck.

Thank you very much, I appreciate it.

• • •

Dusty Rhodes

Dusty Rhodes played only seven seasons in the Major Leagues, all with the New York and San Francisco Giants, making the most of his time in the limelight. In the 1954 World Series against the Cleveland Indians, Rhodes hit a pinch-hit home run in the bottom of the tenth inning to give the Giants an opening game victory. The following day, he came through with a pinch-hit single, and after staying in the game he smacked another home run to help the New Yorkers go up two games to none. The Giants would go on to sweep the heavily favored American League champions, who had won 111 games during the regular season. For his clutch hitting, Dusty Rhodes was presented the Babe Ruth Award, given to the Most Valuable Player in the World Series. James Lamar Rhodes would hit .253 with 54 home runs and plate 207 runs in his career.

This interview was conducted in 1991.

Dusty, you were on center stage appearing in the World Series in 1954, and you came up big. An unbelievable performance that made you a celebrity that appeared on The Ed Sullivan Show.

Well, it is hard to say because you see I came from a farm, and I wasn't used to all that notoriety and all that. So actually, it was a lot of fun, but I'll tell you [it] really hurt your career though because everyplace you go people want you to do this and do that. You don't have any time for to yourself and, and it's hard to stay in condition for the next year.

It was a storybook tale of a player coming out of nowhere to become a star in the World Series. And you also contributed to the success of the Giants during the season.

I came up to replace Monte Irvin, who had his leg broken, so when he got well there was no place for me to play because Mueller was in right, Mays was in center, and Monte was in left. That's where the pinch hitting came in. So Leo used to wait until the last minute in case the game really means something, and it was a challenge going up to bat

Ed Sullivan (left) and Dusty Rhodes, 1954.

when it's the last of the ninth and the bases loaded and we were behind one run. If you got a hit, you win, and if you don't, you say you only get three out of ten hits anyway. So, that is one of the seven. Actually, the pressure was on the pitcher. That's the way I look at it.

Is that the way you approached pinch-hitting in that the monkey more or less was on the pitcher's back?

Always, because he had to get me out or otherwise he's lost. And Leo, that's why I admired him because he used to make me mad, and I always play better when I'm mad. He waited until the last minute when the game meant something, and then he would send me up, and actually during 1954 I think there were about 15 games that I won in the late innings. The winning run batted in today is kinda different from when I played, see if you hit a home run in the first inning and get 15 runs, well you drove in the winning run, well that don't mean nothing.

What about you adapting to the role of a pinch hitter?

Actually, I love to pinch-hit. I didn't care too much about playing nine innings when you could win a ballgame with one time at bat in the ninth inning. You could sit there and watch the whole game. So actually, I really did not care about playing nine innings.

Do you think that players that don't pinch-hit with regularity, maybe they don't have appreciation for the difficulty that's involved?

There is a difference in a pinch-hitter and a guy that knows he is not going to play, but you see I used to get out to the ballpark at 4:00 in the afternoon at the Polo Grounds, myself, Bobby Hoffman, Bill Taylor. I'll tell you, we worked out until about four hours before a ball game. Actually in September we were in better shape than the guys that played all year because we had two or three extra hours a day that we used to get in shape. And I could always tell when I was going to play. Leo always used to put me in with hard throwers. I would know when I was playing because I could hear the guy holler out the window in the Polo Grounds "Hey, you are playing today." You see, I'd be out on the mound pitching, and then I knew I was playing, so they did not want me to use all my energy.

They actually talked to you through the window—that actually happened to you?

Yell out the top window at the Polo Grounds, "Get out of there, you're playing!"

What was the biggest pinch-hit you ever stroked?

We were playing the Dodgers in the Polo Grounds. It was the bottom of the 13th inning and this was going to be the last at-bat. We were behind one run, there was two outs and the bases were loaded, and there were two strikes on me. If I would have walked, the game would have been tied and we'd have played another game the next day. But if I would have struck out, the game was over. So I got a base hit with two strikes on me, and we win 4–3, and I think that was the greatest hit I ever got. Also the next day I got another, I hit the same pitch, the same bases loaded, and we beat the Dodgers. Now if we would have lost that game, we would have been tied and we probably would have never been in the World Series, but we won that game and then we won the next two.

The rivalry between the Dodgers and Giants, was it as intense as people say?

It was worse. It was like you were on pins and needles when you played the Dodgers, and when Campanella caught and Snider was in center and Erskine was pitching and

Hodges was on first, well we knew we had a battle. But when a lot of times Hodges or Campanella didn't play, and if either one of those was out of the line-up, it was just like we was gonna win this game, because I tell you they was four of the greatest players I believe I have ever played against. And when Campy was out of there, that means we was gonna win, and Robinson he could beat you coming out of the clubhouse. To me, I think he started playing baseball when he was 26. To me, I thought Jackie Robinson was the greatest ball player that ever lived. Now that's my opinion.

Could you break that down a little?

Number one, when he come out of the clubhouse, everybody started booing him, and he had that little cocky walk and he could beat you 99 different ways. He could steal on you, he could aggravate you, he could hit, he could just do everything, and he was a good fielder. When he played, you had to be on your toes.

You played with Willie Mays.

Yeah, Willie was great, but I'm talking about the greatest of all time. You see, Willie came up while he was young, and Robinson came up when he was 26, and everything in this world was against him and he still was a star.

That's quite a compliment, especially from someone from a rival ball club. But, if we could just talk about Willie for a moment, were you there when he first broke in with the Giants?

Well, he came up in '51, and then he went in the service '52 and '53, came back in '54 and Willie was one of the best. Well, what I was talking about was a guy that would beat you everywhere when I said about Jackie Robinson, because he had everything against him, and Willie had everything going for him. You know what I mean? Two different ball players. Well, Willie went to the Hall of Fame, you know he had to be good. Willie was great, I mean if I had my druthers, I would say that Jackie Robinson was the greatest.

Keeping in that same line, many people feel that Monte Irvin was a great player.

Now he is a gentleman, now I tell you. You see, when I came up, Monte was just about 35 years old and I can remember one base hit he got up in Milwaukee—bases loaded and we was getting beat 1–0 and he hit a line drive over the shortstop to the fence for three runs. That stands out in my mind more than anything. Monte was some great ball player, but he is in a different category than Willie or Jackie Robinson. You know what I mean.

Everybody has their own distinctive style. Many people believe that Monte could have been the guy to break the color barrier.

Now that is three different personalities all together. Monte is a gentleman, he is well educated, he went to college, and in fact I was over in Bayonne, New Jersey, a few years ago when they honored Monte there. I went over and said a few words, and you see Monte was different than Jackie. In fact I don't think Monte was what you'd call a really close friend to Jackie Robinson, but I know he used to room with Willie. But you see that is three personalities, they're different, and Monte would have been a great man but it is kinda hard to say how he would have took it being the first black.

Allow me to jump to pinch-hitters. During your era, who did you admire or enjoy watching?

Actually, I can't remember too many pinch-hitters because usually when you played, you played nine innings back in those days. Actually I can't recall too many pinch-hitters. Like I said, Leo used to keep me until the very last—the ninth inning, when it really meant something. He would never send me up there five runs ahead or five behind.

Do you think Leo Durocher belongs in the Hall of Fame?

Well, I think he should. You know, he was one of the greatest managers at that time, but you know he could never manage these young kids today, you know with the long hair. Ha—he'd say something to them he'd say "why don't you get lost?" or "I'd buy the club and fire you." You see, it is altogether different. Years ago, Leo could manage—not the kids today, and in fact those kids today, nobody could tell them nothing.

What about in the World Series—the home runs that you hit, you knew you were under pressure? What kind of a thrill was it in the Fall Classic?

Leo started that crap again with making me mad, because that last game in Philadelphia before we had a couple days off before the World Series started, Leo said my starting lineup today will be the persons in the starting lineup in the World Series. So I played in Philadelphia against Robin Roberts, and I tell you that is when Mays got two or three hits and won the batting championship. Robin Roberts walked Don Mueller twice, which he never walked anybody, and Mays was .346 or .344 or something like that. Well, I hit .341 counting pinch-hits, but I didn't go to bat but 182 times. So we're working out in the Polo Grounds on a Monday or Tuesday I think it was, and I'm in the cage hitting, an' you know they had about nine million photographers and sports writers there. They said "okay, the starting lineup over here," and I said, "I'll be with you in a moment." Ha, you ain't a hell playin', so you know I got mad again. So I got showered and I went home.

The next day, actually I wasn't playin', and about the ninth inning Leo says, "Rhodes, grab a bat," so I did and he said "oh, go sit down, I'll let Grissom hit." He was making me mad all the time, and I sit there nine innings watching this ball game, and Leo never called me Dusty, he always called me Jim or Rhodes. Monte Irvin came up and he says, "Rhodes, grab a bat and hit for Irvin," and I grabbed a bat and kinda looked at him because he'd made me sit down again. I drug the bat up to home plate, so actually I was gonna take the first pitch because I ain't never hit Lemon. He had a sinker that went down a foot and a half, so he threw his first pitch and it looked like a hangin' curve ball. I said the hell with it and I swung, and the wind was blowing to right field. Bob Lemon had pitched ten innings of one of the better ball games he had ever pitched, and that little pop fly started out to right field, and the wind took it. It went over Dave Pope's hand when he leaped up, and it landed in the stands. Bob Lemon threw his glove into the stands farther than I hit my ball. HA HA HA. It was unreal. Actually, when I hit the ball, I started trotting to first base and I thought the wind—I thought it was going only 269 feet down the line. It was right there down the line, and Vic Wertz had hit one down to center field 490 feet that Willie caught, and I hit one 269 feet.

Yeah, but you really took advantage of what was there. In the off-season, when you had celebrity status—did you ever think to yourself, "I can't believe I had such a tremendous World Series"?

You know, you're not gonna believe this but actually it never dawned on me.... Once in awhile, like when I got this picture that you sent me from when I was on the Ed Sullivan program with Desi Arnaz and Lucille Ball—you know I was lookin' at it the other night and I was thinkin' hell, I was good, Ha Ha Ha. You know it never dawned on me because that was my job, I loved to play baseball. I would have played it for nothing, and actually I've had a lot of good moments in my life, but it never dawned on me, honest it didn't.

That's surprising, because so many people dream and fantasize about being the hero.
   Well, like I said, I always loved to play the game, and every once in awhile now it dawns on me now what happened back then, but after that it never did. If fact, I got a friend of mine in Montgomery, Alabama, that owned a wine company and he asked me if I would be a public relations man for him. I said yes, so naturally it went around the country that I was a wine salesman, which I wasn't, and I got a couple of letters from a Baptist preacher out in Wyoming or someplace. He said that he was real disappointed in me that the kids looked up to me and I was voted, "Inspiration to the Youth of America."

When you look back at your career, how would you like people to think of you, or how would you like to be remembered?
   I would like to say that I was a pretty good pinch-hitter. I don't care who you mention my name to, they all laugh because I was supposed to be the clown and nothing ever bothered me. I knew nine million jokes, and people used to call me from all over the country tellin' me jokes, and that's the way I was. In a close game, I was still kiddin', but I did get serious once in awhile.

Well, I guess being able to be loose helped you under pressure when you had to go up there and produce?
   Actually, the pressure never bothered me up until the end, when I couldn't hit the real good curve ball. Then it wasn't the pressure that bothered me. Well, hell, I just couldn't hit.

What outside of the World Series would be the most memorable experience in your baseball career?
   I don't know, Jesus, being on the Ed Sullivan program was kinda unique. Well, a lot of things. I met a lot of people. I met the Governor of Arizona, a lot of prominent people. I met Big Jim Folsom, the Governor of Alabama, you know baseball opened the doors to a lot of things.

◆ ◆ ◆

Robin Roberts

   Robin Roberts pitched in the major leagues for 19 seasons, winning 286 games while losing 245. The right-hander finished his career with 2,357 strikeouts, an ERA of 3.41, and 305 complete games. The seven-time All-Star led the league five times in complete games from 1952 through 1956. He was a member of the Philadelphia Phillies from 1948 through 1961, and his number 36 was retired by the ball club in 1962. He later pitched for the Baltimore Orioles and Houston Astros, and completed his career with the Chicago Cubs in 1966. The native of Springfield, Illinois, was elected to the Baseball Hall of Fame in 1976.

Looking back, how has the game changed in your view?

It's so much different than when we played. The hitters when I played were much more disciplined and made you throw a strike, and the whole idea for me was to throw pitches they could hit but not hard if I could, you know. Keep them in good zone areas, and it's changed a little to that extent. They're more involved with fooling them with stuff now than they are with the location of the pitches.

You were never really concerned with the home run.

Not really, with my style of pitching really. I didn't walk many people and I threw pretty well mostly fastballs and I would, when I would get, when I would head into the ballgame, I wouldn't walk people, 2 and 0; I mean if I had a four-run lead in the eighth inning, I threw strikes. I was just a home run type pitcher. I guess Catfish, Ferguson Jenkins, Spahn threw a lot of home runs, of course he pitched a lot of ball, and it was much different then. We pitched with three days' rest, we pitched a lot of daylight ball. There were a lot of different things that were involved in it. In those days, the ballparks were smaller in a lot of cases; but overall I was basically a one-pitch pitcher and I was, I didn't walk people. People were pretty comfortable hitting at me, so it wasn't that big a deal when a guy hit a home run.

The highlight of your career, would it have been getting to the series in 1950 with the Whiz Kids, is that the year that stands out to you?

It sounds crazy. I was 22 at the time. I pitched 17 more years, or 16, but that was really the biggest moment I ever had was walking off the field. I was still, when we had clinched the pennant on the last day, I just never had another feeling that was quite equal to that. I had other moments that were exciting, but that was the biggest moment. Of course, the Hall of Fame election, I had a great feeling for all the people that had contributed towards my career and the hard work I put in. It was nice that it was pulled off with such a high honor.

◆ ◆ ◆

Brooks Robinson

When the name Brooks Robinson is mentioned, the first thing that comes to mind is defense. The third baseman had a fielding percentage of .971 over his 23-year career, all with the Baltimore Orioles. To back up the premise of his superiority at the hot corner, Robinson, or "The Human Vacuum Cleaner" as he was referred to, collected 16 consecutive Gold Glove Awards. He was a member of two World Championship teams (1966, 1970) and was World Series MVP in 1970, when the O's defeated the Cincinnati Reds four games to one. The 18-time All-Star compiled a batting average of .267 and collected 2,848 hits, 268 home runs and 1,357 RBI, illustrating that he was hardly a one-dimensional player. He was inducted to the Baseball Hall of Fame in 1983.

You played in a number of World Series, but 1970 comes to mind with the bat and with the glove. What is the experience of playing World Series, the mystique of it? Can you explain it and why some players come to the forefront and others don't?

Well I think all the, if you're a major league baseball player, the one thing that you want to try to experience is the fact that getting to the World Series, that's really what it's all about. It's so different than playing every day. I mean during the season, you play 162 games day in and day out, and very seldom during that 162 games do you feel it inside; but when you get to a World Series or a playoff or an All-Star Game, just the excitement makes you feel it inside. I guess the old cliché is they say the adrenaline starts to flow, and I think every professional player likes to know how he is going to react when he gets under that kind of pressure. The World Series is probably the greatest pressure for a player because you got millions of people watching, and it's a great feeling to have. It doesn't mean you're gonna play well, because I felt like that and I played lousy, and I felt like that and I played well; but it is a great feeling to have. That's kind of the mystique, I guess players wondering how they're gonna react when you got all the press, all the television watching you. That's the showcase of baseball, the World Series.

When you have that great Series—I spoke with Clete Boyer, and he was saying you just have energy; you don't get tired, you feel like you can just keep going. When you had your exceptional Series, is that what it was like, was it just like you were almost in another gear?

Absolutely. You want to get to a World Series. But after 25 games in spring training, 162 during the season, you play four out of seven in the playoffs, and you get to the World

From left, Brooks Robinson, Larry Brown and the author. Robinson was the best ever at the hot corner.

Series, it's just like you never played before. I mean you are excited and you do have, you're very exuberant and you are, you are like you are on another plateau, and it's a great feeling to have.

Talking just briefly about third base. You're known as the greatest, or one of the greatest to ever play that position. Do you ever think of that; I mean, of all the people that have played this game and the first name that comes to anyone regarding third base, I mean going all the way back, is Brooks Robinson.

Well, it's nice, I do appreciate that. I do when I hear people say that that my name is synonymous with third base, and they mention Brooks Robinson when they talk about third base. It's a good feeling to have, and I really appreciate it. I think that you know that's the great thing about sports, everyone's got their own favorite, everyone's got their own best of a certain position, but to be talked about in the same breath with Pie Traynor or Mike Schmidt or Graig Nettles or guys like that, it's fun.

One of the things that comes to mind with you is durability. You played for so many years and played effectively; you just seemed to go on year after year after year. Where does that come from, are you just blessed with good health, or did you play through injuries?

That is part of it, being blessed with good health. I started playing in 1955, and when I was up and down for a number of years when I, in the early or the late '50s that's really, I had some setbacks. I had a knee operation after making the team in '57, after two weeks I hurt my knee in the '57 season. I had a knee operation. I got dinged three or four times. I got my arm hurt, hung up on a hook in Vancouver and ripped it open; so I had a number of things. But when I started playing, when I came back for the last time to stay, which was June of '59, the only injury I had through 1977 was a broken thumb; I got hit and I missed 18 games, so I played from that time through '76, I played in about 95 percent of the Oriole games. So I was blessed with good health.

What attributes are necessary for a third baseman? I don't mean to generalize, but if you had to, what must one possess in order to be an exceptional player at that position?

I think it's a God-given talent more than anything else. It's not something that you can acquire. I mean you can make yourself better, but I think the thing that separates the great players, the great infielders from the average infielders, is something of a God-given talent that's an instinct, a certain sense of timing that you have to be born with. I have always been able to field the ball. I've always been able to get that extra jump. You know, I signed as a second baseman. I played my first 50 games at second base, and they decided well look, in the long run, this kid looks like he is better at third base. So I moved to third base about midway in my first season, and I was at third base forever. I guess the reason they wanted to move me to third [was] because they could see that I had great reflexes, and third base is a reflex position more than any other position. You don't have far to move; it's either do or don't, and that was probably the best thing that ever happened to me.

You are known as a good hitter, but you're primarily known for your defense. You are probably one of the people most responsible for Cooperstown opening up its doors and having people recognize defense. Are you as proud of that as you are of any other area of your career?

Well I sure am. I think that the big question of Brooks Robinson, would he be able to hit, and it took me awhile to get the hang of it, but I played a long time, almost got 3,000 hits, and I hit much better than I ever thought I would, especially hit with power.

But I think the thing that people are going to remember about Brooks Robinson was the fact that he won 16 Gold Gloves, he was an outstanding fielder, and I think that probably Cooperstown has begun to recognize defense more so than they did in the past. And guys like Aparicio who made it to the Hall of Fame, but he was an outstanding offensive player, stealing bases, getting a lot of hits; but that's nice, and I think that and probably when people think of Brooks Robinson, they always think of defense more than anything else.

• • •

Cookie Rojas

Cookie Rojas played Major League baseball for 16 seasons, primarily with Philadelphia and Kansas City, and was one of the most outstanding players from Cuba. The five-time All-Star was chosen by Phillies fans as the franchise's all-time second baseman during baseball's Centennial. He was also elected to the Royals Hall of Fame in 1987. Rojas later managed the California Angels and the Florida Marlins. In 2011, he was inducted into the Hispanic Heritage Baseball Museum Hall of Fame. For his career, the Havana-born Rojas batted .263, collected 1,660 hits and drove in 593 runs.

This interview was conducted in Pittsburgh, Pennsylvania, in 1993.

Cookie, a long career as a player, 19 years. You played in the National and American Leagues; you excelled in both. In fact, in 1969 the Phillies [fans] voted you the greatest Phillies' second baseman during the Centennial. That had to be a thrill, because that franchise has been around for a long time.

Oh, no question about it. You know after being so many years with the Phillies, there are so many great players that have gone by the ball club. To be selected by the fans as the best second baseman ever was a very rewarding experience that I received, and it was the club that gave me the opportunity to play every day. I came from Cincinnati after, I played in '62 with them, and was traded for Jim Owens and went to Philly, so they gave me an opportunity to play, and I was very pleased by the vote of the fans.

In fact, when you got traded from the Phillies, Curt Flood was part of the deal. It was very historic because of free agency and the reserve clause. What do you remember about that trade and having to leave Philadelphia?

Oh, you know it was Dick Allen and Curt Flood, and of course you know Curt Flood did not report to the Phillies and created a big problem. You know, with a free agency status and actually the player that I was replacing, Curt Flood, was Willie Montanez, who was actually then the first baseman for the Phillies and had a pretty good year for that ball club. So I was along [in] that trade and Tim McCarver also went to the Phillies in that trade, and Byron Browne. It was a big, big trade, and to be involved in such a trade and the meaning of it, you know, behind it was quite something for baseball.

Do you remember when you went over to Kansas in the American League, a tremendous defense, you and Freddie Patek turn in double play after double play. You played on some good teams over there, and it must have been great playing with a guy like Patek, you guys had such a rhythm together.

It was an expansion club, you know, it started in 1969. When I came over from the Cardinals in 1970, June 15 of '70, and see a ball club being built up from the beginning, you know was quite an experience, and all of a sudden they became a contending ball club. On the final [day], they beat the Oakland A's, who had a very good ball club in those years and became the, you know, number 1 club in the West Division. I was there until 1977, and I was with them for two championship series, and both against the Yankees, of course. [I] remember the two home runs, I mean one home run, especially Chris Chambliss, who beat us out of the fifth game because it used to be a five-game series then. And then in the second series in '77, we got beat also in the ninth inning by the Yankees when we had a lead of 5–4. So it was a great experience, though, to see a ball club being built and a unity that was in that ball club. Playing with Freddie Patek, [who] was an outstanding shortstop that had great range with a great arm and a man that could really, you know, play defense, was very, very good.

You were in Philadelphia in 1964 when the Phillies had the lead, and you really didn't have too many losing streaks that year except right near the end. Then it cost you, but everybody always remembers '64, when the Cardinals caught you.

No question about it. But what people don't remember is that the Cardinals and the Cincinnati Reds won ten games also at the same time that we were losing ten. But what happened to the rest of the league, how come the rest of the league couldn't beat those clubs at least one game. We had a great ball club. Nobody gave us a chance to be with any ball club, and we went right to the end. As a matter of fact, then we took Cincinnati out of the pennant. We took the last two games of the series against Cincinnati, and the Mets came over and beat the Cardinals the first two games and they were ahead on the third game, so if the Mets would have won the last game, we would have had a three-way tie and then Monday would have been a deciding series.

Do you remember the great players that influenced you when you were a young man coming up?

Well, I had Willie Miranda, who was one of the best shortstops that came out of Cuba when I started at 16 years old, you know, in the winter league. He had a lot to do with me, he knew a lot about the game and the fundamentals. Of course, Preston Gomez who I played for in 1969 with the Havana Sugar Kings, and then he managed the big leagues. And then after that with Houston, Chicago, and I was with him with the California Angels, and he was one of the men who I respected the most in my baseball career.

◆ ◆ ◆

Al Rosen

In 1950, Cleveland third baseman Al Rosen, in his first full season, led the American League in home runs with 37. The power-hitting Rosen led the league again in 1953 when he stroked 43 to go along with his league-leading 145 RBI and a batting average of .336. Rosen missed out on the Triple Crown when Washington's Mickey Vernon finished the season at .337; however, he was named the AL MVP that year by a unanimous vote. Rosen played on four All-Star teams from 1952 through 1955, finishing his ten-year career with a batting average of .285, 192 home runs and 717 RBI.

This interview was conducted in Cleveland, Ohio, in 1993.

Reflecting on the closing of Municipal Stadium, you've got to have so many memories, even the All-Star Game. What stands out number one?

Well, there are a number of things that stand out. Obviously putting on a major league uniform and playing for the Indians was the biggest thrill I ever had. Being announced Opening Day in 1950 as the starting third baseman, I succeeded a great third baseman by the name of Kenny Keltner. Then I went on to have what I think were seven pretty good years in the big leagues. Unfortunately I got hurt and I had to retire very early, but the years, they were very good to me, the fans were very supportive and I enjoyed every moment I played here.

Nineteen-fifty-four saw the team win 111 games and advance to the World Series. Unfortunately you lost to the Giants. Still you must be very proud of that club.

I was always very proud. When I think about that club, and I said this often, that one year it was probably as good a club [as was] ever assembled. Unfortunately the fact that we lost four straight to the Giants in the World Series sort of dimmed the memory of that team. But it was a great ball club. Al Lopez and his coaching staff did a tremendous job, even with the injuries we had. Some of the people came off the bench and performed admirably. Sam Dente played shortstop in place of George Strickland, and Hank Majeski, who just passed away a couple of years ago, did a terrific job filling in at all positions, and Bill Glynn. I mean fellows just did; it was one of those clubs that just meshed, and everything we did went right. Even as I say, even with the injuries, people came off and did a great job for us. So it was a great ball club, and it was a club that unfortunately did not get the recognition it should have had as a one-year team.

In 1953, you almost won the Triple Crown, just losing out. That was one of the great seasons for you.

Well it was the best season I ever had, and of course I'd like to think about that year because it was such an outstanding year for a player individually and it happened to be me. And again tremendous support from the fans and the ball club and Lopez. I remember when I was going [for] the batting championship, he was nice enough to have me lead off the last few games of the season so I'd get more at-bats in trying to win the Triple Crown. But it was a great year, but you had to have an awful lot of people on base. If you're gonna knock in runs, you know you've gotta have guys out there to. It was one of those clubs that was just, we had so many big players on that club. Larry Doby and Bobby Avila and a host of others.

Did you talk to Mickey Vernon after that?

As a matter of fact, I got even with Mickey because I hired him when I was the president of the Yankees and I put him to work over there for the Yankees. But Mickey and I always remained very good friends. We had known each other for many years, and Mickey was a great ballplayer and certainly losing out to him is not the worst thing in the world. I would have liked to have won it. I needed one more base hit because obviously there are not that many Triple Crown winners, but the fact that I came that close will be forever etched in my memory.

• • •

Joe Rudi

Left fielder Joe Rudi was a member of the great Oakland Athletics dynasty that won three straight World Series Championships (1972–1974). He displayed his great fielding in in his first Fall Classic when he made a game-saving, backhanded catch in Game 2 that prevented a run from scoring for Cincinnati. His home run in Game 5 of the 1974 Series against the Dodgers turned out to be the difference, propelling the A's their third straight World Series trophy. The three-time All-Star and three-time Gold Glove Award recipient played for 16 seasons and batted .264 with 179 home runs and 810 RBI. In addition to Oakland, Joe Rudi played with the Angels and Red Sox.

Joe, you're associated with the tremendous Oakland A's teams in the early '70s or mid '70s. What stands out in your mind? I mean, that team, if they weren't broken up, could have gone on even further.

Oh, I think so. You know, really most of us were still fairly young. When you look back, when we first started winning, most of us were in our early 20s. In 1968, when most of the guys got to the big leagues on a regular basis, the average on the field age [was] 22, and in '76 most of us were not 30 yet. When we all left, you know, Catfish was really the beginning of the downfall when he left. He was the backbone of the ball club. We had a great farm system. You know, guys like Phil Garner and Manny Trillo, a lot of people like that that were in the minor leagues were great ballplayers that could come up and replace guys as they got older. He traded them all away trying to replace Catfish, and of course we all left. But I think the way the organization was at the end of the '74 season, you know we could have won, keeping everybody healthy and all the other variables that are in baseball, another five or six years.

You're always asked about the great catch in the World Series. How many times have you replayed that in your mind?

Well, it's one of those great things that you're able to do the right thing at the right time. When I look back, when I was a kid playing on the sandlots and stuff, you know you do those things so many times when you were a kid, pretending you're a Willie Mays, or a Mickey Mantle or something, to have that happen in the World Series, it's one of the greatest things that has ever happened to me.

Joe DiMaggio, I remember, always said that you were his favorite player in the modern era. That certainly was high praise, but it could be tremendous weight on your shoulder to have a great player express that about you.

I felt very close to Joe over the years. He was a coach with Oakland in '68 and '69. I was fortunate to have some real good people work with me. I first signed as a minor leaguer, I signed out of high school as a shortstop. I played four years as a shortstop; of course they said I was too big. I had Whitey Herzog that first year with Oakland, actually back in the Kansas City days here, aging myself a little bit, work with me as an outfielder, and then my first year in the big leagues in '68, full year, Joe was a coach. I remember in spring training, the first thing he tried to teach me how to go back and make that very play. He'd be out there standing by us and having the coaches, we used to use those air guns that hit the balls where they wanted; so he'd have us standing real close, hit the ball, you know 50 or 60 feet over our head and make us turn, take our eye completely off the ball, and you know, when you turn to your left and peel to go back, you gotta turn back in to stay on line. When we first started doing it, I mean I didn't get within 50 feet of the ball. You know, I'm a shortstop trying to learn how to run 50 feet and catch a ball in the outfield. And he had patience, you know. He worked with me, taught me how to do it, how to stay on line, you know a lot of little things like that people don't realize how hard it is to track a ball. I mean to actually turn, know where the ball is going, and run to that spot and catch it. It takes thousands and thousands of fly balls, practicing, and that very play is one of the hardest things I had to learn that he taught me. And like I said, he stayed with me two years and a lot of fly balls.

Is there one championship that is more meaningful to you than the others?
   I think the first one is always the biggest because it is something that, like I said as a kid or whatever, you're always dreaming about playing in the World Series. To get into the first World Series, win it, have a good Series, hit a home run, make a great catch and all the other things that happened in that first Series with the Reds, and being the tremendous underdogs that we were going into it, I'll never forget it. All the rest of them were great, and winning three in a row, I think a lot of people will never forget that.

Are you guys all close? Because we always hear about the Dodgers in the '50s, the "boys of summer," and now the A's dynasty, you're not that old, but it's been 20 years now. Do you all stay in touch?
   Well, within a degree. You know this old timers' series has been great as far as the guys getting together from time to time. We just had a reunion a couple weeks ago in New York with the '73 Mets and '73 A's. So that's our main way of staying together. Most of us never see each other, other than that type of situations. So it's a lot of fun. A lot of internal benefits of seeing everybody again.

◆ ◆ ◆

Ron Santo

Ron Santo played 14 of his 15 seasons with the Chicago Cubs. His final year was spent with the White Sox. He was an inspirational leader of the franchise and one of the outstanding third basemen of his era, winning five consecutive Gold Glove Awards and posting a career fielding percentage of .954. The nine-time All-Star hit 25 or more home runs eight times, finishing with 342 for his career, with 1,331 RBI and a batting average of .277. In 2011, the Cubs dedicated a statue of the beloved star playing defense at Wrigley Field. Ron Santo battled diabetes for most of his life, and since 1979 the annual Ron Santo Walk in Chicago has raised in excess of $65 million. Ron Santo was elected to the National Baseball Hall of Fame in 2012.

This interview was conducted in Pittsburgh, Pennsylvania, in 1991.

An outstanding career with the Cubs, however, 1969 will always be reflected on, I imagine, because you almost had an opportunity to grab the brass ring.

I always took a lot of pride when I walked across those white lines. You know, I always gave 100 percent, and I loved playing the game. I played hard, and you look back on my career and everybody does bring up '69, but I look at '69 not as a depressing year at all. In fact, it was the most exciting year of my career because that was the closest we ever came to winning a pennant. Everybody says well, we blew it, but we didn't. The Mets won 35 out of 49 ball games, That's hard to beat. If we would have played .500 ball, we still wouldn't have won. They were the team that year. I always said God lived in New York that year.

You played for a man who could be in the Hall of Fame, Leo Durocher.

He very definitely should be in the Hall of Fame as far as I'm concerned. He brought a lot to baseball. A very exciting manager, and he was an exciting ballplayer. The fans loved to come out and watch him. I played six years for the man. I'd say he was a players' manager, a ballplayer's manager. Whatever he said was kept right down on the field. He protected his players. We had our differences, that's for sure, no doubt, but he wanted to win as bad as I did. When you have two guys like that, you're going to have your differences. But I respect him as one of the best managers I ever played for.

Your teammates, Ernie Banks and Billy Williams, are in the Hall of Fame. Do you give thought to joining them in Cooperstown someday?

Well, I still have five years left to get into the Hall of Fame. Ironically, we talk about this, Ron, when I became eligible, I left the game in 1975 and went right into business. I've been out of the game for 16 years, and it probably hurt me leaving the game and not keeping my face in the media. But I couldn't afford to stay in baseball at the time because I had my own business. But what hurt me was the fact that when it came time after five years to go on the ballot, I only got four and a half percent of the vote and you have to get five. Then four years later, they realized it and reinstated me so I still have five years left to get in the Hall of Fame. I feel statistic-wise there's only seven third basemen in the Hall of Fame in all of baseball, and there's probably only one that has better statistics than I have.

You spent your entire career in Chicago, but your final year was on the South Side with the White Sox. Was that difficult for you?

That was a very difficult thing to do. I really wanted to end my career in Wrigley Field, but I had the five/ten-year rule, so I could go to anybody I wanted to. I didn't want to leave Chicago, and the Sox were interested. I had told Chuck Tanner at the time that I wasn't ready for DHing, but he said "Oh no, you'll play a little third, a little first and DH. We'll switch around with Melton and Dick Allen." But when I got over there, it was mainly DHing. I played a little second base and maybe two games at third. But I had a two-year contract, no-cut, but it was very hard to adjust from the National League to the American League. It would have taken me longer, so I decided to retire after the first year.

You played despite being a diabetic. At what age did it affect you?

I had just signed a professional contract with the Chicago Cubs at 18 years old. In those days, they didn't give you a physical so you just went to a regular MD. At home, my mother used to make me go to a doctor every year and get a physical. I found out that I had diabetes and I was an insulin dependent diabetic, what they call a juvenile diabetic. So I had it my whole career, I took a shot every day, and it was hard. The first four years, I had to learn and understand what diabetes was all about, my reactions and everything. But I was very fortunate to spend 15 years in the big leagues with the disease and to play that long.

◆ ◆ ◆

Mike Schmidt

Mike Schmidt is considered by many to be the greatest all-around third baseman in baseball history. The powerful Philadelphia Phillies leader was a 12-time All-Star and three-time winner of the NL Most Valuable Player Award, a record for third basemen. He cranked out 548 home runs, leading the league eight times, and drove in 1,595 runs during his 18-year career. His defense was just as impressive as evidenced by his ten Gold Glove Awards. The Phillies won the World Series in 1980, defeating the Kansas City Royals in six games, and Mike Schmidt won the World Series MVP Award after hitting a pair of home runs and driving in seven runs. He finished his superb career with a batting average of .267 and 2,234 hits. He is a member of MLB's All-Century team and was inducted into the Hall of Fame in 1995.

Mike, after an illustrious career, many people view you as a home run hitter, but you were, in the opinion of many, you were one of the greatest third baseman. You were an outstanding Gold Glove defensive player. Did defense come natural for you or did you work as hard on that as you did on your hitting?

I could never tell you that I worked as hard on my defensive game as I did on my offensive game. My livelihood was driving in runs and hitting home runs, and hitting third and fourth in the batting order for many, many years with the Philadelphia Phillies. Defense was secondary, although I did take great pride in doing my job as a third baseman, and I felt I was a pretty creative third baseman over the years. I had a few tricks up my sleeve down there to find an out somewhere on that field if there wasn't one with the normal play. Never was a consistent third baseman that Brooks Robinson was. I mean Brooks caught everything and threw everybody out at first base. I was more of a flamboyant third baseman, did things a little off-the-cuff, pretty creative down there if you will. I had a lot of fun playing defense. I didn't feel the pressure playing defense that I did with my hitting.

Looking at home runs, I believe 1972 was your first one [against] Montreal, and then you ended up with 548. But the one that stands out to me, the monumental one was the 500th. I guess that put the cap on it; that's the magic number. What do you remember about that?

Well, my 500th home run was pretty exciting because it won a ballgame for us in the town of Pittsburgh. We were in a bit of a bad streak early in the year in April, April 18 to be exact, and we were down by two runs and I hit a three-run homer to win the ballgame in Pittsburgh. I would have loved to have had that happen in Philadelphia, but it just worked out that it was in Pittsburgh. And as far as individual accomplishments go, as I look back in my career, the day that I hit my 500th was one of the big ones.

You never were a guy to show much emotion, and I remember the little chugging down [to] first base; it was kind of a relief to get that over.

Well, it actually happened pretty quick that year. I hit the five home runs that I needed by April 18, which means in the first two weeks of the season I hit those five home runs. Pretty much when you see me emotional on the baseball field, it's just natural. There's no act. I

Mike Schmidt won ten Gold Gloves and had 548 home runs.

always did have a great respect for the opposition when I played. The pitcher who was pitching, in fact Don Robinson, who threw that pitch, is a good friend of mine. I had a great history of battles with Don Robinson at home plate, he struck me out many times. I got a few hits off of him. He was a tough right-handed pitcher, and you know I would never go across the line when it came to emotion or promoting myself on the baseball field at the expense of another player, especially an opposing pitcher.

You played with some great players, Pete Rose, Garry Maddox, great defensive center fielder. Tony Perez came over for a while with Philadelphia. What players stand out to you?

Well, we had some great players over the heyday years with the Phillies. There's no question, Pete you mentioned, is one I happen to remember first, Steve Carlton, Larry Bowa, Gary Maddox, Bob Boone, Steve Carlton at the top of the list. Although John Denny did win a Cy Young Award when he came to the Phillies for a couple of years, Tug McGraw, a great relief pitcher, Al Holland had a couple of great years as a relief pitcher with our ball club. Probably leaving out somebody. Manny Trillo, Dick Allen, in Philadelphia. We didn't have the rich history that maybe the New York Yankees have had or maybe the Cincinnati Reds. In fact, you mentioned the Reds, Tony Perez and Joe Morgan came and played with us for a couple of years. I was very lucky when it came to teammates. It seemed like every year, especially the great years with Philadelphia, all I had to do was look around the locker room and I could see why they were great.

Was 1980 and winning the championship the top year for you?

Nineteen-eighty was the top year in my life, no question about it, apart from [the] World Series championship, the World Series MVP, League MVP; a tremendous offensive year for myself. Everything came together on the baseball field with the team. My first child was born; yeah, I guess that's the icing on the cake and it was the biggest year of my life.

You had three MVPs; you won it back-to-back and then you won in '86 again. That had to be monumental to you.

Well, you know, the three MVP Awards, looking back on my career, probably were the crowning jewel of my career; the other two, Campanella and Stan Musial, are the other two that have had that in their career. That is pretty select company; and I would say that having the two in '80, '81 and then like five years separating the third would say something for my longevity and my consistency. If I could be proud of something in my career, I guess the third MVP is something to really be proud of.

❖ ❖ ❖

Red Schoendienst

Red Schoendienst was happy when he won, and he was a smiling for most of his 19 seasons playing in the Major Leagues with the St. Louis Cardinals, New York Giants and Milwaukee Braves. The ten-time All-Star won the 1950 Midsummer Classic when he homered in the 14th inning in the first All-Star Game to go extra innings. Red Schoendienst played on the 1946 Cardinals and the 1957 Milwaukee Braves World Series champions and managed the Cardinals to a Series win in 1967 and a pennant in 1968. [He] was a coach on two other Redbirds championships. In 1956, the sure-handed fielder set a then-NL record with a .9934 fielding percentage at second base. Schoendienst was a career .289 hitter who collected 2,449 hits. He was elected to the Baseball Hall of Fame in 1989, and his number 2 jersey was retired by the Cardinals in 1996.

Hey Red, 50 years for you in the game, and the majority of your career with the Cardinals. I know you played in the 1946 World Series. I guess that had to the be the first big thrill for you outside of making the club.

Well, anytime you get into the World Series it's a big thrill, and of course when I signed up I have to say one thing, when I tried out with the St. Louis Cardinals, I came in from a little town of Germantown in Illinois, which is only 45 miles from St. Louis, that was a time when they had a tryout camp. They had so many guys there that they had to send the kids from St. Louis back home because they had so many from out of town as well and they came the next day; but they did keep me over for three days, and I think at the time they didn't sign me up. Joe Mathis and Walter Shannon were the two main scouts that were there. They left after three days, and they went to Peoria, Illinois, for another tryout camp. And now when they came back, they wanted to know what happened to me, the skinny, freckle-face kid. And they said oh, they just sent him home. They got my records out and they got the phone number. Of course, we never even had a phone at home, they called next door. I come back into St. Louis, and I think that was about the time when Mr. Rickey, he was with the Cardinals at that time, he and Mr. Breadon. That was the time I think Mr. Rickey came here to Pittsburgh, and it was on his way for the next year. I think he was trying to hide me, really, and then when Joe Mathis and Walter Shannon came back, they called me up. I came back into St. Louis, they signed me to a contract, I went to D-ball, and I was there that half a year. I signed up in July and then I went to B-ball that same year, and the following year I went all the way to Triple A. I led that league in hitting, and then I went into the service for a year, came back out, and then joined the Cardinals and was there for a long time until Mr. Lane traded me after 11 years.

You mentioned you were in the service. You played in the major leagues at a time when the war was going on, and many of the great stars not only from the Cardinals, from all the ball clubs, had been drafted or joined the service. What was the atmosphere playing in the league? We seldom hear much about when the war was going on and a number of players weren't there.

Well, they were trying to, I know a lot of the minor league clubs went down. I played in 1945, and when I came back out of the service, I played in 1945, and then in 1946 they all came back and that was a different thing. That's how I got to room with Musial, you know. We had spring training and we got different roommates and this and that, and you know everybody roomed together in those days when you went on the road. So I wound up, Stan and I roomed together as long as I was in St. Louis while he was playing. But as far as getting back to your question, you know it was, baseball was a little shaky, they didn't know what to do, shut it down [all] the way. They didn't want to do it, and they did keep the big leagues open, which was only eight teams of course at that time through 1945. After that, you know, in 1946 they all came back.

So many players were hurt, they lost four years out of their career, guys like Feller and Greenberg, Dominic DiMaggio. Cecil Travis was never the same, he didn't have the speed it didn't seem.

Well, I don't know, you're getting back to all the great ballplayers you know, and Joe DiMaggio. Ted Williams, you know, he spent his five years, he went to two wars, he spent his best years in the service, no telling what that man would have done as far as his hitting and in baseball. He might have broken every record that was ever put out, and there are so many others. We had young guys with Musial coming back, Harry Walker, Terry Moore, everybody was in the service, Slaughter, and they all came back in 1946, and some of the guys were injured. You know we had a great pitcher by the name of Johnny [Grodzicki]; I can't think of his name, he was from up around here, Pittsburgh, a great pitcher. He was in the paratroopers and he jumped, and he jumped on a mine and shattered his leg. He tried to pitch after that, but he limped so bad that he, he did come back with us and then scouted for the Cardinals for a long time. There's just so many guys that got hurt. Frank Crespi got hurt in the service that I can remember right now, but there's so many that took their careers away from them to a certain extent because [of] being in the service right in the prime of their baseball career.

Albert Fred "Red" Schoendienst. His jersey number, 2, was retired by Cardinals.

You're a player that wasn't known for the long ball, but in the 1950 All-Star Game you took one deep.

Yeah, that was a big thrill. You know anytime you're playing in an All-Star Game, and I was fortunate enough to be on ten, I should've made a few more I thought, but I didn't. I stayed out because I did have a sore arm and I wasn't feeling too good. Eddie Dyer, who was our manager, one year he says, "I'm gonna keep you at home. You should go to the All-Star Game but you're not." But that was a big thrill just to play against all the great stars in the American League, and I always looked forward [to it]. I was happy to be elected to the National League to play against the stars in the American League. And of course that was a big thrill. I wasn't known for hitting home runs. You know, I hit 15 two different years and that was the most, other than that I hit about five, something like that, maybe six, maybe not quite that many in a year. Playing with the ball club in the National League that particular year, I didn't think I was going to get in the game. And then I got in the game right at the ninth inning I think, and then I finally hit in the 14th or 11th inning, whatever it was, I hit a home run that won the ballgame and it turned the National League around. The National League won quite a number of games right after that for quite some number of years, and maybe I ought to go back and do it again, huh?

Maybe. And then of course you had the two years with the Milwaukee Braves, and you appeared in the World Series. You seem to take winning with you.

Well, we had a great ball club in Milwaukee and I was part of it when they got me, and it was just a thrill to leave. I was with the Giants at the time and they needed a second baseman, and I know Duffy Lewis, the old traveling secretary, he was a ballplayer you know also a few years before that, he told me, he said, "listen, I helped to get you over here and"—you know, he says, "oh don't let me down." I says, "well," I says, "I'll give you 100 percent to help you." He was our traveling secretary. I was pretty fortunate to get me on a ball club, such as Eddie Mathews, Warren Spahn, Henry Aaron and Crandall and Burdette and all that whole great ball club that we did have, Mathews. And that ball club we played, I guess there's about five of them that went into the Hall of Fame, so you know they were pretty good ballplayers. I was pretty fortunate to be with a great ball club at that particular time and very happy that I did get over there. I was in nine World Series as a player, manager and coach, so there's a lot of guys like so many great ballplayers that had great careers that never ever made the World Series. You know, you kind of look back and say, oh heck, like Ernie Banks, I think Bob Feller, I don't think he ever made one [Feller pitched in the 1948 and 1954 World Series], and a number of other ones. So it's, it's a thrill to be in an All-Star Game, it's a thrill to be in a World Series. In fact, that's what you go to spring training for, to see how hard you can put yourself together and with concentrating and everything try to help the rest of the boys that are on your ball club, to help win a pennant and then go to the World Series.

Finally, you know this is your 50th year in professional baseball. Do you ever give any thought to hanging it up, or it's just, you having too good a time?

Well, I'm having too good a time right now. You know, I managed for 12 years and then I went to coach, and then after I started coaching, this is it. I hope I can stay around after this year, maybe next year, and then I'll see after next year. I'd like to stay around at least one more year after this and I would like to be into, get another pennant and the World Series, to be in it. It's pretty tough, there's only one winner, and I enjoy the game, I love to see a lot of these young guys. I try to help them as much as possible and to see them playing and of course, [as] you said, this is my 50th year in professional ball. I've seen a lot of great ballplayers. I've seen ballplayers that don't have the real good talent, but are better ballplayers than the guys that have talent. Some guys know how to win, some of them don't, and it's amazing that baseball is not that easy. You know, I sit back and watch, and they say boy, that looks awful easy. It's not easy, this game is not easy, and I realize it. When somebody pops up or makes an error, you know, he said you should have had that, but you don't, I understand the game and their situation. They're tired, some are more at the end of the year, that's when it really counts, that last month when you're playing and you're fighting for a pennant, trying to get in the World Series. You're usually tired, and you really gotta hitch it up and really put it all together, mentally and physically.

Roy Sievers

Roy Sievers won the American League "Rookie of the Year" Award for his hometown St. Louis Browns in 1949, hitting a career-high .306. The first baseman/outfielder was traded to Washington after the 1953 season and blossomed in the nation's capital, making the All-Star team in 1956–1957 and 1959. In 1957, when the Senators finished in last place, Roy Sievers led the AL in home runs with 42 and RBI with 114. However, he missed winning the Triple Crown when Ted Williams finished the season with a batting average of .388, 87 points ahead of his .301. Sievers later played for the Chicago White Sox and Philadelphia Phillies and ended his career batting .267 with 318 home runs and 1147 RBI.

Roy Sievers, Rookie of the Year 1949 with the St. Louis Browns. You have the uniform on and we don't hear too much about the Browns. What was it like playing with that ball club?

Oh it's like anything else, you know, when you play with a last-place club, which the Browns were back then, it was tough going out there every day and battling the rest of the American League. Especially the Yankees, because the Yankees had the good club back then, you know during the '50s, but we had our fun just like anybody else. We beat some of the ball clubs when we had to, you know, the first-division ball clubs. It was just a great experience for me.

There [was] a natural rivalry between the Cardinals and the Browns, no doubt.

Yeah, every year we had the rivalry, you know, spring training the Cardinals would play the Browns opening day, and sometimes the Browns would win and sometimes the Cardinals would win. But Musial always used to say "well, I see we're playing the Browns, I'll get my hitting stroke back in shape for the regular season."

Then you went on to the Senators in 1953. You had some big years there, especially power-wise.

Well, I had a Washington uniform, but the pants were just about wore out, so I didn't bring enough, so I brought the Browns uniform. But from '54 to '59, you know, we had a real good ball club up in Washington. We didn't have much pitching, but we had pretty good hitting. We had Jim Lemon, we had Harmon Killebrew come along, and we had Bob Allison and myself. In the one year we hit about 140 home runs there among us four; but without pitching, you know, it's tough to win.

In 1957, you had a big year with 42 home runs and 114 RBI. However, Ted Williams prevented you from winning the Triple Crown.

Well, I always tell Ted, I should have won the Triple Crown. I hit 301, he only hit 388, he beat me out by about 87 points. But then anyway, it was really an honor for me to beat them two guys, you know a privilege. I was battling Mantle and Williams the whole season up until about the last month, and then I slowly pulled away and beat them out by four home runs; I hit 42 that year.

As a big home run hitter, are there any similarities you see with guys today and players of your era?

Well, the only thing today, you know they say the players are stronger than we were. I sometimes don't believe that. We had guys that were just as strong; but I think what's helped the player today is they do a little more weightlifting, but I don't think the weights really help the players as much as they think. I think it creates more injuries. You know, not being around a major league ballplayer very much today, the only thing that I've heard throughout the years; but we were just as strong and we had some guys hit the ball a long way, like Mantle, Williams, you know, DiMaggio, I played against [them] about three years apiece, and it was just outstanding.

In 1960, I guess with the White Sox and then the Phillies, you did something only Jimmie Foxx had done at that point, you pinch-hit grand slams in both leagues. Many people don't realize that, and that's difficult to do in one league, but in both. Were you aware of that?
Not at the time, but I hit the grand slam off of Jim Maloney in Cincinnati. The following spring, I come up to hit in the first game we played Cincinnati, and he drilled me in the side and broke three of my ribs, and said, "that's for hitting that grand slammer." It's the only one I ever hit off of him.

Unbelievable. What other pitchers were tough on you?
Well, most of them were all pretty [tough]; Drysdale, Koufax; in the American League, you had Whitey Ford, Lemon, Feller; you name it, Score, just everybody, Trucks, Newhouser, they're all tough. It was just a daily battle to go out there every day and fight them guys every day and try and get your base hit.

Did they use a clip of you in the film "Damn Yankees?"
That was me hitting in that. They filmed behind home plate that day, and I hit two home runs and a double off of Whitey Ford during that, and they used it in the movie. So I always tell my grandkids, that's your grandpa up there hitting in the movies [Sievers misremembers here—he hit a pair of home runs and a double off Yankee pitcher Art Ditmar in 1960].

You're retired now and living in St. Louis?
Living in St. Louis, just enjoying life, playing one or two of these old timers' games a year, play a little golf, do a little fishing, and that's about it.

Listen, I appreciate you taking some time. You were one of the feared power hitters of your day and an exceptional ballplayer, and in fact Richard Nixon, you were his favorite player?
Right, yeah back then in the 1950s. He was just on a show the other night with the guy from California, a close-up; you know who I'm talking about?

I'm trying to think, I don't know the close-up, but was he talking about you?
Yeah, well Nixon talked about everybody and he knows quite a bit about baseball, which really surprised me. He knows, he does know baseball real well.

Would you like to see a team come back to Washington?
It was rumored for a while, but I don't think they're gonna make it. I think they would support it if it goes into the National League. Now in the American League I don't know. I would think eventually we would support it, whether it's going to happen. It's been going on and off for about ten or 15 years and nothing has happened, so I don't think it's going to be in the books.

Ted Simmons

Eight-time All-Star Ted Simmons carved out an exceptional 21-year Major League career as a switch-hitting catcher with the St. Louis Cardinals, Milwaukee Brewers and Atlanta Braves. In 1975, the Cardinals catcher set a National League single-season mark for most hits by a backstop with 188, and six times with St. Louis he hit for an average of .300 or better. The Michigan native also caught a pair of no-hitters, one by Bob Gibson in 1971 and the other by Bob Forsch in 1978. His only World Series appearance was in 1982 as a member of the Brewers, who despite his two home runs lost in seven games to the Cardinals. The man called "Simba" ended his career with 2,472 hits, a batting average of .285, 248 home runs and 1,389 RBI. Simmons later became GM of the Pittsburgh Pirates and a scout with a number of teams, and was elected to the Cardinals Hall of Fame in 2015.

You've been in the game what 20 years? It's your 20th season?
This is my 19th full season, parts of 20 I guess, yeah.

Okay, you've had highs, you've had lows, you've been in the National League, the American League. But after all the years with the Cardinals, you were such a popular player, then you were traded over to Milwaukee. What was that like for you?
Well, any kind of guy who spends a long time with one club, as I did in St. Louis, 11 years, and gets traded, it's a little bit like abandonment, but it's overstated. It's like all of a sudden being kicked out of your family, but you come to realize with age that it's not like that at all. It's certainly not intended to be that. You just recognize the industry from a broader perspective, and you realize that if you intend to play a long time, that's going to happen.

When you played in St. Louis, there were memorable moments. In 1971, Bob Gibson's no-hitter against Pittsburgh, was that one of the highlights of your career?
Certainly Gibson's no-hitter had a real impact on me, but at that time in 1971, I was very young, enamored with the whole spectrum of professional baseball, and certainly with Bob Gibson himself. I mentioned that I was young and that I wasn't accomplished and more or less participated in it. Bob Forsch later pitched a no-hitter against Philadelphia, and I guess four or five years later, maybe six years, and I felt integral there. It had more impact on me because I felt, not only did I participate in that no-hitter, but felt like I along with Forsch pitched it.

You're currently with Atlanta. As you mentioned, you were with Milwaukee and of course the many years with St. Louis. When you look back on your career, do you feel like a Cardinal?
Well, certainly having spent as many years as I did and originally signing with them, it's a little bit like the feeling Lasorda talked about in Los Angeles. You know, you bleed Dodger blue and that sort of stuff. You tend to think that once a Cardinal, you're always a Cardinal in that sense. It's like being born in a town and leaving it. You always feel

you're Pittsburgh or Detroit or New York City, regardless of where you end up. So to some extent that's true. But I spent two absolutely magnificent years in Milwaukee, '81 and '82, and those two years exceed all else combined, because we were in the playoffs twice and went to the seventh game of the World Series in 1982.

Was the World Series, when you finally got there, was it everything you expected?

Very much. It was the pinnacle of the industry and why the game is played and why you play today. You get to the end of the season and you find yourself a champion, and then you find yourself a playoff champion, and then you find yourself almost the world champion. We lost in '82 in the seventh game, but there are people who have won world championships, four straight, five games, you still don't know that drama of a seventh game of a World Series. Even having lost it, I felt very special to have participated in one. Because as a boy it's something you dream of your whole life, the seventh game of the World Series.

Ted Simmons: intellect, attitude and ability.

You have seven .300 seasons, you're known as a great clutch hitter, a good, solid hitter. How do you look at yourself as a hitter?

Well, certainly a consistent one. I think you pointed that out briefly by mentioning, you know, the fact that I hit .300 on many occasions, driven a lot of runs, I consider myself a run producer. A lot of doubles. I have I guess a mentionable amount of home runs, but that wasn't much, I never considered myself a home run hitter. But I considered myself very consistent. I considered myself for about four years, when I did hit homers in St. Louis, a feared hitter and certainly a run producer.

You played in Johnny Bench's shadow. I'm not taking anything away from him. Did you ever feel slighted in those years when he was almost an automatic to go to the All-Star game?

Well, Bench earned everything that came to him. He was a very talented player. He was the most accomplished catcher I had seen mechanically in my life. No one could throw like him. He was big in stature and certainly offensively he was feared to say the very least. He had accomplished what he did at the pinnacle. He'd been to playoffs and been successful. He had been to All-Star Games and hit homers. He had been to World Series and he had won them, and in those years of the Big Red Machine in Cincinnati, everyone was in Cincinnati's shadow. When you mention Bench, you have to go to Morgan, Rose, Perez, Foster. These people shed a very bright light throughout all of major league baseball, and to say that I was slighted, for all intents and purposes would, in my mind, simply say we all were.

When you look at yourself, when you look at the numbers that you put down, you did it in a quiet way and you, you did it with ease. I know you worked hard, but it seemed every year you were there, you were there, you were there. Now toward the end of your career, people look at your record, and you are on a pace with many Hall of Fame catchers or anybody. I mean, your numbers speak for themselves. Have you given any thought ever to the Hall of Fame?

Well, I think it's something that certainly passes my mind from time to time, but it's something I dwell on when people focus upon it themselves. Every two or three or four days, someone asks me this question. If the Hall of Fame [is] something you can achieve, aspire to. Certainly it's something I think about, but I think that's more something I harbor for like my grandkids. You know, I'm sitting around 65 years old and got five, six, seven-year-old grandchildren that look to me and say, "hey did you really do all those things?" You know, I'd say, "well, you can check the Hall of Fame and they'll tell you. But it's not something I think one campaigns for, and it's not something I think one should preoccupy their mind with, because those are things that evolve, those are not things that you can create. If it happens, that'd be the last cap on what I consider to be a long and successful career.

This current season, have you given thought to retirement?

Well, I've thought very much about it. For those who watch, certainly Atlanta has not done particularly well. They're in a youth transition where they're trying to get young people to the point where they can be successful on a consistent basis [at the] major league level. That can be very trying and takes some pains, taking work on an everyday basis, and that's part of the reason why I'm here and still playing. Hopefully I can help them in various ways and try to. But retirement is certainly nearing itself and something I think about on a daily basis, and something I think could very well be the case when the season is over.

You're known as a leader on the field and off. I mean you're one of the characters of the game, and I mean that with respect. You're just a guy that keeps people loose. People respect you. The players respect you, the other teams respect you. Has that always been your role since you began in professional baseball, to take that leadership role and plus be there to keep people loose?

Well, I think when I was young I was a physical person to the extent that I was aggressive, played every day, played hurt, did what had to be done when it came my turn to do it. So early in my career, people I suppose attracted themselves to that. But I think leadership is something that develops as knowledge develops. If you run around stark raving crazy, you'll tend to attract the hysterical, the anarchists, the whatever, and you can take them right off a cliff with you if you so choose. But as you mature and you gain knowledge, you tend to lead people with your understanding, and to those who don't understand, your responsibility is to make it clear to them what direction is the most wise to go. I think as I have gotten older, the leadership at least from my perspective is something that says, when it's time to get hysterical, get hysterical. When it's time to show good judgment, you defer to that.

Lastly, you've been known as, after your years as a regular player, as a tremendous pinch-hitter. If you can just briefly tell your approach to pinch-hitting. How do you, what is your attitude? Does the game dictate what you're gonna try to do up there and so forth?

Well, that certainly does have a lot to do with it. If it's a man on first base and you need one run and it's tied in the 15th inning, the object is to get that man to third base if there are less than two outs. So if I were hitting right-handed, they're holding him on at first base and they're playing me for double play depth, there is a very large hole between first and second base. And if I punch that ball through that hole, the man on first base is going to advance to third. You're now going to be in a position to win the game with a man on third base and less than two outs. So certainly that is going to you know dictate how I'm going to approach hitting. If we're down three runs and there's two men on and it's the bottom of the 15th, my object there is to get them all in, so I'm going to look for a ball close to me that I can pull out of the ballpark to tie the ballgame. Because if you don't tie it immediately, you're gonna lose.

Can you think of a hit that stood out, a pinch-hit that stood out and you got the most gratification out of? Maybe it didn't win a game, but something that meant something?

Well, I think the ones that stand out are the ones that did in fact win a ballgame. And I pinch-hit a grand slam, against Pittsburgh as a matter of fact, two years ago and ended up being the deciding factor. I also pinch-hit a homer off of Lee Smith when he was pitching in Chicago. That was the bottom of the ninth inning. He threw me a ball, and I hit it for a homer and the game was over. So certainly the pinch-hit homer has its impact, but I can go back 15 years ago against the Mets, I was playing on a regular basis at that time, and I was resting on that day, I wasn't in the lineup. The bases got loaded, and I was sent up as a pinch-hitter and, Yogi was the manager for the Mets at that time. He brought in a starting pitcher, [Jon] Matlack, who pitched to me and made me hit right-handed. He gave me a slider the first pitch, and I hit a grand slam. So pinch-hitting a homer that means the ballgame for a pinch-hitter is certainly the most memorable.

When you're, as a player, you think a mature player adapts to the role of pinch-hitting better than a younger player can? He's more accepting of that role?

Well, a pinch-hitter in my judgment, he [who] is going to do it every night regularly has to be a veteran player. It's like being on the edge all the time. It's living on the edge; it's like being a short relief pitcher. You go to the ballpark, you don't know if you're gonna play, but you expect that you are, and the circumstances that you're gonna play will either tie or decide the ballgame, whether you're a pinch-hitter or a short relief pitcher. So it's like being on the edge. You got one crack at it, you got to succeed, people expect you to succeed, and when you don't the tendency is to get very low. But over a period of time, the veteran understands that he's gonna have highs and lows. You've got to find that middle ground insanity so you're not at the peak or the depths, depending on what you do one particular time. You know of the long haul; if you have talent and if you have understanding, you'll succeed. That's the only way, you can either pinch-hit and drive in the big runs [so to] speak; or be a short relief pitcher. You must adapt or you'll go crazy.

Why are some veteran players not able to adapt? You know they could be tremendous players, but they just can't adapt to that role?

Usually the problem I've seen there is the player, who is a veteran, that can't handle pinch-hitting, whether they're willing to admit it or not, are still having difficulty coming to grips with not playing every day any more. That's the first prerequisite. If you think you could still be playing every day and are not, and then used as a pinch hitter, you're gonna have real serious problems. You must accept the role for what it is; if you don't, you're not gonna be able to do it. The veteran hitters that I've seen try to become pinch-hitters and are unsuccessful, in the back of their minds aren't giving up the ghost so to speak about playing every day.

Do you think people, the players and fans, don't recognize the difficulty of the art of pinch-hitting. Is it unappreciated?

Well, I don't think it's unappreciated, because certainly when a guy is successful driving in the big run, they're focused upon it and they see how valuable an asset that is. It's just not star-lit in that it doesn't happen that often where a pinch-hitter wins the ballgame or ties it, make it a focus. Everything is focused, and if there's a lot of emphasis on Clemens because he is apt to strike out 15 batters, the ballpark fills up. The ballparks don't fill up to come see a pinch-hitter win the ballgame on any given night, because they don't know if his opportunity is going to present itself.

• • •

Enos Slaughter

Enos Slaughter, referred to as "Country," played from 1938 to 1959 and finished with a batting average of .300. In fact, he hit over .300 ten times in a career that included a mad dash from first base to score the winning run in Game 7 of the 1946 World Series, when his St. Louis Cardinals defeated the Boston Red Sox. The ten-time All-Star played on four World Series championship teams, two with the Redbirds and a pair in New York with the Yankees. The son of North Carolina ended his career banging out 2,383 hits and 169 home runs and drove in 1,304 runs. He was elected to the Baseball Hall of Fame in 1985, and the Cardinals retired his number 9 jersey in 1996.

You had such an illustrious career, and we're at the All-Star Game, you must have some special All-Star memories.

Well yes, I got a lot of them. I played in ten straight All-Star games. My first All-Star Game was in 1941, you know, when the National League was leading in the ninth inning, Claude Passeau's pitching, and then two men on and [Ted] Williams came to bat. So Bill McKechnie goes out and talks to Passeau, and he says he can get him out. He had Hubbell, you know, warming up. Well, the next pitch, you know, the media said that he hit it out of the ballpark; but he did not hit it out of the ballpark. It hit the third deck, came back on the field, and I kept that ball for 44 years. When I was inducted into the Hall of Fame, Mrs. Yawkey convinced Williams to come back to Cooperstown because that's when they unveiled his statue. And when I made my little speech, I called Williams to the podium and I gave him that baseball, and he opened his mouth and couldn't speak. And I remember my last All-Star Game was in 1953, which was my tenth All-Star Game. Pee Wee Reese and I beat the American League single-handed in Cincinnati, 5 to 1. I got my last hit off of Satchel Paige, stole second, and then made a diving catch off Harvey Kuenn in right field to end the ballgame.

You're known for the mad dash for home in the World Series. Do you ever get tired of talking about that?

Well, I get tired of hearing it because it seems like every time somebody introduced me, that's the only thing I did in my career, which I thought I had a nice career. I hit 300 ten times or better, I wound up with a lifetime average of .300. I played in ten straight All-Star Games, five World Series, and four World Championships. But every time they introduced me, the only reason I got in Cooperstown [was that] I scored from first. To me, they tried to make Pesky a goat, but what was wrong with Bobby Doerr and Pinky Higgins? Pesky had his back to the outfield and when he turned, I think I caught them all by surprise. See, people don't realize in an earlier game I had a triple, and Mike Gonzalez stopped me at third and we lost the ballgame. So Eddie Dyer came to me and he said, "from now on with two men out if you think you got a chance to score, you go ahead and gamble, and I'll be responsible," and that's just the way it happened.

Enos Slaughter, winner of the mad dash home in the 1946 Fall Classic.

Forty-one years after your last All-Star Game, you still enjoy it all.

Well, it's nice to come back and see the fellows, but the majority of these boys now, they were not playing when I was playing.

Do you still get excited?

Well, I enjoy it because I come back and see a lot of players. I see Feller and people like that, you know. The rest of them, they came along after I retired. I was very fortunate. I broke in with the Gas House Gang in St. Louis in '38 with the Deans and Medwick, Mize and Pepper Martin, and then I ended up with the Yankees in '59; so I had a nice career and I enjoyed every day I put on the uniform.

◆ ◆ ◆

Hal Smith

Hal Smith hit what is probably the most dramatic World Series home run that many casual observers of the game never heard of. It was the bottom of the eighth inning of Game 7 of the 1960 World Series, with the Pittsburgh Pirates trailing the mighty New York Yankees, 7–6. Hal Smith readied himself with two strikes and two outs and smacked a drive off pitcher Jim Coates, over the 425-foot left field wall to put the Bucs up by a pair heading to the ninth inning. The only problem was the never-say-die Yankees tied the game in their half of the ninth, setting up Bill Mazeroski's walk-off homer in the bottom of the inning to give the Pirates their World Series triumph. Smith played for five different teams, batting .267, and hit 58 home runs while driving in 323 runs.

Your Game 7 home run, it was in the eighth inning. You had come in the inning prior.

I think I came in the sixth inning; I can't remember now. I know we used a pinch-runner for Smoky Burgess that particular game, then I came in and was catching.

You hit a three-run homer to put the Pirates up. What do you remember? Obviously you remember everything.

Well yes, I remember that when I hit the ball, all I was trying to do was to get a base hit to at least tie the ballgame. When I hit it there were two outs, two men on first and second, and I knew when I hit it, it was a home run. But it didn't really strike me until I rounded second base what had happened, because I looked up and the people in the stands were on the dugout and going crazy. All of a sudden, as I rounded third, I passed the Yankee dugout and saw the expressions on their faces. People like Gil McDougald, Whitey Ford, Casey Stengel, Bobby Richardson, their mouths were open, they were sad, and I realized that I had done something that looked like you might win this ballgame.

When I was speaking with Bobby Richardson, I asked him what he remembered about that. He said that, I remembered he swung real hard and missed the first time. It stuck out in his mind, and of course then you went up there and you hit it out.

Right, the first pitch he threw me may not have been the first pitch or the first ball I swung at. I think the count was two strikes and one ball. Yes, it was two strikes and one ball, and at the time, I usually had a good cut before that, and he threw another one in the same spot. This time I didn't miss, I made contact.

It was a storybook year for the Pirates in 1960. When you think about that ball club and that year, what comes to your mind?

The way each player took it upon themselves to help do their own job. We had eight players who played every day, and any one of [the] eight could get a hit to win a ballgame. We took turns that year winning ballgames. We started out, I think the first game of the season I pinch-hit a double to win a ballgame. The first game I'd ever played with the Pirates. I'd been in the American League for a lot of years, but I said then, after about the second week of this happening, I said well, it looks to me like we need to start ordering our World Series tickets. I never played on a pennant contender before, it had always been on last-place ball clubs. It was quite a thrill for me to be able to spend the season battling for first place. It was great.

You've gone over in your mind obviously so many times that historic time at bat. Do you ever discover anything different about it because you've analyzed it so much?

Well, not really. I guess, I guess they have an unsung hero videotape that they play all of the time. As a matter of fact, the home run that I hit is on television five or six times a year. I have people coming up to me all of the time saying well, I saw you again last night, and I'd say well that's great. I never see it, but I do have videotape of it. In that particular interview that I was doing on the unsung heroes, one of the things that came out that I remember was after the Yankees tied it up in the top of the ninth, Bob Skinner and I were talking. I told Bob, I said, "well Bob, it looks as though I won't be a hero." And then the following, as soon as we got them out, as soon as Mazeroski came to bat, he hit about the first or second pitch over the wall. Then he became instantly a hero, a national hero, and still is because of that. He's the only player that has ever ended a World Series with a home run.

Do you remember when you came back into the dugout, what the atmosphere was like? Anyone in particular stand out, what they said?
You mean as we, when I hit the home run?

Yes.
Well, no, not really because it was chaos; everybody had gone crazy. Murtaugh, bless his heart, he has since passed away, and everyone, we were all, it was just chaos all over the ballpark; it was chaos. You know I couldn't think. I was getting really, actually, it hadn't sunk it what the heck had happened at that time.

Do you ever feel in some respects though maybe a little bit shunned because it wasn't quite as dramatic; although it still was a monumental blow?
Oh, not really. I've gotten everything I, after playing on second-division ball clubs for about six years and coming to a chance of playing in the World Series, I have no regrets at all. It was wonderful, and here I am talking to you today about it. Probably if I hadn't hit that home run, I may not even have been here today, so I'm happy about it.

◆ ◆ ◆

Willie Stargell

Willie Stargell played his entire 21-year career (1962–1982) with the Pittsburgh Pirates. The outfielder/first baseman became one of baseball's most feared power hitters, pole-axing 475 home runs to the deepest recesses of National League stadiums. The left-handed powerhouse batted .282 over his career, drove in 1,540 runs, and displayed leadership in the franchise as they captured World Series championships in 1971 and 1979. 1979 was a magical year for the 39-year-old called "Pops" by his teammates, as he shared the NL MVP Award with Keith Hernandez and was named the NLCS MVP and the MVP in the World Series. The seven-time All-Star joined baseball's Hall of Fame in 1988, and in 2001 a statue of him at bat was unveiled in front of PNC Park in Pittsburgh.

This interview was conducted in Pittsburgh, Pennsylvania, in 1999.

We are having a year-long celebration for Henry Aaron. You were one of his contemporaries. During that historic season that he broke Babe Ruth's all-time home run record, do you remember what he went through that year? It must have been a joyous occasion but also very sad at times for him because of racism.
Well, it's unfortunate that he had to do that because all he was doing was going out there doing the best that he could on a day-in, day-out basis, not just for a couple of years, but year after year after year. So there was a lot of blood, sweat and tears that Hank had put forth to be able to accomplish what he did. When you look at all those offensive statistics, I mean he's in the top three in every conceivable category, so he's just not a home run hitter. He has a lifetime .300 [average]; his hitting is probably 1–2 with a lifetime

RBI, total bases, doubles, triples, and he was a very good outfielder as well defensively. Because you know when you talk about assists, putouts and things in that category, he was right there again at the very top. He didn't have the flair that Mays had, but he was very consistent on a year-out basis, stealing bases. He has a tremendous percentage in all these different things. So I think the spotlight should stand throughout his offensive category. Not just the fact that he did a miraculous thing with hitting home runs, which is unbelievable. You know for him to have achieved that, I take nothing away from Mark McGwire and Sammy Sosa last year because they certainly deserve all the accolades they got, but when you talk about a man who has been hitting for 20 years consistently, where does that put him when it comes to receiving tremendous accolades? It shouldn't have taken this long and for what reason I don't know, but I guess the fact is that it is being done while he is still alive, number 1. And the fact that people that really admire and respect Hank like myself, no one has achieved those milestones that he has done. I mean everybody who has played the game—I played 20 years and I have what you call a good career—but it still doesn't compare with what Hank has done. So it's just unbelievable how this man was able to do all the things he did, and when you talk about the pinnacle of any and everything that a man certainly does, he needs exceptional recognition.

You mentioned your career, you had a Hall of Fame career, 475 lifetime home runs. You played at Forbes Field. You could have very well, if you played in a smaller park, had conceivably hit 600 or more home runs lifetime.

Well, that's true, but I wanted to play baseball here and I had my dreams fulfilled

From left, Vada Pinson, Willie Stargell, and Maury Wills. Pinson was underrated, Stargell was a beloved Pittsburgh slugger, and Wills stole 104 bases in 1962.

by getting an opportunity to play. Just putting on a Major League uniform, I wasn't interested in records and statistics and things like that. All I wanted to do was be the best player I could, Monday through Sunday, and learn how to win, and then make sure on a consistent basis that we did win. So that to me was a real joy of my life, to be able to say that I was in two World Series and never lost one. There's still so much that I can say that I have fond memories about, and I can't say that I would do anything any differently than I did.

You talked about the two World Series, of course 1971 where you played with the great Roberto Clemente; but 1979, this is the 20th anniversary, that had to be an incredible, incredible achievement, and you were the elder statesman on the ball club and the great Series you had, and the MVP.

There's no question. I think that we did in '79 as a unit, it just seemed like everybody in every category knew their responsibility and tried to make sure that when it was time to execute, everyone did what they were expected to do. As a result of that, we gained a tremendous amount of chemistry and a fondness for each other, because we could lean on each other. If one guy wasn't doing it, somebody else would come along and do it. There was never really a down moment, because we knew everybody was trying, and if they weren't doing well on offense, then they would do well on defense and intelligently play the game if they were on the bases or whatever. These are things that you saw because so many little things that took place in order to achieve the formula for winning, and then that's exactly what [we] needed to do. Those were very fond memories, and I can say that each and every one of the guys that I played with in '79, I would not mind them being in my foxhole if I was at war.

What year, and that might be the year, but for you personally what was the greatest memory that you have in your career? Was it your first game, or maybe it's some obscure thing that happened to you that the general public doesn't know about.

Well, my first at-bat was against Stu Miller, and he was with the Giants. He was known for having an exceptional change-up, and I remember I went up to pinch-hit and I must have swung at the ball three times until it got to the plate. And I never will forget that, because the guys never let you forget about it. It was something I can laugh about now, but at the time I just felt that this guy was not going to throw no fastball, by then it wasn't a fastball, it was a change-up one. Me personally, I think the times in 1971 I got off to a really good start and I set some high goals for myself, I felt I was on my way to achieving some outstanding things until August, when I hurt my knee down in Houston. The doctor wanted to operate at that time, but we were doing so well and we felt good about the fact that we would possibly be going to the playoffs and then on to the World Series. I told them I would do whatever I could to make it through the year and participate in my first World Series. I was really moving, I had 30 home runs and 80 RBI, so I'd like to think that, you know, if I hadn't gotten hurt and playing in the second half with being in pain and agony, just getting up every day and trying to get through nine innings. As a result, I just felt that I can really do something to help the ball club, even though I wasn't there, or at least not as well as I would have liked to have been. I still have no regrets.

Well, we'll end it there on no regrets. You had a tremendous career. You are one of the statesmen of the game. We appreciate you taking the time and wish you and the Pirates' organization all the best, Willie.

Thank you, Ron. It's always a pleasure being on your show.

Ron Swoboda

The year was 1969, and the Miracle New York Mets were supposed to be rolled over by the highly favored Baltimore Orioles in the World Series. After dropping Game 1, the Mets won Games 2 and 3. In Game 4, Baltimore was trailing, 1–0, but mounting a threat with one out and runners on first and third. Brooks Robinson was at the plate and hit a line drive that was curving in right fielder Ron Swoboda's direction. The 25-year-old made a diving backhanded catch that prevented the O's from taking a lead. The runner from third scored, but the Mets won the game, 2–1, in ten innings. The Amazin' Mets would win Game 5 and the Series thanks in part to an eighth-inning double by Ron Swoboda that drove in the winning run. Swoboda finished his nine-year career with the Mets, Yankees and Montreal hitting .242 with 73 home runs, 344 RBI, and one moment in time as a World Series hero.

This interview was conducted in Pittsburgh, Pennsylvania, in 1989.

This year is the 20th anniversary of the Miracle Mets season. You were one of those players in the fall classic who came up big. You were a good ballplayer, but probably not someone that people would have thought to have been a hero of a World Series, and yet you were with that great catch.

World Series are made for average ballplayers because you don't have to be a great ballplayer for a whole season, you just have to get up and do it for a short series. That's why I think you'll see average players spark in a Series. I was lucky. It was the only one I was ever in. I had a good one and we won it. You know it was a great experience for me and the rest of the guys because [for] most of us that was the big flash in our career.

When you look back at that ball club, nobody at all took you guys seriously. Did you feel the momentum growing?

Yeah, I mean it was an asset to be a little better than people thought you were. Not to have the responsibility of winning, and no one should have thought we were ready to make that kind of a move. What happened is we kind of started out haltingly and then our pitching got together, we picked up Donn Clendenon, got a little more smack with the bats. And that staff came together, Seaver, Koosman, Gentry, Ryan. I mean, after awhile McGraw was on that staff, Ron Taylor. I mean it became a pretty good pitching staff. We had, we played .750 ball our last six weeks of the season, so it caught on fire. We hit some turbo there.

When you look back on it now, does it have more meaning now as opposed to when you first won it?

I'll tell you what, I don't know that I've spent 20 years thinking about it. Off and on, you know, obviously when that's the only thing you've ever done of that magnitude in your career, you're reminded of it quite a bit. But you're going to look at everything 20 years later from a different perspective and we do now. I mean we're former players now, coming down here to have a little fun, play old timers' days, which is a treat. At the time, you were an athlete who knew right then he may have done the unsurpassable. You know

From left, 1969 Series hero Ron Swoboda, Felix Mantilla, Johnny Callison, Gene Bearden, Ron Hunt, Ralph Branca, Gene Tenace, Carl Erskine and Jim Maloney.

at 25 years old, even then you knew you may have done the unsurpassable. Moments like that are few and far between, much better ballplayers than me never had a moment like that in a Series, never got to a Series, never won a Series. So you don't have any of that coming. So it, I think at the time I think you're pretty, I was pretty aware of what this could mean. Now 20 years later I realized that was it, and you know how fortunate we were to be there and be the master of those times.

◆ ◆ ◆

Gene Tenace

Oakland A's catcher Gene Tenace became the first player to hit home runs in his first two World Series plate appearances, but that was just a sampling of what was to come for the man who would end up being named the 1972 World Series MVP, helping Oakland defeat Cincinnati in seven games. All told, Tenace, who seized the moment, was Dave Duncan's backup for the 1972 season and his replacement in the post-season. [He] went 8-for-23 in the Series with four home runs and nine RBI. For his career, he batted .241 with 201 home runs and drove in 674 runs. The 1975 All-Star also played for San Diego, St. Louis and Pittsburgh in the NL.

Gene, you had a long career, 15 years. You're known for something extraordinary in the World Series with the A's in 1972. That year, you weren't a regular. Dave Duncan, the catcher, got hurt or went into a slump actually, and then you took over and magic seemed to happen in the World Series. What happens to somebody when you just get in a groove?

You just hit the nail right on the head there. I just got in a groove. I had seen the ball extremely well, and it's just one of those situations where you know the hitter can get into a hitting groove where you see the ball so well. It seemed like, everything looks like it's right down the middle of the plate to you, 'cause your timing is so perfect. It doesn't matter what pitch they are throwing you, it seemed like you are right on it, and basically that's just exactly what happened to me. Fortunately it happened, you know, in the World Series.

That's the extraordinary thing, because it seems like there is so much more pressure on people to perform. You can have tremendous ball players during the regular season, but they don't come up big in the post-season.

Well, I have no answer to that, but you know like I said, it was just a unique situation for me, you know, not playing a whole lot that season. Duncan, like you said he was our number one catcher, and I took over the number one job in late August. I caught the remainder of the season through the playoffs, and you know then I'm in the World Series. I started seeing the ball really well in the playoffs. Unfortunately I only got one hit in the playoffs, and it happened to be the hit that drove in the deciding run in the fifth game in Detroit. But up to that point, which nobody remembers, I do personally because I was seeing the ball so well. I was hitting the ball extremely well, but it seemed like it was going right at somebody. All of a sudden I got into the World Series, and I maintained that same mental approach and consequently everything seemed to fall in.

You know you guys ran off the three world championships, and Lord knows how many more there could have been, but the team was broken up. But we heard so many stories about that team. It's legendary now. You guys walked to the beat of your own drum. Some people said you didn't all get along, there were fights, but when you got on the field you won. How would you characterize that team?

Well, we had 25, obviously 25 different individuals, different personalities. We also had 25 guys who could play the game of baseball. Even taking away the starters, we had a great bench. And our bench, you know, played a big part in our success along with everybody else. But our bench enabled the manager to maneuver the line-up around where you give a guy a day off here and there for a couple of days, and was able to put a guy out there and feel confident in him contributing, which you know which they did. That's the kind of ball club we had. Sure you know when you get that much talent under one roof and you are together for approximately 162 games of the regular season, and then you got about 30-some exhibition games and the playoffs and World Series, so you're roughly getting in the neighborhood of 200 days a year with a person, so it's just like a marriage. You know, even though you and your wife are not going to get along every day, so basically what happens when you get that kind of talent and the kind of personalities we have, you're going to have a little friction. But the key word, you know, you mentioned by asking me that question, was that we were able to separate the problems that we had maybe off the field and in the clubhouse. Once we got in between the white lines, we were able to pull together as a unit and play together.

When did it sink in with the players? Was there a certain turning point when you knew that this was a special team, because of what the A's accomplished? I don't know when we're ever going to see it again, especially today; but was there a point when you said, hey there's something going on here?

Yeah, when they hired Dick Williams. We always felt we had a lot of talent, you know. I got to the big leagues in '69, and of course I started putting things together in '70. Then '71, we got into the playoffs and lost to Baltimore three straight, and we knew then, you know, that we had a nucleus of a lot of talent. But when Dick Williams came over and was named manager, he saw the talent, but he also saw a piece of the puzzle wasn't quite there, and that was a fundamental execution. He got a hold of us in spring training, and he pounded fundamentals into us in spring training. Sure enough, we went out there and we executed fundamentals as well as anybody. You know, you're talking about the rundowns to the moving runners over, manufacturing runs, hitting a cutoff man, all phases of fundamentals. We never beat ourselves, and that's the key to our success that was the last piece of the puzzle. Because the pitching was there, the offense was there, we had good team speed, we had a good bullpen, and we had depth on the bench. But we made a lot of mistakes, fundamental mistakes, and that was the main reason why we weren't winning. When Dick came in there and was able to put that together, the last piece of that puzzle, all of a sudden we took off as a club.

◆ ◆ ◆

Bobby Thomson

It was 3:58 p.m. on October 3, 1951, at New York's fabled Polo Grounds, when Bobby Thomson hit a Ralph Branca fastball that would forever be known as "The Shot Heard Round the World." The shot would not only win the National League pennant for the Giants, but allow the Polo Grounders bragging rights over rival Brooklyn. The dramatic home run capped off a three-game playoff between the Giants and Dodgers after the teams split the first two games. In the third and final game, the Giants trailed 4–1 going into the bottom of the ninth inning, and after scoring a run to make it 4–2, with two runners on base Brooklyn skipper Charlie Dressen called on Ralph Branca to replace starter Don Newcombe on the mound and face Bobby Thomson. Ironically, Thomson had hit a sixth-inning home run in the first playoff game off of Ralph Branca. On this day, Branca's first pitch was a called strike. His second offering would set into motion one of baseball's most shocking and dramatic moments.

Bobby Thomson played a total of 15 Major League seasons with the New York Giants, Milwaukee Braves, Chicago Cubs, Boston Red Sox and Baltimore Orioles. For his career, "The Staten Island Scot" batted .270 with 1,705 hits and 264 home runs.

This interview was conducted in Pittsburgh, Pennsylvania, in 1989.

You are known for the "Shot Heard Round the World," and I'd like to address, that but you also hit a dramatic home run the last game of the year. Were you playing the Braves to get you into a tie?

Yes. Actually, I hit three in the last four games I played in. We were behind up in

Boston that last game, and I guess we were behind a run. I hit a home run, and I think it tied it up. I don't think there was anybody on. Then I happened to hit one in the first playoff game. We were behind one nothing, and I hit one with a man on, whenever, the fifth inning or something like that, and then the third one I guess you heard about.

About that third one. I was reading Leo Durocher's book, and he said that you two had a conversation about what Branca would throw you, because you had hit one in the first game. Can you recall the conversation?

Well, I don't recall the conversation he said we had. We apparently have two different opinions or we remember two different things, you know, which is fine, I could be wrong. All I remember was after they carried Mueller off the field, he put his arm around me and said, 'Bobby, if you ever hit one, hit one now, and I thought to myself Leo, you're out of your mind. I didn't, I didn't even answer him, you know, I just headed for home plate. That's my version.

I think Ralph Branca said he was trying to waste a fastball up and in on you.

Yeah, he had a strike and why I took the first pitch right down the middle. Well, I was all the way home, you know, we were down there at third, as I said with Mueller hurt, and it seemed a pretty long walk from third base to home plate in that situation. I just kept telling myself to wait, wait, wait, wait and watch, wait and watch. Don't get overanxious and get out on your front foot. So I sat back, and I was waiting and watching and took the first pitch, I guess right down the middle. It was a great pitch to hit. He came inside, up and in, it was bad but it wasn't that bad. I had been pretty quick with my hands inside, and I remember getting a glimpse of it and I just jumped on it.

Did you know it was going to go? It was like a sinking line drive.

No, [when] it started out, I thought it's gone upper deck, and immediately home run. And then I watched the darn thing after about a second it seemed, it must have had tremendous overspin, and I could see it start to sink. I thought to myself, it's not a home run, it's just a base hit. I think I wasn't even running, I don't know, normally when you hit the ball you're supposed to get going. I watched the ball, but I couldn't help myself [from] watching that one. And as the pictures of the tape showed afterwards, I was only halfway to first when I saw the ball disappear.

These many years later, how did that home run change your life?

Bobby Thomson, 1951 miracle worker.

Well, it hasn't changed my life after baseball in terms of me to go out to work and earn a living and get into something other than baseball, which I'd been in all my life since high school. But obviously my name still comes up because of it, and it's nice to be remembered. Let's face it, I still have to get out of bed in the morning and get to work. So that's it. I don't think there's anything more to it than that. You know I get invited out once in awhile and heck, everybody likes to get invited out.

The player that replaced you in New York was Willie Mays, and later in Milwaukee it was Hank Aaron.

Yeah, two pretty good ones. Yeah, I guess when Hank came up in '54, they just brought him to spring training I guess to just have a look at the young man and let him see what big league spring training was like, 'cause they had just traded for me to play left field. And of course I broke my ankle and Charlie Grimm said, "Henry there it is, you know, it's yours till something happens to get you out of there." So I've always kidded Hank about that, I said "Hank, do you realize if I hadn't broken my ankle, you might never have made it." Of course that draws a big laugh from old Hank.

The shot that you hit, as a professional ballplayer it's almost the pinnacle of what someone could do. Where could you go as a player as far as heroics or drama after that?

Well, I know that Durocher said the next spring, he said, "Bobby I just feel you're going to hit one every time up." Of course, everybody knows I didn't. When that happened, really all it meant to me and to the Giants I'm sure was that we beat the Dodgers. We had a real rivalry, second to none it would seem to me, and that's all it meant. Never in the world did I think they'd still be talking about it years later. So that's how it goes, it's Mickey Owen's third strike, missing the third strike, and so as I say it's nice to be remembered.

◆ ◆ ◆

Cecil Travis

Cecil Travis performed with grace and expertise on the playing field and the battlefield. He played his entire 12-year career with the Washington Senators and represented his country by fighting for it during World War II. On the diamond, 1941 was his signature year as he hit .359 with 101 RBI and 106 runs scored while collecting a league-best 218 hits. The three-time All-Star finished with a batting average of .314, 657 RBI and 1,544 hits. However, had it not been for his time lost during the war (4 years) and injuries sustained (frostbite), there is no telling what he would have accomplished in the game. Still, there have been many in the game who believe his sacrifice off the field should have provided him entry to Cooperstown.

This interview was conducted in 1990.

Nineteen-forty-one, what a dominating season. You had what people refer to as a career year.

Well, I mean I had a better year all the way around, but really usually I always hit pretty high, you know, every year. It went from .320 on up to you know, .340 something, but that was the best year. In other words, I knocked in more runs and got more hits and things than I did in any other year. It just happened to be one of the years, and I guess, what you call reaching your prime, you know, about that time.

You were playing with the Senators, and it seems that that season, even though the players that played with you and against you, you certainly had their respect and admiration; you weren't able to grab the headlines like some other guys.

Well, no, no. When you're on a losing club, it's sort of that way. DiMaggio was having that streak, and Williams having that year, that just you know, really overshadowed everybody. So I wasn't disappointed in that.

You posted averages of .319, .318, .317, .344. What stands out about you as a ballplayer, especially as a hitter, is consistency. What do you attribute that to?

Well, I always stayed in good shape. In the winter time I kept, I did a lot of hunting and was in shape. I was really in shape when spring training started. I never gained a lot of weight or anything like that, you know, and I always was sort of a type hitter that, I didn't go for the long ball. I wasn't like a lot of them, but more so just meeting the ball, you know, and there's a lot of hitters, and I was no guess hitter. A lot of these people are guess hitters, you know, I usually decided to hit what I saw.

You have here, 1,544 hits in your career, which is phenomenal for the number of years that you played. In 1941, you ended up with 218 hits.

Yeah, I got over 200 something in that year. That's just one of those years you know everything goes, it's gotta go right for you, you know. The ones you're hitting hard are dropping in [as] hits, and the ones you're not hitting good drops in and that, that's what you gotta have. You know if you have an outstanding year, you gotta be lucky too with it.

Then along came the war, and a number of big-name major league ballplayers were drawn into the conflict. You lost four years of your career.

Yeah, but a lot of other people did the same thing. A lot of people did the same thing. Even if they're not ballplayers, I mean they lost time too, you know, which it's just one of those things.

I know you don't want to attribute to your service time the struggles that you had when you came back, because I know you had mentioned about getting older and so forth; but you were in the Battle of the Bulge, and I guess that you developed frostbite on your feet?

I had that, I got the frostbite really right before that in France. Our Division was sort of a green division, a new division. It followed right behind to Bastogne, Battle of the Bulge. You know, we weren't right in that fighting. We just followed in. That's the way you do it, you got these different divisions, you know, falling right along behind. You know, you['re] moving. At that time, things was moving fast, you know, after that. So we didn't get into that, the bad fighting, like they had, no.

I seemed that when you served, the atmosphere in the country was ballplayers were no different than any other people, they served their time. I'm sure it was tough on you physically. What was it like being inactive and trying to come back?

No, the first two or three years I was in the service, I got to play some ball when I was down at Camp Wheeler down in Macon, Georgia; and when I went to Camp McCoy, Wisconsin, that's where the 5th and 6th infantry division was about a year before I went overseas, I got to play some ball. But as I say, after I went overseas I didn't play, you know, in the last year at all. When I got out, I hadn't played any at all, in other words when I got out of the Army, they let me out. I knew that I was gonna get out and practice around here with the Atlanta Crackers. You know, at that time I went up there a few days before Washington, but no, I hadn't had any playing at all that year.

Regarding the men that served, like the Fellers or Ted Williams and so forth. Was there a closeness that you felt afterward when you were playing back in the states again?
Well, probably so. I ran into some of them when I was in the service. One of the years before I went overseas, you know, they had that All-Star game. Mickey Cochrane, I think he was the manager, it was then at that time we went up to Great Lakes Naval Station and trained about two weeks for it. I saw a lot of players then that I played with.

I know you are a very modest person. There are players like you and Dominic DiMaggio who many believe should be given consideration for the Hall of Fame.
Well, you take him, now he probably didn't get the publicity and things that he deserved, because he was, I think really you know one of the best all-around players. He was a great outfielder. He had a good arm and always gets the, I don't know what his average at all was, ended up or anything, but he was consistent every year. He was the brother of Joe too, you know, and then it sort of, they talked about Joe too, which he deserved it too, but I don't think Dominic received what he should have.

What about yourself, because so many people seem to feel that Cecil Travis was certainly on a path for a Hall of Fame career, and of course losing those years, it to me seemed to hurt you.
Well, it could have been if I'd have continued on and was lucky to have the same kind of years I had before I went in. I mean it might have, could have happened or something, but I don't know. I just figured it was just a lot of players deserved it as much or more than I do. There's a lot of them that's not in there, so that, that don't worry me one bit, I'll tell you.

So when you look back over your career, are there a few highlights that you pick out that stand out to you more than others?
Well, the first one was my first game. You know I got five hits. In other words, I had never seen a big league ball game or nothing, and I was playing at Chattanooga. The Washington, infielder got hurt, they happened to call me up one day, and to be up there the next day. I got in at I think around 12:30 or 1:00 and started to play. I got off to a good start, so that was the biggest thrill, and also playing in maybe one of the All-Star Games in Detroit when Williams, you know, hits the home run and we won that game. I think those would be the two main things that I remember most.

Do you hear from any of your former teammates?
Not too many of them. In other words, Mickey Vernon and Buddy Lewis; I haven't seen him in quite a few years. A few of them when they come through here. Some of them scout, you know every time they come to Atlanta they would call. During spring training we used to go to Florida to see some of them, but not too many of them. You know, I['ve] just sort of gotten away from it.

Is there any way you would like the people who saw you play or the fans of baseball to remember you? Is there any way that you look at yourself and would like to be remembered?

Well, not particularly, I just hope they think I did my best. That's the only thing. I hope I tried to do that and just let it go at that.

I certainly appreciate you taking your time and speaking with me.

You're quite welcome. I don't value my time too much.

Well I certainly do, but I just want to tell you that after reading about you, I have a great respect and admiration for you as a player and as a person. You and your colleagues, you never complained about what you had to do. You didn't mention yourself as being any different than anybody else and you're, you know, I think people of your era were an inspiration to many of us, and we appreciate you.

I appreciate being thought of that way. That's the main thing anyway in life.

❖ ❖ ❖

Johnny Vander Meer

Cincinnati Reds pitcher Johnny Vander Meer is the only pitcher in major league history to throw back-to-back no-hitters. The accomplishment was as clear as day and night, as on June 11, 1938, in the Queen City, the man known as "The Dutch Master" shut out the Boston Braves, 3–0. In his next start four days later, in the first night game at Brooklyn's Ebbets Field, he blanked the Dodgers, 6–0. He completed his career with a record of 119–121, an ERA of 3.44 and 1,294 strikeouts. However, he will best be remembered for his two consecutive no-hit games in that magical year of 1938.

The year was 1938. It just seems to be the most unbelievable pitching feat to accomplish, back-to-back no-hitters. To throw one no-hitter, it takes great pitching and a lot of breaks.

Well, I think the best way to explain that is you gotta go through two ball games that everybody is in the right position at the right time. The old saying, you know, you're there at the right time, it helps a lot. That's about the best way to explain it.

Were there close calls in either of those games for you?

No, there was only one close call. There were a lot of ground balls in both ball games. The closest call was in the second game, when a line shot [was] hit back to the box at me. I knocked it down and threw the hitter out at first base.

The second one, was that the first night game ever in Ebbets Field?

That's right. That was a dedication of the lights in Ebbets Field that night.

What was it like pitching under the lights in Brooklyn?

Well, we had lights in Cincinnati but we only played each team once, and of course

The "Dutch Master," Johnny Vander Meer (center), with two unidentified men. He pitched back-to-back no-hitters in 1938.

MacPhail put them also in Cincinnati and then he went to Brooklyn, so he put them also in Brooklyn. Of course, in Brooklyn they started playing more games, but the lights were better in Brooklyn than they were in Crosley Field because they were put in ten years later, and also the fact that they have the high stands in Brooklyn all the way around. The higher the lights are, the better the lights are.

Now in 1938, of course, you were "Player of the Year," I think The Sporting News *named you that. That was really only your first full year as a major leaguer. Do you think that hurt you later on, because my God what do you do after you've come through with a great performance like that?*

No, I don't think it hurt me. Of course, in '39 I hurt my arm and I was out the rest of '39 and almost all of '40, except for the last month of '40 when I came back and won four games. I think that was a bad period, and then of course I had to put my three years in the service on the top of that, and right in my prime years. So there's a build-up in there that is not in the stats, as everybody reads, you know, what everybody studies, everybody votes by them.

When people think of Johnny Vander Meer, how would like them to think of you as a player?

Well, all I can say is that everything I start I like to finish; I had above 50 percent finishing all my games I started, I think it was about 62 percent. I'm proud of that, and I was dedicated to the ball club, and I'm still dedicated to the game [according to Retrosheet, Vander Meer completed 46 percent of his starts].

Mickey Vernon

Mickey Vernon competed in four decades (1930s–1960s) in the Major Leagues and won a pair of AL batting titles in 1946 (.353) and 1953 (.337). He earned the reputation of being one of the best fielding first basemen and played the position in a record 2,237 games. The seven-time All-Star, who served two years in the Navy during World War II, played the majority of his 20-year career with Washington and was named the Senators' all-time first baseman in 1969. Mickey Vernon completed his big league tenure batting .286 with 172 home runs and 1,311 RBI, along with accumulating 2,495 hits.

This interview was conducted in Cleveland, Ohio, on August 22, 1987.

Mickey, a great career, a long career, 20 years, and most people associate you with the Washington Senators and as being one of the great-fielding first baseman. Why did you have such great hands, is that something that came natural?

Well, I think so. You just don't, as you play as a young fellow you kind of develop it, I guess, and maybe just one of those things I was blessed with.

Because you were so exceptional on defense, did you get as much pleasure out of that aspect as when you got a big hit?

Maybe it looked that way, but I would get more pleasure out of a game-winning hit or a home run here or there, I think, than making some play with the glove, although I'm sure the pitchers think of it the other way. They would rather have the guy make a good play for them once in awhile.

You had 2,495 hits in your career and very well should have been elected to the Hall of Fame. Is it something that you think about or concern yourself with at this stage?

No, not, the only time I think about it is when I get mail once in awhile that says they think that I should be in it. Otherwise I don't give it much thought, because my name has been through the process and it hasn't gotten there yet, so I just don't think about it.

You look back on your years in Washington, you know they're talking about getting another ball club there. Did you enjoy playing ball in that city?

I enjoyed playing period. Whether it would be Washington or Hoboken, but naturally it's tough when you go out day after day and you know you're not going to be up there in the World Series come October. But like I said, it was a dream come true. I always can go back to when I was 12, 13 years old, I wanted to be a major league ballplayer. I realized my dream, so that's why I say it didn't make any difference who I was playing for as long as I was playing in the major leagues. Washington wasn't that bad really. Mr. Griffith was a great man to work for, and even though the saying [that] Washington, you know, was always last in the American League, well it really wasn't the time I played with them. I don't think we ever finished last. I think the St. Louis Browns or Philadelphia A's were always down below us, so there's a misconception there. Maybe it was back in the 1900s when they were finishing last. But the period I was with them, it wasn't a last-place club.

Mickey Vernon (left) and Al Kaline. Vernon won two AL batting titles.

The batting titles in 1946 and 1953, were those the highlights of your career?
    Yes, they had to be. Yeah, they'd be highlights of a lot of players' career, I think. If you win the batting title two years, yeah they were highlights, yes. Of course I never got the opportunity to play in the World Series, so they had to be.

Listen, I appreciate you taking the time. Wish you the best.
    Okay, Ron, thank you.

Bob Watson

Bob Watson had a 19-year playing career in Major League Baseball. He played with the Houston Astros, Boston Red Sox, New York Yankees and Atlanta Braves. On May 4, 1975, Watson scored the one millionth run in baseball history when he scored from second base on a three-run home run by Astros teammate Milt May at Candlestick Park in San Francisco. Years after this interview, Watson's millionth run would be disputed. The power-hitting Watson was also the first Major Leaguer to hit for the cycle in both leagues, first doing it with Houston in 1977 and for the second time with Boston in 1979. After his playing days, Bob Watson became the first African American GM to win a World Series when he accomplished it with the Yankees in 1996. He batted .295 with 184 home runs and 989 RBI.

This interview was conducted in Pittsburgh, Pennsylvania, in 1994.

A very stellar career, 15 years, almost a .300 hitter, I believe .295. You were always known as a great clutch hitter. You also scored baseball's millionth run. I suppose that gets mentioned to you frequently.

Oh, a lot of people ask me about that. They also ask me about being the only player to hit for the cycle in both leagues. You know, scoring that millionth run was a thing where it's something that you don't plan, I just happen to be in the right place at the right time and very fortunate I think when that happened. My fan mail increased, I don't know, by leaps and bounds, a hundred-fold. The thing that is positive for me out of that, I wouldn't have been in the Hall of Fame or anything, my shoes are there and my uniform is in the Hall of Fame now, I guess in a section for special achievements. I'm proud of it. You know some years before that, a black man named Jackie Robinson scored number 500 thousand and something run, and some years later I scored a millionth run, and I'm just pleased to be that guy.

Bob, you mentioned hitting for the cycle in each league. You did it in the American League with the Red Sox and with Houston in the National League. Was there any fanfare when you pulled it off the second time in Boston?

No, the only thing in Boston that I was proud of, I hit it in order; a single the first time, double second time, triple the third time. I hit a home run when I tried to hit a home run,

Bob Watson, one in a million. Baseball giveth and taketh away.

and I can tell you sitting here with 8,000 at-bats in the big league, I only hit maybe one or two home runs when I tried. That was one of them, and that was, you know, something special.

Your career primarily with the Houston Astros, many of those years the team wasn't a contending ball club, and you didn't have players around you that could protect you as a hitter. Did you ever feel that it hurt you as a hitter?

Oh no, in those years it was Cedeno and myself were the two main guys; you know, off and on we had Lee May, and Jimmy Wynn was there for a while and Doug Rader was there in and out. But it was mainly Cesar Cedeno and myself, and you know we knew we couldn't do anything about it, so you just went out and did your job. You know my main goal as a player was to be consistent and be a guy that you can count on day in and day out, game after game at game time, and I took a lot of pride of driving in runs with two outs. I can sit here and tell you, 40 or 50 RBI a year, would come with two outs, letting Cedeno steal a bag and getting a base hit to knock him in.

You played with the New York Yankees in 1981 and competed in the World Series. That had to be one of the highlights, I would imagine?

Oh, without a doubt playing in the World Series. But you know the best club I ever played with was the '80 club. We won 105 or 106 games and lost in the playoffs to the KC club, but the '81 World Series was definitely a highlight of my career. My first at-bat, I hit a home run off of Jerry Reuss, a three-run homer to put us in the lead, and we won that first game. I think the second game I got the game-winning hit in that game, and those were the only two games we won in the World Series, but by far, you know, playing in the World Series was a highlight.

You're the assistant GM with Houston. Your name has been mentioned in many quarters [as] becoming a GM. I don't know, are you being considered for the league presidency possibly? Many people feel that Bill White did an excellent job and are sorry to see him stepping down. What are your feelings on that?

I feel the same way, I'm very sorry that he is stepping down because I think he's done the best job possible given the situation that he's in. On the other hand, I'm flattered that he mentioned my name as being a possible successor. You know, it remains to be seen if I become that guy. I haven't been interviewed. I don't even know when I'm going to be interviewed, and you know my main goal though, why I'm in the position I'm in is to be a GM. The people that do the interviewing there also are people who hire GMs. So I think it's a plus situation for me. A situation that I can let some people know what my thoughts are and my philosophy on baseball and on life.

◆ ◆ ◆

Billy Williams

Nearly a half-century ago, "Sweet Swinging" Billy Williams held the title as the National League's Iron Man (1963–1970), playing in a record 1,117 consecutive games.

The six-time All–Star and 1961 "Rookie of the Year" won the NL batting crown in 1972, hitting .333. He was quiet and unassuming but wasn't shy when he stepped into the batter's box, finishing with a lifetime batting average of .290 with 426 home runs and 1,475 RBI. Williams played with the 1969 Chicago Cubs team that came ever so close to winning the pennant, featuring future Hall of Fame manager Leo Durocher, position players Ernie Banks, Ron Santo and pitcher Ferguson Jenkins. Williams was elected to the Hall of Fame in 1987.

This interview was conducted in Pittsburgh, Pennsylvania, in 1987.

A long, storied career for you, ending with of course the Hall of Fame. When people remember you, the first thing that comes to mind is the great swing, the sweet swing of Billy Williams. Now I know you made it look easy, but you probably put many hours into developing it.

Well certainly. I remember when I first started playing baseball, when I found out I had a quick bat. I know it's raw talent, but with my [being] willing to work and willing to perfect it and to meet up with a guy in 1958 or 1959, a guy by the name of Rogers Hornsby. So we worked, and we worked, and we worked until we perfected the swing. I think a lot of people in baseball saw me play in the big leagues and they said sooner or later, you know, with that swing, making good contact, he will eventually win the batting title. Of course I did in 1972, but I put in some long hours, you know, trying to perfect the swing. I think one of the most important things was being able to hit strikes, one in the strike zone, the ball coming over home plate.

Billy, you were a guy that played with the great Ernie Banks; you played with some great ballplayers on the Cubs. Did you ever feel that throughout your career you didn't get the respect? You were steady and consistent.

"Sweet Swinging" Billy Williams, 1972 NL batting champion.

Well, sometimes if you do things on a steady basis, a lot of people take you for granted. But you know, playing in Chicago, and I know that when I first came to the big leagues, myself and Ron Santo, Ron Santo came in 1960, of course. I came in 1959 but I came to stay in 1961. But Ernie had been there for about five or six years, and I mean every year he's doing it. He hit 35 or 40 home runs, winning the Most Valuable Player in '58 and '59. Certainly you know the fans are going, you know he's gonna be one of the favorites of the fans in Chicago, and I could live with that. I think one of the things why we all didn't get recognized a little bit more is not having to play in the World Series. I know that we played, we were exciting six or seven years through 1972, and we almost won the division in 1969, which the Mets won. They were destined to win because they went on to beat Baltimore. I think if we had won that particular year, you see guys like Fergie, just recently went into the Hall of Fame. You see myself, you know who was on the ballot for about six or seven years and finally going in to being installed in the Hall of Fame, and my teammate who played third base, Ron Santo. I think if we had been in the post-season play, I think people would realize the type of ballplayers that we were; it's tough to get the recognition if you don't play in October.

Well, you're right, and you know that's the showcase and everyone takes notice. But you were the ironman for so many years. What is it, today we see so many injuries. What happens to a guy like you that just goes on playing year after year?

I think at that time, Ron, when I played, I think the majority of fellows, they wanted to stay in the lineup to play. I know there were only 16 teams in the Major League, eight teams in the National League and eight teams in the American League, so you had to be a good ballplayer and you had to stay out there every day. You know the secret of playing 1,117 games, a lot of people don't know that when I first came to the big leagues, I was concerned about people coming up. Just like I was a young player and I came up to the big league and took "Moose" Moryn's job, so I was concerned about young people coming up to the big league and taking my job. And I guess it was after about five or six years, after I found myself, you know, on a steady pace that I could hit major league pitching. I found that a lot of players that came through with me in my first couple of years in left field, I moved them to center field or they went to right field or someplace else. They were like vultures. But I think one of the most important things is I got enjoyment out of playing baseball. I wanted to be out there, and of course I felt if I was on the ball field I was going to do something to help my ball club win. So far as hitting a home run, hitting a double, maybe getting a walk to score a run and stuff like that, I think, you know, this is one of the reasons why Jack Lang called me and said you [were] inducted in the Baseball Hall of Fame. If I hadn't been in those line-ups and playing, you know, I wouldn't have had the 426 home runs.

The high point obviously is the Hall of Fame for you. I don't want to haunt you with the question, but in 1969 it appeared that the Cubs were on the doorstep of going to the World Series.

Well, I think any player, you know, what you go to spring training for is to get yourself in shape or is playing in the World Series; and of course I never did get there. I got a chance to play in the playoffs when I went to Oakland in 1975 or '76; 1975, we were in the playoffs. But I think every player who puts on a major league uniform wants to get in the World Series, and of course 1969 seemed like we were destined to go there. Of course we played baseball three-quarters of the season, but the last quarter of the season I think the Mets took over. But anytime in the later part of the season, if you got pitchers like Tom Seaver, Gentry, and Koosman, those particular individuals, and they were putting it on. They were pitching real well, and I think that was the biggest heartache of all my years in the big leagues. I thought for sure we had the ball club, I thought sure we had the pitching, I thought sure we had the defense, and we had the personnel to go all the way. When we started losing those ball games, it's tough if you hadn't been there before, and trying to regain your composure, regaining the play that you had been doing all year; but we just couldn't do it. We had a bunch of players that had never been there and we didn't know what it was like, you know, when you're playing in the pennant race and you gotta win a big ball game and stuff like that. So I think, you know, if we had won that particular year we could have won about five or six more, because we were all young and we were sound players. I think the whole infield was on the All-Star team through the '70s; you know, '73, '74 and '75. But we had a good ball club and one of the most agonizing things, and I hear about it all the time now, because we didn't win. I like to say that we played good, sound baseball, but the Mets played better. I think they, they played, they would have beat anybody.

What was the best year, the one that gave you the most satisfaction?

Well, I think my best year was 1970, although I won the batting title in 1972. It was satisfying to me when you win a batting title, that's knowing you were consistent all year. But I think insofar as producing runs, 1970 was the year, because that year I hit 42 home runs, I scored like 130 runs. You know I drove in 129 runs. So I think any player who hit where I did in the lineup, I hit third, and every year I wanted to hit better than 30 home runs. I wanted to drive in 100 runs. I wanted to score 100 runs. So those are three things I wanted to do, and I surpassed all those marks by a long shot; insofar as having good years, I think this was the most productive, this was a career year for me in the 1970 season.

Well, you could have said that almost about any year with Billy Williams. You are enshrined in Cooperstown, what else can we say? But you're one of the players, a lot of people they say, well they're in but maybe they shouldn't be; but in your case, there is no question. You are where you belong. The only other place you belong is on the ball field. I thank you for taking time out, Billy.

Well, thank you very much, Ron, for having me on your show, and good luck to you in the future.

• • •

Dick Williams

In his first season at the helm, Dick Williams guided the Boston Red Sox to the American League pennant in 1967. He went on to lead the Oakland Athletics to back-to-back world championships in 1972–1973. He would later manage the California Angels and Montreal Expos before taking charge of the San Diego Padres and leading them to the NL Pennant and a World Series appearance in 1984. He would finish his career in the dugout with a stint as skipper with the Seattle Mariners from 1986–1988. Williams finished his 21-year managing career with a record of 1,571 wins and 1,451 losses. He was elected to the Baseball Hall of Fame's class of 2008. He was also inducted into the Boston Red Sox and San Diego Padres Halls of Fame.

Many think of you primarily as manager of the great Oakland A's teams. They had the three straight championships, and you were there for two of them.

Show you how smart I am, I resigned from Oakland, I was going to go with the Yankees. I was leaving Charlie to go with Steinbrenner, but I mean, George is a good friend of mine and all he wants to do is win. You know, he gets a lot of bad press and all of that, but he's fighting a bunch of things in New York. You know, he was fighting the Mets as well in order to get that back page as far as journalism goes on those newspapers, so George is all right.

What do you remember about the great Oakland teams, because I don't know if people appreciate it enough. It was a dynasty, and we're always trying to look for another one. There really hasn't been one, and you guys had the pitching, you had everything. What stands out to you?

Well, I'll tell you one thing, and we'll go back to Charlie Finley. If I needed a player, that next day there was always, I had my choice of one, two or three different players. That's how he operated. He knew baseball very, very well. But that organization, we had great players coming up, we had a great pitching staff, we had great camaraderie and we had great teamwork on the field. They talked about us fighting all the time. Well, we didn't have any more brawls than the eighth-place club, except we were in first place and they're writing about it. But it was best ball club I have ever been associated with.

I know you were gone after the second year, Al Dark came in, and the team was....

That was my club. I left there, but they won five divisional titles. We won 101 ballgames in 1971, and Baltimore beat us three straight in the playoffs. Then we won the next two years I was there, won it all, the World Series. Then the next year after I left, they won it hands-down again and beat the Dodgers in five. That may have been the best ball club of all of them. Most of them say the '71 club where we didn't win, when we won 101 ballgames was the best club. My '73 club, with all the turmoil we had when he fired Andrews, and we had a few other mishaps and all that. Reggie and him got in a big argument. I consider that the best ball club, but maybe '74 was even better, and then they won in '75 after Hunter left, to show you the depth they had in pitching.

But then Finley, for money reasons, he broke the club up. It could have gone on even longer.

Well, now free agency is happening. He lost three players that he could have got $2 million for. In fact, he tried to trade them during the year, and he had Fingers and Rudi in the Boston uniform on the Boston bench, but they couldn't play; and he had Vida going to the Yankees. Now is he going to get a million for Fingers and Rudi, and is he gonna get a million for Vida? But he feuded with Bowie Kuhn, and he stopped it, and he ended up getting nothing for those players because they all went different places at the end of the year.

With the Red Sox, from last place to the first place. That has to be very special to you.

Oh well, that was my first year in the major leagues as a manager, and they had finished I think a game and a half ahead of the Yankees in ninth place in a one-division ten-team league. Well, I had a one-year contract and if I'm going down, I'm gonna go my way. I stepped on a lot of toes, got a lot of my players mad, and they didn't especially like me, but they busted their tail for me. That was my job, to win, and we won that thing on the last day of the season. There were four clubs going for it the last week, and three clubs the last day, so it was a great experience, it was unbelievable.

As a manager, you've seen many changes in the game. It seems that you can't take an iron hand. You were a guy that people didn't fool around with. You know, you have to be more diplomatic today. I'm not saying you couldn't manage today, but it has changed.

Well, we'll find out what's going to happen with the New York Mets, because they've

Dick Williams, old school skipper, leader of the A's dynasty.

got a guy, Dallas Green, who is basically the same way. Now you have another guy managing in the major leagues and their club is in first place in the National League East in Philadelphia, Fregosi. He's the same way I am, or Dallas Green. He's got a bunch maybe, I guess you'd call them rednecks over there, sloppy-looking guys like we had at Oakland, and they're doing a hell of a job and they govern themselves. My Oakland club, they governed themselves. In fact, I probably had the easiest time of my career when I managed for Charlie at Oakland because they were, my players were never mad at me. They were always mad at Charlie, and I was like one of the guys. Still I had a stern hand on what was going on in the field, and my players respected me for that.

◆ ◆ ◆

Maury Wills

Maury Wills will always be associated with the stolen base, and why not? Over his 14-year career, mostly with the Los Angeles Dodgers, he brought the art of base stealing back into the game, stealing a total of 586. In 1962, the seven-time All-Star broke Ty Cobb's stolen base record of 96, set in 1915, by finishing with 104. However, an asterisk was placed beside the record due to an increase in games played from 154 to 162. Wills was presented with the first-ever All-Star Game MVP Award in 1962 and later that year won the NL MVP Award. He led the league in stolen bases from 1960–1965, won two Gold Glove Awards at shortstop, and played on three World Series championship LA Dodgers teams in 1959, 1963 and 1965.

When the subject of base stealing comes up, you are one of the first in modern history that people remember because of your record-setting pace. To begin with, you played almost nine seasons in the minor leagues. How did that impact you as a player?

Well, Ron, I spent 8½ years in the minors. I'm not a big guy, I never have been, never will be, so I had to do the things, in order to compete in the major leagues and stay there, I had to do the things that I did well and that I was gifted with, which were the ability to run, I had a good arm, and I had to hit line drives and be an expert runner, okay. So working on those few things, I made myself a pretty good baseball player. I came into the major leagues in the middle of 1959. That year Willie Mays, I believe it was 23 stolen bases and he led the National League. My first full year in 1960, I stole 50 bases;

I grabbed the bag out of the ground at the Colosseum in Los Angeles, unheard of. So, it was a home run game then. So in 1962, when I stole 104 bases and we had a great season and everybody saw what the Dodgers were doing with speed, Maury Wills stealing bases, and the team taking extra bases, running the bases well, running, squeeze plays, hit and runs. Then with spring training, they started briefing their speed guys on the art of base stealing, and the game has changed since then. So it's a running game now. Ty Cobb's record was 40 years old when I broke it.

We heard so much about tailoring the field in Los Angeles, well not only there but everywhere, for each particular team. They must have been waiting for you during the heyday of Maury Wills and the running Dodgers.

Well, in San Francisco they watered the field down to the point where I was up to my ankles in mud, but that was after infield practice. During batting practice, the field was great. And they let the infield grass grow high by three to four inches so our ground balls couldn't go through. Hey, you know, the umpires had them clean it up and they put sand down and made it worse. But the teams can normally tailor fields to this, as long as they stay within some kind of foul lines, to coin a phrase. But in Pittsburgh, one day we were playing, I tried to take a lead off first base and I was down below my ankles in sand, I was trying to get some traction. Finally the umpire after the second time on first base in the ballgame, the umpire called time out and had them take the sand up. Harry Walker was managing the team then, the Pirates. It took three wheelbarrow loads of sand off of the base paths between first and second. So, but see that was flattering to me. I remember spending 8½ years in the minor leagues, nowhere, not even a dream again of being in the big leagues. So now they doing that stop Maury Wills, it was flattering.

Finally, when you are watching a guy like Rickey Henderson today, what goes through your mind when you see a base stealer of his talent?

Just, it causes me to reminisce and appreciate what he is going through. Stealing bases, it takes a lot out of you. You have to be durable, you're on the ground a lot, you don't have many friends on the other team because stealing a base against you is kind of humiliating. So I really admire Rickey Henderson, I think he is perhaps the best all-around baseball player in the game today.

◆ ◆ ◆

Jimmy Wynn

Jimmy Wynn was compact and strong, blasting 291 home runs over a 15-year career spent mostly with the Houston Colt .45s/Astros. Wynn became the first Houston player to hit three home runs in a game (June 15, 1967) at the Astrodome against Cincinnati. The man known as "The Toy Cannon" because of his tremendous power and short 5'9" stature, quickly became the face of the franchise. He was named to three All-Star teams and had his number 24 jersey retired by Houston. Jimmy Wynn finished with 1,665 hits, a .250 batting average and 964 runs batted in.

I assume because of the power that you possess that you got the nickname "The Toy Cannon." Who gave that to you?

It was a sports writer by the name of John Wilson, who was with the Houston Chronicle, and he gave me the nickname mainly because of my size. I'm only about 5'9" tall and weigh 165 pounds.

How were you able to generate such tremendous power?

Well, with a lot of help from my father. He told me, you know, when I was playing with him in high school, you want to drive a Cadillac or do you want to drive a Chevrolet? So I wanted to drive a Cadillac, so he taught me to hit with my upper body. And of course I went to the gyms to build my upper body strength up, but that's how I can generate a lot of power.

You played in Houston, and that was a tough park, the Astrodome. It was difficult to hit home runs in.

It was, it was the toughest ballpark to hit a home run in because there was no wind. It was closed and indoors. I was very fortunate, I was one of the fortunate guys, you know, who can hit home runs in the Dome.

The "Toy Cannon," Jimmy Wynn, the Eighth Wonder of the World's power-source.

Looking back on your career, it was very successful. Things that stand out that you are most proud of as a player?

For number one, for hitting the ball in the upper tier in the Dome stadium, 540 feet away. The only player in Astros history to hit three consecutive home runs in the Dome. The only player to hit 30 or more home runs three years in a row. So those are some of the proudest moments that I like.

When you were traded from Houston, how tough was that on you?

It wasn't tough at all. I was happy about it. As a matter of fact, it was a good Christmas present. I was taking my wife out to dinner and just as we were walking out of the door, the phone rang. There was the general manager, Spec Richardson, [who] said, "Jimmy, how would you like to be traded?" I said, "now you cannot trade me without my consent," and he said, "well, the Dodgers are interested in you, would you like to go to the Dodgers?" I said sure. So five minutes later, he called back and I became a Dodger.

How did those years compare, though, with the years in Houston for you?

Well, 1974 was the best year all-around that I've had. In Houston, of course, I hit 37 home runs, but in 1974 we had a team that played together and consequently I hit 34 home runs, had a .279 batting average and 109, 110 RBI. And plus the most important thing is that we went to the World Series [Wynn hit 30 home runs twice, in 1967 and in 1969. In 1974, he hit .271 with 32 home runs and 108 RBI].

How would like people to remember you as a player?

As a little guy that stood up for the little people, who could not have been prouder than to be a ballplayer.

Index

Aaron, Hank 1–7, 12, 16, 56, 85, 102–3, 108–9, 149, 159–60, 167
Adcock, Joe 85
Allanson, Andy 9
All-Century Team 3, 11, 144
Allen, Dick 138, 143, 146
Allen, Mel 91
Allison, Bob 99, 150
Alou, Felipe 34
Alou, Matty 34
Alston, Walter 9, 126–27
Altman, George 98
American Flag 113
Amoros, Sandy 127
Anderson, Sparky 7–9
Andrews, Mike 179
Aparicio, Luis 138
Arnaz, Desi 133
Arroyo, Luis 93
Averill, Earl 106
Avila, Bobby 2, 10, 140

Babe Ruth Award 52, 130
Back to Back No Hitters 170
Baker, Dusty 71
Ball, Lucille 133
Baltimore Elite Giants 15
Bando, Sal 47
Bankhead, Sam 65–66
Banks, Ernie 11–12, 61, 88, 98, 121, 143, 149, 176
Barber, Red 88
Barger, Carl 97
Bartell, Dick 13–15
Baseball Assistance Team 16, 95
Baseball's Millionth Run 174
Battey, Earl 79, 99
Battle of the Bulge 95, 168
Bearden, Gene 19, 163
Beckert, Glenn 98
Bell, Cool Papa 120
Berra, Yogi 40, 93, 113, 127, 155
Bessent, Don 58
Big Red Machine 7, 153
Birmingham Black Barons 64
Black, Joe 2, 15, 66
Blackwell, Ewell 17–18
Blue, Vida 47, 179
Boo Ferriss 55
Boone, Bob 146

Borowy, Hank 102
Boswell, Kenny 39
Boudreau, Lou 19–20, 103–4
Bowa, Larry 146
Boyer, Clete 136
Boyers, Clete, Ken 56, 93
Bragan, Bobby 61
Branca, Ralph 20–22, 124, 163, 165–66
Breadon, Sam 147
Brock, Lou 23, 57, 121
Broglio, Ernie 23
Brown, Gates 1, 24–27, 78
Brown, Larry 136
Brown, Raymond 96
Browne, Byron 138
Buck, Jack 41, 88
Buhl, Bob 28, 84
Burdette, Lew 27–28, 77, 84, 109, 149
Burgess, Smokey 25, 48, 84, 158
Burke, Richard 66
Burleson, Rick 95
Burris, Ray 114
Byrne, Tommy 40

Callison, Johnny 163
Camp McCoy 169
Camp Wheeler 169
Campanella, Roy 60, 126–27, 131–32, 146
Campaneris, Bert 47
Campbell, Jim 94
Canseco, Jose 109
Cardenal, Jose 115
Carew, Rod 29–31, 99
Caribbean Baseball Hall of Fame 34
Carlton, Steve 146
Carter, Gary 32–33
Carter, Joe 80, 121
Carty, Rico 33–35, 37
Casey, Hugh 90, 123
Cash, Norm 26
Cedeno, Cesar 175
Cey, Ron 114
Chambliss, Chris 1, 36–37, 139
Charles, Ed 37–38, 87
Charleston, Oscar 121
Chicago American 13

Chris Chambliss Rule 36
Clark, Jack 80–81
Clark, Jerald 82
Clemens, Roger 156
Clemente, Roberto 56, 161
Clendenon, Donn 57, 87, 162
Coates, Jim 157
Cobb, Ty 23, 180–81
Cochrane, Mickey 124, 169
Colavito, Rocky 69
Coleman, Jerry 39–40, 114
Collins, Joe 42, 60
Colombia 66
color line 5, 53–54
Comorosky, Adam 14
Conley, Gene 56
Cooper, Cecil 68
Cooperstown 67, 98, 137–38, 143, 156–57, 167, 178
Craig, Roger 9
Crandall, Del 29, 149
Crespi, Frank 148
Crosetti, Frank 1
Crosley Field 171
Cuba 66, 123, 138–39
Cuban Winter League 15
Cy Young Award 72, 98, 108, 146

Dahlgren, Babe 1, 41–44
Daily, Bill 128
Dandridge, Ray 96
Dark, Alvin 45–46
Davidson, Donald 6
Davis, Tommy 1, 47–49
Dawson, Andre 114
Day, Leon 2, 49–50, 96, 120
Dean, Dizzy 105–6, 157
Denny, John 146
Dent, Bucky 1, 51–52
Dente, Sam 140
Devine, Joe 14
DH 8, 48, 99, 143
DiMaggio, Dominic 55–56, 147, 169
DiMaggio, Joe 1–2, 40, 55, 77–78, 91, 93, 105, 141, 147, 151, 168
Ditmar, Art 151
Doby, Larry 2, 20, 53–54, 65, 140
Doerr, Bobby 54–55, 157

183

Index

Dominican Republic 34, 66, 116
Doyle, Brian 52
Dressen, Charlie 20, 22, 60
Dreyfuss, Barney 14
Drysdale, Don 56–58, 99–100, 151
Duncan, Dave 163–64
Duncan, Frank 63
Durocher, Leo 166
Dyer, Eddie 148, 157

Easter, Luke 10
Eckersley, Dennis 35, 67, 114, 129
Ed Sullivan Show 133–34
Elston, Howard 93, 127
Enright, Jimmy 13
Equitable 95
Erskine, Carl 59, 163

Face, Elroy 60–61, 68, 128–29
Feller, Bob 10, 19–20, 40, 62–64, 89, 105, 147, 149, 151, 157, 169
Ferguson, Jenkins 98, 135
Ferrell, Wes 103
Fetzer, John 95
Fingers, Rollie 1, 12, 47, 57, 66–68, 76, 129, 179
Finley, Charlie 67, 69, 141, 178–80
Fisk, Carlton 95
Fitzsimmons, Freddie 124
Fletcher, Art 42
Flood, Curt 138
Folsom, Jim 134
Ford, Whitey 40, 93, 151, 158
Ford C Frick Award 39, 87
Forsch, Bob 152
Fosse, Ray 47
Foster, Rube 120
Foxx, Jimmie 41–42, 151
Francona, Tito 69–70, 104
Furillo, Carl 78, 127

Gagne, Eric 67–68
Galbreath, John 102
Garcia, Mike 10, 32
Garner, Horace 5
Garner, Phil 141
Garrett, Wayne 39
Garvey, Steve 1, 70–71, 114
Gas House Gang 157
Gehrig, Lou 41–45, 91
Gentry, Gary 162, 177
Gibson, Bob 1, 57, 72–76, 108, 152
Gibson, Josh 65–66, 96, 120
Gibson, Kirk 114
Gilliam, Jim 11, 127
Gionfriddo, Al 1, 77
Globetrotters 76
Glynn, Bill 140
Gomez, Preston 139

Gonzalez, Mike 157
Gonzalez, Tony 29
Gordon, Joe 19–20, 69
Gossage, Goose 67, 71
Grant, Mudcat 78–79
Green, Dallas 180
Greenberg, Hank 44, 102, 147
Greyhound Corporation 16
Griffith, Clark 172
Grimm, Charlie 167
Grissom, Marv 133
Grodzicki, Johnny 148
Grotes, Jerry 87
Guidry, Ron 52
Gustine, Frankie 61
Gwynn, Tony 30, 71, 80–82

Haddix, Harvey 28–29, 83–84
Harder, Mel 8
Harrelson, Bud 39, 85–86
Harris, Mickey 55
Harris, Vic 66
Hartung, Clint 46
Harwell, Ernie 87–88
Havana Sugar Kings 139
Hegan, Jim 10
Hemus, Solly 73–74
Henderson, Rickey 120, 181
Henrich, Tommy 1, 40, 89–93, 123–24
Herman, Billy 102–3
Hernandez, Keith 159
Herzog, Whitey 142
Higgins, Pinky 157
Hill, Calvin 16
Hispanic Heritage Baseball Museum 30
Hodges, Gil 38, 86, 127, 132
Hodges, Russ 87, 91–92
Hoffman, Bobby 131
Holland, al 146
Holtzman, Ken 47
Homestead Grays 64–66, 96–97, 120
Hornsby, Rogers 176
Horton, Willie 25–26
Houk, Ralph 93–95
Houston, Tex 55
Houston Chronicle 182
Houtteman, Art 102
Howard, Elston 93, 127
Hubbell, Carl 156
Hundley, Randy 98
Hunt, Ron 163
Hunter, Catfish 47, 135, 141, 179

Indianapolis ABCs 121
Irvin, Monte 2, 11, 65, 95–97, 130, 132–33

Jackie Robinson Foundation 16
Jackson, James 66
Jackson, Jesse 5
Jackson, Reggie 47, 65–66, 179

James, William 27
Jay, Joey 28
Jenkins, Ferguson 176
Jethroe, Sam 65
Jimenez, Manny 34
Johnson, Lou 121
Johnson, Walter 58, 105–6
Jordan, John 120
Jorgensen, Mike 33

Kaat, Jim 79
Kaline, Al 25, 173
Kell, George 105
Keller, Charlie 40
Keltner, Ken 20, 140
Kennedy, Bob 20, 71
Kessinger, Don 98
Killebrew, Harmon 79, 99–100, 150
Kinder, Ellis 55
Kiner, Ralph 101–2
Klieman, Ed 19
Korean War 2, 39
Koufax, Sandy 56, 58–59, 74, 99, 127, 151
Kramer, Jack 55
Kranepool, Ed 87
Kubek, Tony 93
Kuenn, Harvey 156
Kuhn, Bowie 179

Labine, Clem 58, 127
Landis, Judge 92
Lane, Frank 147
Lang, Jack 177
Lasorda, Tommy 71, 77, 115, 152
Lemon, Bob 10, 19, 52, 56, 73, 103–5, 108, 133, 151, 158, 174
Lemon, Jim 150
Leonard, Buck 65–66
Lewis, Buddy 169
Lewis, Duffy 149
Lewis, Rupert 65
Lindblad, Paul 47
Littell, Mark 36
Lockman, Whitey 46
Logan, Johnny 109
Lopat, Eddie 40
Lopez, Al 105–6, 140
Lou Gehrig's Disease 41
Louis, Joe 93
Lowenstein, John 35
Lynch, Jerry 48
Lynn, Fred 95
Lyons, Ted 91

Mack, Connie 41
MacPhail, Lee 171
Mad Dash 156–57
Maddox, Garry 16, 146
Maglie, Sal 57
Majeski, Hank 140
Malcolm X 5
Maloney, Jim 151, 163

Manning, Max 65–66
Manning, Rick 35
Mantilla, Felix 5, 163
Mantle, Mickey 40, 60, 93–94, 129, 141, 150–51
Marichal, Juan 34, 106–8
Maris, Roger 93
Marsalis, Wynton 5
Marshall, Mike 67
Marshall, Willard 18
Martin, Billy 52, 176, 178
Martin, Pepper 157
Mathews, Eddie 56, 108–10, 149
Mathewson, Christy 20
Mathis, Joe 147
Matlack, Jon 155
Matthews, Gary 16
May, Lee 175
May, Milt 174
Mays, Willie 3, 46, 56, 102, 121, 130, 132–33, 141, 160–61, 167, 180
Mazeroski, Bill 1, 61–62, 83, 110–13, 157–58
McCarthy, Joe 44, 89
McCarver, Tim 138
McCovey, Willie 49
McDougald, Gil 40, 158
McGraw, John 14
McGraw, Tug 146, 162
McGriff, Fred 80–82
McGwire, Mark 160
McKechnie, Bill 156
McKinney, Frank 102
McLain, Denny 73–74
McPhail, Andy 95
McReynolds, Kevin 71
Medwick, Joe 157
Melton, Bill 143
Mexican Baseball League 10
Mexican League 11, 35, 95
Mexico 10, 35, 64, 66
Miller, Stu 161
Minoso, Minnie 49, 69
Miracle Mets 38, 85, 162
Miranda, Willie 139
Mitchell, Dale 10, 20
Mize, Johnny 40, 92, 124, 157
Molitor, Paul 68
Monday, Rick 71, 113–15, 133, 139, 161
Montanez, Willie 138
Moon, Wally 127
Morgan, Joe 146, 153
Mota, Manny 34, 116–18
Mueller, Don 46, 130, 133, 166
Murtaugh, Danny 159
Musial, Stan 3, 6, 18, 40, 56, 62, 110, 146–48, 150

National Baseball Hall 7, 19, 39, 105, 143
National Basketball League 20
Necciai, Ron 118

Negro American League 120
Negro League World Series 64, 95
Negro Leagues 2, 11, 15, 49–50, 53–54, 63–65, 95–97, 120
Negro Leagues Baseball Museum 120
Nelson, Thomas 32
Nettles, Graig 48, 52, 71, 137
Newark Eagles 50, 65, 95
Newcombe, Don 126
Newhouser, Hal 151
Nixon, Richard 151
Northrup, Jim 25

Ogilvy, Ben 68
Oliva, Tony 79, 99, 121–22
O'Neil, Buck 2, 120
Owen, Mickey 1, 28, 89, 123–24, 167
Owens, Jim 138

Page, Joe 40
Paige, Satchel 62–63, 120–21
Painter, Doc 45
Parker, Dave 11
Parnell, Mel 55
Partlow, Roy 96
Pascual, Camilo 79
Passeau, Claude 156
Passed Ball, World Series 118, 123
Patek, Freddie 138–39
Perez, Tony 146, 153
Perranoski, Ron 127–28
Perry, Gaylord 125–26
Perry, Jim 79
Pesky, Johnny 157
Phillips, Adolfo 98
Piersall, Jimmy 69
Pinch-Hitter, Greatest 116
Piniella, Lou 7, 23, 42, 44–45, 91
Pinson, Vida 160
Pope, Dave 10, 133
Puerto Rico 66

Radatz, Dick 128–29
Radcliffe, Ted 50
Rader, Doug 175
Raines, Tim 114
Randolph, Willie 52
Raschi, Vic 40, 60
Reardon, Jeff 129
Reese, Pee Wee 127, 156
retro-sheet 171
Reuss, Jerry 175
Reynolds, Allie 40
Rhodes, Dusty 129–33
Richardson, Bobby 93, 158
Richardson, Spec 182
Rickey, Branch 101, 147
Rickey Henderson 181
Rijo, Jose 107

Rivers, Mickey 51–52, 90, 93–94, 124, 140, 172
Rizzuto, Phil 40, 92
Roberts, Robin 29, 133–34
Robinson, Brooks 135–38, 144, 162
Robinson, Don 145
Robinson, Eddie 19–20
Robinson, Frank 53
Robinson, Jackie 5, 15–16, 20, 53, 96, 127, 132, 135–36, 174
Roebuck, Ed 58
Rogers, Steve 114
Rojas, Cookie 138
Ron Santo Walk 143
Rosar, Buddy 92
Rose, Pete 91, 110, 146
Roseboro, John 127
Rosen, Al 10, 139–40
Rudi, Joe 47, 141, 179
Ruth, Babe 2–3, 13, 15, 20, 44, 93, 96–97, 120, 159
Ryan, Nolan 58, 87, 162

Sain, Johnny 101
Samuel, Amado 34
Santiago, Benito 80–82
Santo, Ron 38, 142–43, 176–77
Savage, Ted 98
Schaefer, Phil 35
Schmidt, Mike 108, 137, 144–45
Schoendienst, Red 102, 146–49
Schrieke, Brian 92
Seaver, Tom 38, 87, 162, 177
Shamsky, Art 87
Shannon, Walter 147
Sheely, Earl 14
Sherry, Larry 127
Sievers, Roy 150–51
Silvestri, Ken 92
Simmons, Ted 152–55
Simpson, Harry 10
Singleton, Ken 33
Sisler, George 91
Skinner, Bob 158
Skowron, Bill 40, 93
Slaughter, Enos 57, 156–57
Smith, Hal 61, 157–58
Smith, Lee 129, 155
Smith, Mayo 26
Smith, Ozzie 121
Smith, Reggie 71
Snider, Duke 127, 131
Sosa, Sammy 160
Spahn, Warren 28–29, 56, 135, 149
Spencer, Jim 52
Stanley, Mickey 25
Stargell, Willie 56, 159–61
Stengel, Casey 93, 124, 158
Strickland, George 10, 140
Sullivan, Ed 95, 130

Sutter, Bruce 67
Suttles, Mule 96
Swoboda, Ron 162–63

Tanner, Chuck 143
Tatum, Art 5
Taylor, Bill 131
Taylor, Ron 162
Tekulve, Kent 129
Templeton, Garry 71
Tenace, Gene 47, 163–64
Terry, Bill 14
Terry, Ralph 21–22, 95, 103, 110
Thomas, Gorman 68
Thomson, Bobby 1, 20–22, 28, 46, 59, 87, 113, 124, 165–66
Tiant, Luis 128
Torre, Joe 37
Torrez, Mike 33, 51
Tovar, Cesar 99
Travis, Cecil 1, 147, 167–69
Traynor, Pie 14, 137
Trillo, Manny 141, 146
Trouppe, Quincy 96
Trout, Dizzy 90
Trucks, Virgil 151

Valenzuela, Fernando 71, 114
Vance, Dazzy 105
Vander Meer, Johnny 1, 17, 170–71
Veeck, Bill 19
Veracruz 10
Vernon, Mickey 140, 169, 172–73
Versalles, Zoilo 79, 99
veterans, U.S. 33, 62, 123, 155
Viola, Frank 127–28

Wagner, Honus 80
Walker, Dixie 34
Walker, Harry 148, 181
Waner, Lloyd 14
Waner, Paul 14
Watson, Bob 174
Wells, Willie 96, 120–21
Wertz, Vic 10, 46, 133
Wheeler, Lonnie 3
White, Bill 175
Whiz Kids 135
Wilhelm, Hoyt 67, 128
Will, George 100
Willey, Carlton 28

Williams, Billy 143, 175–78
Williams, Dick 46, 67, 74, 165, 178–80
Williams, Ted 16, 27, 34–35, 39–40, 55, 89, 98, 103, 105, 147, 150–51, 156, 168–69, 176, 178
Wills, Maury 23–24, 160, 180–81
Wilmer, Fields 2, 64–65
Wilson, John 182
Wonder Boys (film) 111
Wooden, John 20
World War II 2, 39, 50, 64–65, 89, 95, 167, 172
Wright, Glenn 14
Wyatt, John 128
Wynn, Early 10
Wynn, Jimmy 27, 71, 175, 181–82

Yankee Clipper 1
Yawkey, Tom 156
Yawkey family 95
Young, Cy 108
Yount, Robin 68

Zimmer, Don 127